C0-ATQ-416

Dimensions of United States-Mexican Relations

Volume 5

Foreign Policy in
U.S.-Mexican Relations

Dimensions of United States-Mexican Relations

a series

Series editors:
Rosario Green and Peter H. Smith

E
183.8
.M6
F67
1989

Foreign Policy
in U.S.-Mexican Relations

edited by
Rosario Green and Peter H. Smith

Dimensions of U.S.-Mexican Relations, Volume 5
papers prepared for the
Bilateral Commission on the Future of United States-Mexican Relations

Published by the
Center for U.S.-Mexican Studies
University of California, San Diego
1989

HORN LIBRARY-BABSON COLLEGE

ISBN # 0-935391-82-7

Table of Contents

SECTION I

FOUNDATIONS

SECTION II

INSTRUMENTS

SECTION III

CASES

Dimensions of
United States-Mexican Relations:
Series Introduction

Rosario Green and Peter H. Smith

This volume is part of a five-volume series, *Dimensions of United States-Mexican Relations,* consisting of selected background papers originally prepared for the use of the Bilateral Commission on the Future of United States-Mexican Relations.

Appreciation of the series must begin with an understanding of its origin. The Bilateral Commission was formed in 1986 as an independent, privately funded group of prominent citizens who were seeking to make a contribution to the improvement of U.S.-Mexican relations. Early in its deliberations the Commission agreed to produce a book-length report in time for consideration by incoming presidents to be elected in 1988.

With a two-year schedule, the Commission decided to seek the opinions of expert analysts on a variety of issues—specifically, on economics (including debt, trade, and investment), migration, drugs, foreign policy, and cultural relations. In addition, of course, Commissioners read a great deal of already published material and heard testimony from numerous government officials in both Mexico and the United States.

As staff directors for the Commission, the two of us assumed responsibility for coordination of the research activity. With the assistance of an Academic Committee,[1] we organized an intensive series of workshops and solicited papers from leading experts on each of these broad topics.

Our principal purpose was to provide the Commission with a broad range of informed perspectives on key issues in U.S.-Mexican relations. We wanted to introduce its members to the terms of current debates, rather than buttress conventional wisdoms; we sought to acquaint them with the broadest possible range of policy alternatives, rather than bias the discussion in favor of any particular view.

As a result, many Commissioners do not agree with the opinions expressed in these papers—just as some of the authors may disagree with parts of the Commission's report, published in English as *The Challenge of Interdependence: Mexico and the United States* (University Press of America, 1988).[2]

Accordingly, the publication of this series does not necessarily represent the viewpoints of the Commission or its members, and the papers herein do not simply provide supporting documentation for positions and recommendations of the Commission. The *Dimensions of United States-Mexican Relations* series represents an outgrowth of the same initiative that resulted in the Commission's report, but in other senses it is separate from it.

As we developed our research program on behalf of the Bilateral Commission, we nonetheless sought to make useful contributions to scholarly discourse on U.S.-Mexican relations. In this regard we had three goals:

One was to encourage the application of *comparative perspectives* to the study of U.S.-Mexican relations. Much of the work in this field has tended to concentrate on properties of the bilateral relationship alone and to assume, and often to assert, that the U.S.-Mexican connection has been "unique." It goes without saying, however, that you cannot determine the uniqueness of a relationship without comparing it to others. This we invited our authors to do.

Second was to encourage appropriate *attention to the United States*. We believe that much of the literature tends to concentrate

---

[1]The members were: Jorge Bustamante, John Coatsworth, Wayne Cornelius, William Glade, Guadalupe González, Cassio Luiselli, Carlos Rico, and Marta Tienda.
[2]The Spanish-language version appeared under the title *El desafío de la interdependencia: México y Estados Unidos* (Mexico: Fondo de Cultura Económica, 1988).

too much on Mexico, on Mexico's problems, and on Mexican contributions to the state of the relationship. We wanted to correct that
imbalance and, at the same time, to promote the study of the United
States by Mexican students and scholars.[3]

Third was to encourage analysts to spell out the *policy
implications* of their work. Academic investigation and primary
research have enormous value, of course, but we hoped to provide
an opportunity for scholars to speak as directly as possible to the
policy-making community. Accordingly, we asked each contribu-
tor to provide practical policy recommendations; in addition, we
obtained some papers from specialists with policy experience and
authority.

With such criteria in mind we solicited and obtained forty-eight
papers that were presented at about a dozen workshops in 1987
and early 1988.[4] These presentations proved to be of great use to
the Bilateral Commission. With the aid of the Academic Committee, we then defined a set of topics for the volumes in this series.
We selected papers for inclusion in the series primarily on the basis
of their relationship to these particular subjects. This led us,
regrettably, to exclude many fine papers from this collection. But
our purpose has been to produce anthologies with thematic coherence as well as substantive originality, and we hope to have
achieved that goal.

We conclude with an expression of thanks to all of our authors,
especially to those whose papers are not in these volumes; to
members of the Commission and its co-chairmen, Hugo Margáin
and William D. Rogers; to our colleagues on the Academic
Committee; to officers at the Ford Foundation who made possible
this enterprise. Sandra del Castillo, Lee Dewey, Will Heller,
Blanca Salgado, Gerardo Santos, and Arturo Sarukhan all made
invaluable contributions to the editing and production of these
volumes; to them our heartfelt gratitude.

Mexico City

La Jolla

---

[3]Indeed, one of the most alarming findings of the Commission relates to the decline
of U.S. studies in Mexico. See *Challenge*, ch. 6.
[4]A complete listing of all papers appears in Appendix II of the Commission's report,
The Challenge of Interdependence. Papers not included in this series may be published elsewhere and are available upon request; please send written inquiries to
the U.S. Office of the Bilateral Commission, Institute of the Americas, 10111 North
Torrey Pines Road, La Jolla, CA 92037.

1

Foreign Policy in U.S.-Mexican Relations: Introduction

Peter H. Smith and Rosario Green

Foreign policy has become a prime source of contention between Mexico and the United States in recent years. In addition to such long-standing issues as economics, migration, education, and drugs—explored in other volumes in this series—foreign policy questions have come to the forefront of the bilateral relationship. There have been disputes over substance as well as style. The U.S. Department of State and the Mexican Ministry of Foreign Relations (SRE) have come to regard one another with deep-seated suspicion and sometimes hostility. Ambassadors, especially U.S. emissaries to Mexico, have become highly controversial figures, and politicians in both countries regularly denounce the other's foreign policy. How has this come about?

As with so many aspects of the U.S.-Mexican relationship, foreign policy has a *double entendre*. On the one hand, it refers to the management of the bilateral relationship itself—how the two governments conduct business with each other. And on the other hand, it refers to the respective stances of the two governments toward third-party and multilateral issues, ranging from Chile to South Africa to Nicaragua. Along both dimensions, directly and indirectly, foreign policy concerns have added complexity and importance to the governance of the relationship. They have also expanded the range of possible grounds for disagreement.

What are the root causes of such conflicts? What are the dynamics underlying foreign policy problems between Mexico and the United States? What are the options—and the prospects—for the future?

ANALYTICAL PERSPECTIVES

Much of the scholarly literature stresses the "uniqueness" of the U.S.-Mexican relationship and tends to adopt an essentially descriptive mode. Nonetheless we think it is possible, and useful, to derive several distinct analytical frameworks from the existing body of literature.

There is a paradigm, for instance, that focuses on the presidents themselves. With reference to Mexico, this often means that foreign policy is identified with the personality of the president himself: books and articles speak of "the Echeverría policy" toward the Third World, the "López Portillo policy" toward El Salvador, and so on. Often this tendency reflects not a deliberate interpretation of the decision-making process, but an unthinking extrapolation from the assumption that *presidencialismo* prevails in Mexican politics—external as well as internal.

With reference to the United States, this orientation can focus either on the individual president—Jimmy Carter versus Ronald Reagan, for instance—or on the party that he represents. One often hears about the difference between "Democratic" and "Republican" foreign policies, particularly in the 1980s—and especially with regard to Central America. (Perhaps in tacit recognition of this reality, politicians respond with labored pleas in behalf of a return to "bipartisan" stances.)

As applied to both Mexico and the United States, this framework tends to emphasize the *changeability* of foreign policy processes and policies. New presidents, or new parties, can come into power and impose sweeping changes on the country's policies. The inference is that U.S.-Mexican relations are subject to periodic, predictable, and significant alterations.

Other positions stress elements of continuity rather than change. One interpretation stresses the more or less inevitable dynamic of historic and cultural factors. The United States and Mexico are so fundamentally different—in background, outlook, philosophy—that they will remain at odds with one another. As two prominent experts have argued, there will always be "limits to friendship" between the two nations. Improved communication and understanding can soften the impact of these national differences, but it is the differences that will continue to define and determine the nature of the relationship itself.[1]

An alternative framework emphasizes not national history but the development of the relationship, especially the *dependency* of Mexico on the United States. According to this view, Mexico's economic subordination to the United States—like that of other "periphery" countries to the "core" of the capitalist world-system—has established and defined the terms of discourse between the two countries. We do not here intend to rehearse long-winded and well-known debates over the question of *dependencia*.

Nonetheless we are tempted to observe that the dependency arguments, so triumphant in the 1970s, have never achieved quite the status or currency with regard to U.S.-Mexican relations that they acquired throughout the rest of Latin America. This strikes us as a rather conspicuous silence. It may be due in part to the diversity of the Mexican economy, which never fit the prototypically monocultural mode; and it may be due to the fact and the legacy of the Mexican Revolution, a monumental upheaval that bequeathed its citizens a much more autonomous and powerful state than elsewhere in Latin America.

And it may reflect the fact that the United States has at times applied direct political and even military pressure to Mexico, instead of relying on the economic influence of foreign investors and transnational corporations. As a result many analysts, especially from Mexico, have stressed the concept of *asymmetry*—a somewhat broader notion than *dependencia*. Despite its seemingly euphemistic quality, the idea of "asymmetry" is rather sweeping: it implies that imbalances in national resources tend to be *cumulative* and mutually reinforcing, not just drawn from economic inequalities, and it suggests that the more powerful country—in this case the United States—may at times employ brute force.

---

[1] Robert A. Pastor and Jorge G. Castañeda, *Limits to Friendship: The United States and Mexico* (New York: Alfred A. Knopf, 1988). As though in demonstration of their own thesis, these two authors take implicitly different approaches toward the relationship: Castañeda focuses on historical-structural matters, while Pastor employs psychological and cultural arguments.

In apparent contradiction to this image is the more recent idea of "interdependence." Politicians and promoters have sometimes used this phrase to describe utopian schemes of collaboration and cooperation, ranging from diplomatic agreements to free-trade zones to common-market arrangements; others have used it to de-emphasize imbalance and asymmetry.[2]

Strictly speaking, however, the idea of interdependence does not imply advocacy. It simply reflects a recognition that the two nations have become interconnected to a considerable degree, that the fate of each is contingent upon the fate of the other. It is in this sense that the Bilateral Commission on the Future of United States-Mexican Relations addressed itself to "the challenge of interdependence."[3] And it is in much the same, value-free sense that one thoughtful observer has chosen to use the phrase "asymmetric interdependence" to describe the U.S.-Mexican relationship.[4]

Yet another body of literature addresses itself not so much to the structure of the relationship as to the decision-making proc-esses behind it, especially in the United States. Some of the most sophisticated writing of this genre has argued that Latin American policy tends to result from the interplay of "bureaucratic" politics within the U.S. government. It is the pulling and hauling among different elements in the governmental bureaucracy, rather than the grand pursuit of national purpose or the ignoble defense of private interests, that characterizes and dominates U.S. policy toward the region.[5] Though the argument is not without its crit-ics, it helps explain the chronic confusion and inconsistency in Washington's stance toward Mexico—which involves a myriad number of agencies while remaining an issue of low-to-medium priority for the White House. The implication of this outlook is that

---

[2]See Carlos Rico F., "The Future of Mexican-U.S. Relations and the Limits of the Rhetoric of 'Interdependence,'" in *Mexican-U.S. Relations: Conflict and Convergence,* ed. Carlos Vásquez and Manuel García y Griego (Los Angeles: UCLA Chicano Studies Research Center/UCLA Latin American Center, 1983), pp. 127-174.
[3]*The Challenge of Interdependence: Mexico and the United States* (Lanham, Md.: University Press of America, 1988).
[4]Mario Ojeda Gómez, "Mexico and United States Relations: Interdependence or Mexico's Dependence?" in *Mexican-U.S. Relations,* ed. Vásquez and García y Griego, pp. 109-126; see esp. p. 112.
[5]See Abraham F. Lowenthal, "United States Policy toward Latin America: 'Liberal,' 'Radical,' and 'Bureaucratic' Perspectives," *Latin American Research Review* 8:3 (fall 1973): 3-25; and Lowenthal, "'Liberal,' 'Radical,' and 'Bureaucratic' Perspectives on U.S.-Latin American Policy: The Alliance for Progress in Retrospect," in *Latin America and the United States: The Changing Political Realities,* ed. Julio Cotler and Richard Fagen (Stanford: Stanford University Press, 1974).

U.S. policy toward Mexico is unlikely to undergo dramatic change because bureaucratic rivalries and fiefdoms will neutralize presidential initiatives or other outside influences.[6]

A useful extension of this perspective stresses the importance of domestic political considerations and regards U.S. policy toward Mexico as an expression of "intermestic" concerns (*inter*national and do*mestic* at the same time). The concept implies that American governmental agencies are responsive to domestic constituencies, if not to exalted visions of national purpose, and that decision-making toward Mexico reveals the continuing importance of these internal considerations. Political factors (such as the fate of tomato-growers in Florida) thus tend to govern the relationship. And as the adage has it, "all politics is domestic politics."

We do not seek to reconcile these differing perspectives or to provide an overarching theory of our own. We both believe, with slightly different emphases, that these perspectives are by no means mutually exclusive; in view of the complexity of U.S.-Mexican relations, we suspect that the most useful explanations will emerge from the creative integration of some of these divergent paradigms. (Indeed, that tends to be a common characteristic of the essays in this volume.) For the moment let us turn from these scholarly debates to recent trends in the relationship itself.

DEVELOPMENT AND TRENDS

Since World War II profound changes in the national and international arenas have led to important modifications in Mexico, in the United States, and in their places in the world. These shifts have also had decisive impacts on their foreign policies.

While the United States entered the postwar period with a nuclear monopoly and with economic predominance, its supremacy in these areas is now being contested by various nations as the twentieth century draws toward a close.[7] There is a growing

---

[6]See Abraham F. Lowenthal, "Ronald Reagan and Latin America: Coping with Hegemony in Decline," in *Eagle Defiant: U.S. Foreign Policy in the 1980s,* ed. Kenneth Oye (Boston: Little, Brown, 1983), ch. 10.

[7]For example, see Abraham F. Lowenthal, *Partners in Conflict: The United States and Latin America* (Baltimore and London: Johns Hopkins University Press, 1987), esp. ch. 2 on "hegemony in decline"; and Paul Kennedy, *The Rise and Fall of the Great Powers: Economic Change and Military Conflict from 1500 to 2000* (New York: Random House, 1987), esp. ch. 8.

realization that the United States is increasingly limited in its capacity to impose its unilateral will on military or financial aspects of global affairs.[8] Moreover, current transformations within the Soviet Union may herald a significant advance in superpower détente, which might in turn prompt modifications in the U.S. concept of national security. In this sense, a favorable evolution in superpower disarmament talks could lead to a genuine relaxation of East-West tensions and thus pave the way for an improvement of inter-American relations.

It should be remembered that it was in the postwar context of rivalry with the Soviet Union that the United States articulated its definition of hemispheric security. Every challenge to this notion was seen as emanating from the Socialist bloc and, more concretely, from the expansionist designs of the Soviet Union. The emergence and development of the Cuban revolution introduced a specifically *continental* dimension to the concept of security.[9] The argument stressed that threats could emerge even within the U.S. network of military alliances, especially through the penetration of alternative ideologies and forms of social organization.

The subsequent consolidation of East-West détente would lead not only to some redefinition in the concept of security and in the political, economic, and military relationship between the superpowers. It would also produce a different (or more nuanced) role for the United States in the maintenance of that security. Some observers even surmise that the United States will in the future have to exercise a more subtle kind of leadership than in the past, concentrating as much on the definition of threats (past and potential) to its alliances as on enforcement.[10]

According to this scenario the United States would reduce its own international activity and encourage its allies to assume an increasing share of the financial and other burdens required for the maintenance of security, especially in light of the growing difficulties of the U.S. economy. This does not mean that the United States will have to abandon its commitments, but rather that it will

---

[8]Henry Kissinger and Cyrus Vance, "Bipartisan Objectives for American Foreign Policy," *Foreign Affairs* 66:5 (summer 1988): 900.
[9]See Lars Schoultz, *National Security and United States Policy toward Latin America* (Princeton: Princeton University Press, 1987); and, more broadly, Stephen E. Ambrose, *Rise to Globalism: American Foreign Policy, 1938-1980*, 2d. rev. ed. (New York: Penguin Books, 1980).
[10]Kissinger and Vance, "Bipartisan Objectives," 900.

have to specify them in a more realistic way if it seeks to continue its central role in the changing world scene. Nonetheless it must be recognized that U.S. foreign policy—perhaps more important to the rest of the world than to the U.S. public and its leaders— has tended to focus on East-West relations and on the "containment" of communism; this has not provided a clear set of principles or strategies for dealing with the Third World.[11] From its position as a global power, the United States has not only acted on behalf of national and global interests, but has also drawn itself into numerous armed conflicts throughout the world—sometimes without a coherent sense of purpose (ideological, economic, military, whatever) and sometimes without a clear definition of the enemy, frequently mistaking a simple difference of opinion as hostility.

By contrast Mexico, from a diametrically opposed economic and military stance, has pursued its national interests with the support of a solid set of norms derived from international law. Foreign policy is not, for Mexicans, the result of improvisations or conjunctures or conveniences. Foreign policy is one of the grand national traditions, sustained and upheld throughout the country's history in the most trying of circumstances. Moreover, the history of Mexico demonstrates how the guiding principles of foreign policy emerge and develop through the traumatic experiences of threats to national sovereignty. Conspicuous among these episodes have been, in the nineteenth century, the loss of half the nation's territory to U.S. expansionism (1848) and the imposition of a foreign emperor by the invading armies of Napoleon (1861-67); and, in the twentieth century, foreign pressures on the Mexican Revolution, from the American invasion of Veracruz (1914) to the punitive expedition under General John Pershing (1916) to the subsequent opposition to the nationalization of oil companies by Lázaro Cárdenas (1938).

In the face of such violent confrontations Mexico has always given the highest priority to the observance of key principles: nonintervention and self-determination, the use of reason over force, the importance of political negotiation and compliance with the norms of international law. This emphasis reflects the conviction that respect for the international juridical order is the most effective means of defending the sovereignty and integrity of Mexico and of other nations, especially the weaker countries of the world.

---

[11]See George Kennan's famous article, "The Sources of Soviet Conduct," *Foreign Affairs* 25:4 (July 1947): 566-582.

In view of such stark differences in philosophy and ideology—and style, the United States being much the more pragmatic of the two—it is hardly surprising that conflicts have from time to time arisen between Mexico and the United States across the entire span of political, social, and economic relations. Yet when frictions occur over questions of foreign policy, it is not because Mexico has intentionally sought conflict with the United States. Such differences have been, instead, a secondary consequence of Mexico's projection in the world and, above all, a natural result of the fact that national interests of the two countries may not always converge.

Mexicans insist that the motives behind their foreign policy are "reasons of state" (*raisons d'état* or *razones de Estado*) that reflect the traditions and the interests of the Mexican state, and that have acquired strength and durability through strict adherence to the international juridical order. Apparently this argument has not always been accepted in the United States, where some sectors seem to be convinced that Mexico uses its foreign policy to irritate the United States—either because of excessive and unrealistic nationalism or because of alleged concessions to the domestic left. Such perceptions impede a better understanding between the two nations, confuse the relationship, and overlook the countless occasions when U.S. and Mexican policies have agreed with one another.

To be sure, Mexico has raised protests when the United States, either alone or with others, has intervened in the political affairs of sovereign nations, as in the CIA-supported overthrow of Jacobo Arbenz in Guatemala in 1954; the invasions and campaigns against the Cuban revolution; the dispatch of the "inter-American peacekeeping force" to the Dominican Republic in 1965; the pressures against Chile under Salvador Allende and against Nicaragua under the Sandinistas; the military assault against Grenada; the opposition to Panama; and so on. In support of the principles of nonintervention and self-determination, Mexico has also, over the years, challenged the Italian invasion of Ethiopia (now Eritrea); the Japanese invasion of China; the German annexation of Austria; Russian designs on Finland; the Soviet invasion of Afghanistan. In short, Mexico has consistently opposed attempts by powerful nations to justify the violation of the rights of sovereign states and thereby to weaken the bases of comity among nations.[12]

---

[12]See Mario Ojeda G., *México: el surgimiento de una política exterior activa* (Mexico: Secretaría de Educación Pública, 1986).

PROSPECTS FOR NEW RELATIONSHIPS

Notwithstanding historical disagreements, it is also true that Mexico and the United States have shared common interests, objectives, outlooks, and concerns—within and beyond the field of conventional diplomacy. To begin, the two nations share a general aspiration for world peace and international security. Both signed the Charter of San Francisco, creating the United Nations. Both have an interest in the economic development and peaceful evolution of other nations within the hemisphere. Both nations encourage the diplomatic settlement of disputes within the region and, even as they disagree about means to achieve this goal, on the insulation of the Americas from East-West conflict.

In the bilateral arena, both countries have gained enormous benefits from peace along their common border, one of the longest in the world (3200 kilometers = 2000 miles) and a uniquely abrupt separation of one of the world's most highly developed countries from a nation in the process of development. Over the last half century there has been only occasional conflict and a good deal of cooperation and collaboration. There has not been any military action since 1917; neither country has had to assign substantial military resources to the defense of the border for more than sixty years. The border has thus been a benefit for both countries; both should want to keep it that way. For there exist, along the length of the border, a great variety of crucial interests—ranging from protection of the environment and the control of cross-border pollution, to restrictions on drug trafficking, to the question of labor migration. As such the border has the potential for provoking conflict as well as cooperation, and for this reason it deserves constant attention from the two nations.

Mexico and the United States have a mutual interest in each other's economic recovery and growth (as shown by another volume in this series),[13] and also in each other's political stability and development. In practice this usually reflects North American concern about Mexico,[14] itself a relatively recent phenomenon. Not too long ago, Mexicans point out, academic specialists in the United States tended to celebrate the virtues of the Mexican political

---

[13]William Glade and Cassio Luiselli, eds., *The Economics of Interdependence: Mexico and the United States*, vol. 2 in *Dimensions of United States-Mexican Relations*.

[14]Mexican concern about the United States tends to focus on the possibility of nuclear catastrophe, rather than internal upheaval, and this leads to efforts on behalf of disarmament and arms control.

system,[15] and these favorable assessments were more or less shared by the U.S. government. Starting with the Carter administration, however, there began to appear critical judgments about the nature of power in Mexico, its representativity, its orientation, and the policies that it produced.

We see at least three reasons for this change in the mid-to late 1970s. First there was, toward the end of the Echeverría period, the appearance of an economic crisis that spawned doubts in the United States about Mexico's capacity to govern itself. Second was the discovery of vast petroleum deposits, just as revolution was mounting within Iran and prompting fears about the security of U.S. oil supplies. Third was Mexico's posture toward the Sandinista revolution in Nicaragua.

Thus emerged within the U.S. government and some other circles a negative picture of Mexico—as inefficient, anti-democratic, and prone to support "totalitarian" movements. During the 1980s this image found indirect reinforcement in the waves of "democratization" that swept over other parts of Latin America; in comparison with Argentina under Alfonsín or Brazil under Sarney or Uruguay under Sanguinetti, Mexico no longer looked so impressive. For such reasons Mexico and its political stability took a prominent place on the national security agenda of the United States, a position it still holds.

Multilateral as well as bilateral disagreements have increased in recent years. There were sharp differences during the 1950s and '60s over U.S. (or U.S.-supported) interventions. In the 1970s and '80s frictions have multiplied and tended to focus on two key issues: Mexican policy in Central America, including Panama, and Mexico's position in international forums.

The latter question is of recent vintage. Before the 1970s Mexico's stance in regional and multilateral forums had never caused serious tension in the bilateral relationship. Mexico customarily exercised what José López Portillo would later call "the right to dissent" (el derecho de disentir) and the United States accepted this practice. The surge of multilateral activism under Luis Echeverría brought an end to U.S. tolerance; Mexico's support for Third World causes, particularly its sponsorship of the Charter of Economic

---

[15]See, for example, Robert E. Scott, *Mexican Government in Transition* (Urbana: University of Illinois Press, 1959), and Frank R. Brandenburg, *The Making of Modern Mexico* (Englewood Cliffs, N.J.: Prentice-Hall, 1964).

Rights and Responsibilities, led North American representatives to conclude that Mexico was openly hostile to the United States and that it was advocating a "tyranny of the majority" within the United Nations.

From this time onward multilateral issues proceeded to "contaminate" the bilateral relationship between Mexico and the United States. At the behest of Congress, the U.S. State Department began to compile data on U.N. voting records that documented emerging differences between Mexico and the United States.[16] Mexico, for its part, became fond of citing studies showing that the United States was either becoming isolated within the U.N. or staunchly opposing multilateral initiatives.[17] The Mexican government further argued that a vote on behalf of its national interests should be seen as such and should not be construed as a vote against anyone else.

Central America has been a continual source of discord ever since the late 1970s, when Mexico first began to take a position differing from that of the United States. Mexico severed relations with Somoza's Nicaragua in 1979, withdrew its ambassador to San Salvador in 1980, and joined with France in calling for the recognition of the Salvadoran insurgent movement as a "representative political force" in 1981. Later, in 1983, Mexico founded the Contadora Group, together with Colombia and Panama and Venezuela, and has consistently lent its support to that effort— notwithstanding the resistance of some elements within the U.S. government that regarded the Group as pro-Nicaragua and therefore sought to obstruct its efforts.

More recently these disagreements have come to embrace Panama as well, where U.S. policy has been perceived in Mexico as openly interventionist. Leaving aside any judgment one might have about the leadership of Panama, Mexico insists on respect for the sovereignty of the Panamanian people. Challenging the North American argument about "the promotion of democracy in the Americas" (a frequent refrain in the past), Mexico upholds the principle of nonintervention. Interests and principles come into conflict; under such circumstances dialogue becomes practically impossible.

---

[16]For example see U.S. Department of State, *Report to Congress on Voting Practices in the United Nations* (Washington, 1987).
[17]Planetary Citizens, "Voting in the General Assembly of the United Nations: 1970-1985" (San Anselmo, Calif.: 1985).

PROSPECTS AND ALTERNATIVES

The intensification of the relationship between Mexico and the United States and the expansion of the bilateral agenda have created a long-term basis for continuing conflict. Nonetheless we firmly believe that conflict is not necessarily inevitable, and that (when it occurs) it need not inflict irremediable damage on the bilateral relationship. We believe that both countries, Mexico as well as the United States, have plausible options for the conduct of their foreign policy and its bearing upon U.S.-Mexican relations.[18]

Options for the United States

The United States has three broad options for dealing with Mexico and, in particular, with foreign policy questions. One would be to adopt a laissez-faire attitude: to ignore Mexico and Mexican foreign policy, letting Mexico conduct its own foreign policy without any special input or communication from the United States. This would satisfy Mexico's long-standing insistence on sovereignty, one might argue, and it would avoid unnecessary arguments over inconsequential diplomatic niceties.

The difficulty with a laissez-faire posture is that Mexico and Mexican diplomacy have become too crucial to U. S. national interests. This is especially true in light of the increasing importance of regional, hemispheric, and Third World concerns. Ignoring Mexico would mean ignoring one of the most visible and significant actors in the international arena. It would also forgo opportunities for constructive collaboration.

A second option would be for the United States to take a hard line, as it has sometimes done in the past, attempting to use the asymmetry in the bilateral relationship as a means of forcing compliance in the multilateral arena. There is a broad range of instruments—economic, social, political—the United States could use for this purpose. It might, for instance, threaten to impose an economic boycott on Mexican products unless Mexico falls into line on some contested international issue (one imperfect but nonetheless telling illustration came in the mid-1970s, when the U.S. Jewish

---

[18]Our opinions tend to agree with the detailed analysis and recommendations offered by the Bilateral Commission on the Future of United States-Mexican Relations in *The Challenge of Interdependence,* ch. 5. As volume editors we function here as individual scholars, however, not as spokespersons for the Commission.

community prompted a tourist boycott after Mexico voted in favor of the "zionism as a form of racism" resolution in the U.N.). And as a constant reminder, the United States could sustain a constant campaign of harassment and intimidation in order to exercise its domination. This option draws special support from the American right and had powerful advocates within the Reagan adminstration. In late 1984, for example, President Reagan signed National Security Directive 124 ordering the State Department to pressure Mexico to cooperate in Central America.[19]

Such coercion would be unethical, in our view, and it would cast a pall over U.S. bilateral relations with other less powerful countries throughout the world. It would also be unworkable. If history conveys any lessons at all, it demonstrates that Mexico (and other nations in similar positions) remains fiercely proud of its integrity and autonomy. Heavy-handed attempts to impose obedience would meet with resistance, defiance, and resentment. In the end, the United States would simply add to its own problems in the world.

The third option for the United States would be to establish a constructive collaboration and communication with Mexico. The United States should, we think, show utmost respect for the sovereignty and logic of Mexican foreign policy, but also feel free to communicate its concerns about foreign policy questions clearly and candidly. Mexico is too important to ignore and, at the same time, too important to coerce. The United States should strive to have in Mexico a strong and independent partner, rather than a weak and subservient client. This means, above all, full and frank communication.

Options for Mexico

If proximity and importance generate conflict in U.S.-Mexican relations, the solution for Mexico is not to be found in an aloofness or distancing from the United States. In fact Mexico could not do so even if it wanted to: the country finds itself within the orbit of U.S. security concerns, like it or not, and can do little to change this position. The most constructive alternative is to take advantage of the situation and turn it to the benefit of Mexican interests.

---

[19]On CIA Director William Casey's views about Mexico see Bob Woodward, *Veil: The Secret Wars of the CIA, 1981-1987* (New York: Simon and Schuster, 1987), esp. pp. 339-346.

To be specific: U.S. concerns about political, social, and economic stability in Mexico should make it possible for Mexico to
seek conditions for a bilateral and international climate that will
contribute to that stability. Mexico could therefore request that the
United States open its markets to Mexican products; encourage its
banks to recognize its share of responsibility with regard to the
debt; persuade its investors to accept the integrity and logic of
Mexican laws; and adopt a constructive stance toward the problem of drugs, including a campaign against consumer demand in
the United States. In general, the U.S. government should take every
possible step to promote a constructive, positive, and responsible
atmosphere for the conduct of the relationship.

Such a policy would of course entail risks and costs for Mexico.
A close relationship with the United States could reduce Mexico's
legitimacy in the diplomatic arena; it could provoke nationalist
resentment from within; and it could mean excessive reliance on
an undependable partner. But the existence of these possibilities
should not lead to a retreat from the United States. Rather, they
should encourage a clear assessment of the risks and costs that
Mexico should be prepared to accept and to pay. That is to say,
while a good understanding between Mexico and the United States
would come from mutual concessions, these trade-offs do not have
to mean surrender (*cesiones*) by Mexico. Sacrificing positions and
stances is not the answer. For example, Mexico has sustained its
role in Latin American diplomatic cooperation (*concertación*) and
in other efforts toward regional integration.

It would be just as illusory to assume that exclusive cooperation with the United States would solve all of Mexico's problems
as to suppose that bilateral collaboration would bring nothing but
aggravation. As the world moves toward the consolidation of
regional powers and partnerships in Europe, the Pacific Basin, and
elsewhere, an excessive reliance on the United States would bring
many more costs than benefits to Mexico.

Options for Mexico and the United States

For reasons already explained, we do not anticipate that foreign policy differences between Mexico and the United States will
come to a prompt end. But we think that the two countries can
and should make deliberate efforts to draw clear distinctions between disagreements that are more profound and those that are
less profound. On less important issues, they should look toward

grounds for compromise; that is, they should try to accommodate their positions in favor of an agreement that serves the interests of both countries.

On the more important disagreements, we think the only viable option is to resuscitate the time-honored formula of the "right to disagree"—that is, letting the other country formulate its foreign policy freely but not letting disagreements in substance cast shadows over the relationship as a whole. This seems to be the only workable recommendation: preventing contamination of the bilateral relationship by multilateral considerations; learning to accept and to manage discord; maintaining a clear distinction between the political, economic, and social core of the U.S.-Mexican relationship and the foreign policy area where tension sometimes predominates. An "agreement to disagree" would create the basis for a more fluid and flexible relationship.

Regional issues have a special bearing on the bilateral relationship. The creation of a new basis for a system of inter-American collaboration will be a major challenge in the years ahead. If it proves impossible to resuscitate and reinvigorate the Organization of American States, we would urge the formation and consolidation of informal regional groupings throughout the hemisphere.[20] This is particularly evident insofar as the national interests of Mexico and the United States become involved in conflicts in Central America and elsewhere. So if the multilateral agenda between Mexico and the United States can be isolated and insulated (even quarantined) to some extent, and if the bilateral agenda can be negotiated, the regional agenda will require consultation and communication. The United States should see in Mexico a valid bridge to the rest of Latin America; and Mexico should deal with the United States directly and forcefully, without turning its back on the rest of Latin America.

IN THIS VOLUME

To explore such issues we here present a selection of essays prepared for the Bilateral Commission on the Future of United States-Mexican Relations. The first section examines the basic premises of foreign policy. In her study of Mexico, Guadalupe

---

[20]See Inter-American Working Group, *Collective Security in the Americas: New Directions* (Boston: World Peace Foundation, 1988).

González seeks to analyze, on the one hand, the historical determinants of Mexican foreign policy and, on the other, the patterns
that shape both continuity and change. She argues that the policy
environment of the 1980s is extremely complex and poses new
problems and challenges for foreign affairs, especially given the
convergence of economic crisis with political transformation within
the context of regional and international crisis. She suggests that
Mexico may have to reorient its development strategies and sharpen
its definition of national goals in the short and medium term—
without departing from the traditional bases of Mexican foreign
policy—and thus develop an agenda that is more in keeping with
new realities and national interests.

Lars Schoultz, in his essay, traces the connections between basic
trends in U.S. foreign policy and its relationship with Latin America
and especially Mexico. He demonstrates that the postwar policy
of containment, which defines almost every conflict as an
expression of Soviet expansionism, has now become outmoded,
especially in view of the new era of détente and great-power
accommodation. Given the interdependence of international
relations, Schoultz argues that this new phase will have profound
impacts on Latin America, most notably in regard to the peace and
security considerations that have so long caused preoccupation in
Washington. He thus concludes that Latin America will continue
to hold a high priority on the U.S. security agenda, but that the
relaxation of security concerns may open new political and diplomatic space for Mexico and other countries.

Our second section deals with decision-making processes in
the bilateral arena. In a path-breaking essay, Jorge Chabat describes
how Mexico makes its foreign policy toward the United States.
Offering an analytical picture of long-term trends in policy-making
patterns and of specific transformations during the 1980s, Chabat
catalogs the attributes and jurisdictions of governmental agencies
involved in foreign policy. His essay reveals an apparent lack of
coordination between the decision-making arenas, which tend to
be more concentrated at the cabinet level than in the presidency
itself, and it suggests that the traditional agents of foreign policy—
such as the Secretaría de Relaciones Exteriores—have lost a good
deal of room for maneuver with regard to such crucial issues as
the debt and foreign trade.

Carlos Rico then raises the question of how, and to what extent,
Mexico might increase its influence on Washington—in other
words, how Mexico might improve its capacity for negotiation with

the United States. He stresses the importance of identifying potential points of access into U.S. decision-making processes with regard to Mexico, and of maximizing the utility of those access points through structural changes in the Mexican government and its diplomatic missions. Through his demonstration that there is no single decision-making process within the United States, where non-governmental actors as well as governmental agents play important roles, Rico underscores both the growing complexity of the policy environment and the differing priorities that Mexico receives at different times from different U.S. agencies.

Beginning with a similar set of observations, Cathryn Thorup raises the counterpart question: whether bureaucratic reorganization within the United States might lead to an improvement in the quality and conduct of the bilateral relationship. Good process is no substitute for good policy, as she clearly points out, and the U.S. government must first define exactly what it wants from the relationship before designing a bureaucratic structure to achieve its goals. For this reason long-term national interests should take precedence over the short-term demands of special interest groups within the U.S. political scene. For Thorup, the deterioration of U.S.-Mexican relations from 1973 to 1986 reveals the dangers and disadvantages of a fragmented decision-making process. She therefore proposes ways to design a mechanism to enhance the coherence of U.S. policy and the conduct of the relationship, to avoid unnecesary conflict, and to increase the prospects for bilateral cooperation.

The third and final section deals with multilateral cases of policy conflict. Comparing U.S. and Mexican postures with regard to Central America, Claude Heller explores the differing perceptions and actions of the two governments. Within this framework, he gives a detailed—and first-hand—description of the formation of the Contadora Group in 1983. To this he adds a thorough and thoughtful examination of the efforts of the Group and of the differences that emerged between Mexico and the United States and that appeared in various international forums, including the United Nations. Heller thus confronts a crucial question: Will it really be possible for Mexico and the United States to reach a better understanding over Central America?

William H. Luers concludes the volume with an arresting comparison between the U.S.-Mexican relationship and U.S. relations with the Soviet Union. He reveals the central role that each interaction has had in the formation of U.S. foreign policy as a whole, both during and after the revolutionary eras in the two countries. During the postwar period the Soviet Union has been the principal rival and adversary of the United States; Mexico has been its initial and principal window on the Third World. Both societies are now in the midst of profound socioeconomic and political transformations that the United States must take great pains to understand. While the U.S. government has had a fairly coherent (if not always friendly) policy toward the Soviet Union, its policy toward Mexico has been incoherent and uncoordinated. Stressing the global importance of U.S.-Mexican relations, Luers concludes with a visionary proposal for a new institutional mechanism for the management of the bilateral relationship.

With this collection of fine essays we, as editors, hope to have made a contribution to the understanding of the logic behind U.S. and Mexican foreign policies, of the reasons behind disagreements, and of the prospects for agreements. We also hope to stimulate further research and reflection by other scholars on these important subjects.

SECTION

I

FOUNDATIONS

2

The Foundations of Mexico's Foreign Policy: Old Attitudes and New Realities

Guadalupe González

This essay delineates the interacting ideas, perceptions, and general attitudes that underlie the historical development of foreign policy in Mexico. The identification of these various elements derives from an analysis of the overarching tendencies in Mexico's international behavior. Concrete problems and the specific policies designed to address them are considered only when they illustrate the steps on the road toward a particular historical pattern of foreign behavior,[1] or movement in a divergent direction. This essay, then, emphasizes general trends over particular policies in its search for patterns of continuity and permanence.

This paper does not aspire to present an analytical framework which can explain why Mexico has or has not adopted a particular policy in a given international issue area or to explain why Mexico's foreign policy approach has varied in parallel situations. Much less would I assert that the categories appearing below would be useful in predicting future positions. I merely hope to clarify

---

[1]The distinction between the general (patterns of historical behavior) and the particular (concrete decisions and actions) in the study of foreign policy seems to be a correct analytical point of departure because it elucidates the kind of phenomenon that we will try to study. This conceptual distinction is supported by Baghat Korany, "Foreign Policy Decision-making Theory and the Third World: Playoffs and Pitfalls," in *How Foreign Policy Decisions Are Made in the Third World. A Comparative Analysis*, ed. Baghat Korany (Boulder, Colo.: Westview Press, 1986).

the concepts, images, and attitudes about what the international reality *is* and *should be* that have provided the foundation for Mexico's international behavior. Thus, the analysis will focus on the study of the general reference framework of Mexico's foreign policy and not on the particular perceptions and concrete issues of the regional or world stage.

In the case of Mexico, the decision to focus our analysis on general trends and not on particular issues is not totally arbitrary. One element arguing for a more global approach is the fact that, unlike other Latin American countries, Mexico has, throughout this century, developed a foreign policy marked by a high degree of continuity. Many scholars have characterized it as "state," as opposed to "government," foreign policy.[2] This conceptual distinction emphasizes the structural and functional relationship between a country's foreign policy and the character of its political regime, such that the basic orientation of the country's foreign policy remains firm through changes in administration, regardless of the degree of divergence between successive administrations. Viewed as a state policy, Mexico's foreign policy has built upon the ideological and political elements contained in the national project which emerged from the Mexican Revolution. Additional factors which contribute to the high degree of continuity characterizing Mexico's foreign policy and which enter into any study of its general trends are the country's long-term political stability and the permanence in power of a single political elite, identified with the Partido Revolucionario Institucional (PRI). In pointing to the continuity and coherence in their country's foreign policy, Mexico's leaders have been joined by Latin American and U.S. observers:

> Mexico's foreign policy, in its approach to broad international issues, has been remarkably stable and consistent since its basic tenets were implicitly codified in the 1917 Constitution and explicitly enumerated by President Carranza in his 1918 Report to the Congress.[3]

---

[2]See Carlos Rico, "Common Concerns and National Interests: The Contadora Experience and the Prospects for Collective Security Arrangements in the Western Hemisphere," Documento de Trabajo, no. 8 (México, D.F.: Programa de Estudios de América del Norte, ILET, 1987).

[3]John F. McShane, "Emerging Regional Power: Mexico's Role in the Caribbean Basin," in *Latin American Foreign Policies: Global and Regional Dimensions*, ed. Elizabeth G. Ferris and Jennie K. Lincoln (Boulder, Colo.: Westview Press, 1985), p. 191.

And

Compared with other Latin American countries, Mexico's foreign policy shows itself stable and foreseeable.[4]

Most historical analyses offered by Mexican scholars have determined that this element of continuity dates from the time of Mexico's independence and can be seen even in historical periods such as the *porfiriato*, which were less suspicious of the outside world and favored opening Mexico's borders to external.[5]

According to this interpretation, the Mexican Revolution merely enriched and articulated a tradition of Mexican foreign policy which had prevailed throughout the country's uneasy relations with the outside world during the 19th century. True, it placed this tradition within a new framework, but it did not destroy it. This widely accepted idea was expressed by former minister of foreign relations Antonio Carrillo Flores:

Fortunately—repeating the obvious—Mexico's foreign policy has old and strong roots which start with Morelos, reach their momentum with Juárez and continue with Carranza, Calles and Cárdenas; to be fair—excepting Santana—with all the Chiefs of State that have ruled us.[6]

Even though this convergence of academic and political viewpoints on the continuity of Mexican foreign policy reaffirms the validity of this essay's focus on the forest, rather than the trees, a detailed analysis demands that we examine the problem in a different way. Actually, continuity as a characteristic of Mexico's foreign policy is relative; continuity does not imply a total inability to move away from fixed points of reference, but rather that foreign policy in practice has evolved within historically narrow parameters. If this is the case, by determining the amount of flexibility which could be achieved and by identifying its historical

---

[4]Alberto Van Klaveren, "Mexico: principios y pragmatismo en la política exterior," in *Las políticas exteriores latinoamericanas frente a la crisis*, ed. Heraldo Muñoz (Buenos Aires: GEL-PROSPEL-CERC, 1984), p. 39.
[5]For a good example see Rosario Green, "Vigencia de las raíces históricas de la política exterior de México: Estados Unidos-Centroamérica," mimeograph, 1985.
[6]Antonio Carrillo Flores, "Reflexiones acerca de la política exterior y la diplomacia mexicanas," *Diálogos* 120 (November-December 1984): 11.

limits to foreign policy behavior, we can find the connecting thread for a reinterpretation of the development of Mexican foreign policy. In accordance with previous studies, we could say that Mexico's foreign policy has moved between two extreme positions: in the words of Poitras, from legalistic passivism to reformist activism.[7] The limits to change would be defined by two basic objectives: internationally, to avoid a direct confrontation with the United States, and, domestically, to maintain political legitimacy and stability.[8] This will be examined in depth later in this paper.

Mexican foreign policymakers of the postrevolutionary period have repeatedly insisted on defining it as a "policy of principles," whose basic postulates are an invariable and integral element of the nation's historical tradition. As pointed out by former minister of foreign relations Bernardo Sepúlveda, Mexican foreign policy's close adherence to principles has been both a moral commitment and a response to reality:

> Another feature of Mexico's foreign policy is that it must be considered as a policy of principles, both out of conviction and necessity. Mexico has sustained all along its postrevolutionary historical path a set of principles that have always guided its foreign policy. However this policy doesn't rest on abstract notions. These principles are an integral response to the most legitimate interests of the nation.[9]

Although this quotation explicitly denies that Mexican foreign policy rests on abstract notions, official insistence on ritually declaring the immutability of the basic principles,[10] as well as the official tendency to define the national interest solely in normative and doctrinaire terms, seriously complicates efforts to elucidate the real and concrete meanings of Mexico's foreign actions. Sometimes official arguments seem to reduce basic foreign policy

---

[7]Guy Poitras, "Mexico's Foreign Policy in an Age of Interdependence," in *Latin American Foreign Policies*, p. 103.
[8]See Jorge Chabat, "Condicionantes del activismo de la política exterior mexicana (1960-1985)," in *Fundamentos y prioridad de la política exterior de México*, ed. Humberto Garza Elizondo (México, D.F.: El Colegio de México, 1986) pp. 89-108.
[9]Bernardo Sepúlveda Amor, "Reflexiones sobre la política exterior de México," *Foro Internacional* 24:4 (April-June 1984): 409.
[10]Jorge A. Lozoya, "México y la diplomacia multilateral," *Foro Internacional* 24:4 (April-June 1984): 437.

positions to a simple enumeration of principles, such as peoples' right to self-determination, the political sovereignty of all countries, nonintervention, the legal equality of all countries, international cooperation, peaceful resolution of conflict, and the respect of human rights. This tendency makes Mexico's foreign policy seem "ambivalent and open to interpretations that create doubt and confusion in other countries about the real purposes of this policy."[11]

What are the ideological assumptions, the historical contents, the concrete interests, and the world perceptions and political premises that underlie the doctrinaire foundation of policy to which official discourse always alludes? Their identification is the precise objective of this analysis. To this end, let's consider the historical, geopolitical, and political factors that have forged Mexico's particular view of the world on the assumption that these principles and their management have responded to concrete national interests.

That policy of principles, despite its overall historical continuity, has not been identical over time. The real meaning of each of these principles, its assigned priority, and its relationship with the country's concrete interests in specific periods have varied under different historical conditions.[12] The analysis of these variations that produced different degrees of passivism and activism in the international arena will also be addressed.

The fact that Mexican foreign policy has developed primarily in a political, juridical, and institutional environment has led a good number of Mexican and U.S. scholars and observers of Mexico's reality to question whether the country's foreign policy is really intended to promote national interests abroad or to serve as an instrument of domestic policy. If the latter is the case, the logic of a specific foreign policy action in addressing an international issue will be reduced as it seeks rather to respond to the requirements and demands of domestic politics. As a notable American citizen queried: "In addition to principles, what else is there in Mexico's foreign policy? Has Mexico only principles, and no interests?"

---

[11]Humberto Garza Elizondo, "Desequilibrios y contradicciones en la política exterior de México," *Foro Internacional* 24:4 (April-June 1984): 446.

[12]For a rejection of the so-called "myth of the mechanical use of the principles of foreign policy," see Ricardo Valero, "La obligación del exterior," *Nexos* 102 (June 1986): 42.

This kind of question is neither wholly unjustified nor the result of ethnocentric attitudes. These questions underscore the need to delve deeply into the analysis of the real interests of Mexican foreign policy as they have been defined by foreign policy makers and the basic perceptions which guide them.

Unfortunately, the undervaluation of the legalism of Mexico's foreign policy has reduced scholarly interest in this topic. In the theoretical literature on foreign policy, studies of the international behavior of small or developing countries have appeared only recently. The assumption in the past has been that the foreign policy of such countries, given their low profile on the world scene, merely "reflects" the policies of the major countries or represents a set of futile reactions to the international dynamic. The Third World's emergence as a world political force in the 1970s modified this image and gave rise to the proliferation of studies about the foreign policies of these small and developing countries.

Based on the preceding, the present essay focuses on three tasks:

• To describe and characterize the premises (conceptions, views) on which Mexico's foreign policy has been founded (an effort of historical interpretation).

• To identify the factors which led Mexico to adopt these premises, the so-called "roots of foreign policy."

• To determine whether the conditioning factors of foreign policy which prevail in both the international and domestic arenas have altered during the 1980s. That is, have changes in its political system, its development model, and the world context led Mexico to reexamine the basic premises that have guided its international behavior. To this end, the paper considers the impact of the current debate promoted by the Salinas administration on the need to modernize foreign policy.

To return to our first objective—to describe the premises underlying Mexico's foreign policy—many Mexican and North American scholars (Ojeda, Astiz, Bender, Green, Pellicer, and Shapira, among others) have identified and analyzed the convictions that have traditionally underlain Mexico's foreign policy. Thus, a significant portion of our analysis is based on previous works and on a review of the official foreign policy record.[13]

---

[13]For this task the review of the four volumes that conform the work *Política exterior de México. 175 años de historia*, edited by the Foreign Relations Ministry in 1985, was of great help.

In this case, the starting point is not a detailed historical research, but rather a general interpretative effort to grasp the implicit and explicit foreign policy premises prevailing to the present.

In relation to the second objective—why Mexico adopted certain premises rather than others—within the broad spectrum of theoretical approaches and analytical perspectives that have been developed to study the international behavior and foreign policy of medium and small countries, we find constant references to three determining factors at the macrostructural level.

The first factor—or, more appropriately, set of factors—derive from the country's geopolitical reality, especially if this reality is viewed as relatively permanent. This factor gains importance in defining maneuvering space, and restrictions on it, in countries which find themselves in markedly asymmetrical or unstable geopolitical contexts.

The second set of factors pertain to the economic realm: The degree to which a country is integrated into the world economy and its overall model of economic development go a long way in determining that country's sensitivity, or vulnerability, to the outside and its goals in the foreign policy field.

Third are those factors relating to the historical and institutional "forging" of the country's political system and that system's success in preserving internal political stability. Together, these factors exert an intense and direct impact on foreign policy. It is within the domestic arena that the content and scope of a country's national interest are defined. And these two determinants, in turn, define the logic of foreign policy.

Turning to the third objective—to determine if changes have occurred—I would suggest that the new conditions which emerged in the early years of this decade—in both the domestic and international arenas—will force a reevaluation of some of the basic assumptions on which Mexico's foreign policy has rested. Substantial changes in the attitudes toward Mexico's ties to the world economy have produced commercial opening and rapprochement with the United States, Canada, and Japan. These changes make it more difficult to articulate the political and economic dimensions of Mexican foreign policy. The current transitional process in internal politics, along with the economic modernization project, are factors which may well modify the basic terms of reference for Mexico's international behavior, particularly its element of traditional nationalism.

BASIC FOREIGN POLICY THESES

I will discuss two general elements of Mexico's international profile before undertaking a more thorough characterization of the premises upon which Mexican foreign policy rests, as well as of the determining factors that have shaped it:

First, Mexico is an inward-looking country. It has no expansionist ambitions or program to promote its political and economic values abroad. Thus, its national project has not been conceived in terms of a need or ability to project beyond national borders, nor has there been a practical need to undertake permanent and continuous foreign activity. Ideas such as territorial expansion and the foreign promotion of political values have been absent from Mexican conceptions of foreign policy. The idea of creating a national zone of influence emerged briefly during the nineteenth century in relation to Central America. But what has been a crucial element is Mexico's desire to provide political leadership in promoting certain shared values among specific groups of countries. Witness Mexico's efforts to organize a community of Latin American countries, and its recent activities to promote Third World interests.

Because Mexico has tended to look inward—an orientation imposed both by the magnitude of its domestic problems and its limited room for maneuver externally—its foreign policy was not designed as a mechanism of entrenchment (to stop the enemy, to isolate Mexico from the negative impact of foreign factors). Essentially, it has been a *defensive* policy. It has declined to define interests beyond its borders, although these may be deduced from Mexico's international behavior, a feature shared by other countries. Mexico has always focused its attention on domestic concerns; when it looked beyond national borders, it did so with great caution:

> Instead of looking outward, Mexico turned inward toward achieving a rather impressive record of political stability and economic development. The outside world was regarded as a hostile and dangerous force and the role of foreign policy was to insulate the internal efforts to make Mexico a viable nation from the Cold War and global conflict.[14]

---

[14]Guy Poitras, "Mexico's Foreign Policy in an Age of Interdependence," p. 103.

This view, which recognized the importance of the external—but more as a source of evil than of opportunities—has persisted throughout Mexico's history. Why has this "negative-pessimistic" view predominated? This question permeates much of the following discussion.

A second element of Mexico's international profile is that in its scope, its foreign policy assumes a restrictive view of the methods and instruments to be utilized and of the foreign arena of action in which to operate. This restricted view derives from Mexico's tacit acknowledgement of its structural limitations, most the result of its geopolitical context.

This explains why Mexico's foreign policy comes into play almost exclusively in the political, juridical, and institutional realms of foreign activity, and within the framework of hemispheric relations. It is a *regional*, rather than *global*, actor, which considers diplomacy as the basis or core of its foreign activity: promoting guidelines for coexistence, downplaying the use of economic instruments, and completely rejecting the option of military force.

CONDITIONING FACTORS

Geopolitical Foundations

Mexico's foreign policy principles and foundations can be best understood in the context of geopolitics. It is hard to comprehend Mexico's noninterventionist zeal and historical insistence on self-determination without taking into consideration the difficulties inherent in undertaking and carrying out an autonomous, sovereign national plan on the doorstep of the world's most powerful nation.

Since attaining independence, Mexico has carried out its domestic and foreign programs while always bearing in mind the proximity of a militarily stronger country that, from its beginnings, held expansionist ambitions. The 1848 war with the United States, the loss of half of Mexico's territory to the United States, and the threatened use of force which continued into this century during the Mexican Revolution illustrate clearly that Mexico's national plan cannot depend on the use of force to any significant degree.

If we consider Mexico's geopolitical borders, both on land and at sea, we find that since the nineteenth century they formed part of a much larger geopolitical border, part of a global project which has historically limited any expansionist aspirations that Mexico might have had.

Convinced by the forces of history, Mexico has been a peaceful, pacifist country. Her foreign policy has traditionally espoused peaceful settlement of disputes and nonuse of force in international relations. It could hardly be otherwise for a state, wise enough to survive, whose expansionistic adventures in any direction would immediately be curbed and blocked by far superior forces and would almost certainly cost more than they were worth. Self-determination, nonintervention, peaceful settlement of disputes, and nonuse of force in international relations have therefore become constants in Mexico's foreign policy that historically are more than justified.

For many analysts, Mexico's traditional adherence to international legal standards is but a reflection of intrinsic weakness in the face of threats which, if carried out, would be almost impossible to confront with any reasonable expectation of victory. The fact is that the best weapon is the one that works for the purpose for which it is brandished. In this sense, international policy based on these principles has certainly proved effective in safeguarding the sovereignty and territorial and political integrity of the Mexican state since the second half of the nineteenth century.

In general terms, Mexico's geopolitical standing has conferred three central and constant traits on its foreign policy. First is the absence of a military component in conceptions of national security and in strategies for dealing with other countries. This is explained, on the one hand, by the impossibility of winning a military confrontation with its powerful neighbor to the north and, on the other, by the protective coverage of the U.S. security umbrella in case of extra-hemispheric threats. This geostrategic situation and the low military profile in Mexico's foreign presence account, in part, for its interest in promoting regional and international détente and disarmament.

Second is the impossibility of developing expansionistic geopolitical interests within what is the country's only natural sphere of influence, since this is encompassed by the geographic perimeter considered to be a "strategic imperative" of the security system of the United States as a world power. Any attempt to expand Mexico's economic and political presence in the Caribbean and Central American region faces the inevitable risk of competition and confrontation with the United States.

The third trait of Mexico's foreign policy is the decisive impact of proximity to the United States. This factor has shaped not only the order of priorities and the high degree of concentration of Mexico's foreign relations but also, and perhaps more importantly, the country's economic development process and the internal structuring of its national political plan.

Convergence and Coincidence

Administering foreign policy became more complicated for Mexico with the emergence of the United States as the most powerful country in the world. Mexico remained neutral during World War I, with no important implications for the U.S.-Mexican relationship. The armed revolution in Mexico was at its peak, and economic interaction was limited to certain specific fields in which there were large U.S. investments.

By World War II, scenarios were very different. Mexico was entering a period of political and social organization that, up to a point, was consolidating the gains of the Mexican Revolution; meanwhile the United States was developing as the foremost world power. On the one hand, Mexican neutrality would have been politically inadequate. On another, taking part in the Allied cause opened channels of economic interaction that would be highly beneficial for Mexico. The war facilitated very astute political actions such as the expropriation of the oil companies. It invigorated important sectors of the economy that complemented and covered areas of production that concentrated on the war supply effort in the United States. The need for labor led to the first agreement on migratory workers. In exchange for its alliance, the United States tolerated certain Mexican acts of sovereignty, such as refusing entry to troops who were to install U.S. military bases in Mexico. In spite of U.S. displeasure over the oil expropriation, four years later Mexico was able to restructure her debt—outstanding for several decades—under very favorable terms and shortly thereafter received the first credits from the U.S. Eximbank, as well as major financing for agricultural and infrastructural projects, including some in the oil sector. Perhaps the most important element produced by the context of world war was the laying of a foundation on which to build a permanent accommodation between the U.S. and Mexican governments after the Revolution. It was in this context that the economic and political transformations launched by the revolutionary process in Mexico under the model of a mixed economy and a strong reform state—quite a different approach from prevailing U.S. political trends—were recognized as irreversible facts.

From then on, the dynamics of interplay between the two economies became an ever-present constant at the top of the bilateral agenda. Mexico found in the United States its main export market and chief source of financing. For the United States, Mexico became a natural sphere of economic expansion, one of its primary customers and an attractive destination for new investments. Mexico's economic development plan needed a protective shield to nurture its budding industry, but the dynamism of the U.S. economy was so wide-ranging that this did not become an obstacle to emphasizing and, gradually, to deepening the process of interaction. The United States found an important market for its capital goods and a supplier of raw materials and cheap labor.

By the late forties, the compatibility between Mexico's development style and the buoyant U.S. economy was evident to any observer. Politically Mexico, as a sovereign state, maintained its margins of independence. The country's international policy, considered "passive" by many analysts, avoided trouble, quarrels, or confrontations with the United States. The Mexican political system, although already considered imperfect by the doctrinal purists of U.S. democracy, proved to be perfectly operative for the relationship between the two nations, a practicality which took precedence over quibbling about nuances.

New Scenarios, New Problems

In the seventies, a new stage began in the relationship between the two countries. The golden years, the years of the misnamed "special relationship," clouded over, thanks to both internal and external factors. At the beginning of the decade, the United States experienced its first postwar economic crisis; among the measures to counteract the crisis was a special import duty which seriously affected Mexican exports. The Mexican government decided to regulate foreign investment, particularly targeting U.S. firms; and the United States, for its part, multiplied nontariff restrictions on Mexican products. Migratory workers came to be viewed as a problem in the United States, and the issue of drug trafficking took on political overtones and became an instrument of pressure.

Mexico, for the first time, undertook a global foreign policy with strong Third World rhetoric. Although this move did not produce spectacular results or accomplish the basic objective of diversifying economic relations so as to decrease dependence on the United States, it did manage to plant the seeds of political friction and divergence. The golden years of the "special relationship" faded into the past.

Mexico's economy grew and developed. The political system, with its quirks and unique features, had achieved a high degree of consolidation. Caution and prudence, characteristic of the governments of the previous two decades, were cast aside to make way for greater boldness, reflected in the economic plan and in greater foreign policy activism.

Mexico's administrations thought that the country was now strong enough and had the international standing to carry out its more active policy—which not only consolidated its principles with highly symbolic political actions, such as its traditional position on Cuba, but also sought to increase its actions' impact on international events. This position was applied to global and multilateral problems as well as to its geopolitical borders, especially at sea, with Mexico's more active involvement in the crisis in Central America as the Sandinista revolution was about to triumph in Nicaragua.

Then Mexico's economic plan got out of hand. Based on discoveries of extensive oil deposits, Mexico wagered on the permanence of this asset as a multibillion-dollar source of outside resources. While the world economy was going through a serious recession, Mexico grew at the brisk clip of 8 percent, for which purpose it could count on abundant financial surpluses in the international market. A heady Mexico operated with enormous flexibility in regard to debt limits, overvaluation, unbalanced budgeting, and overheating of the economy. By 1982, with the decline in oil prices, Mexico's trump card vanished and the avalanche of economic growth ended in an unprecedented balance of payments crisis: depletion of international resources, a current account deficit, a plunging exchange rate, mass capital flight, and a historically unimaginable budget deficit.

The Changing Economic Environment

The main challenge facing the administration entering office at the end of 1982 was to overcome modern Mexico's most acute economic crisis ever. By that time, the era of the "special relationship" was not just a vague memory; there was even doubt as to whether it had indeed ever existed. To resolve the crisis, the Mexican government had to resort to an unparalleled internal adjustment as almost the sole available instrument. Economic growth ground to a halt. Before getting back on the road to growth, Mexico has had to make far-reaching structural adjustments aimed at a structural change in the economy. This has been deemed the only viable means of regaining a growth track without falling back into the structural problems which sparked the crisis. External circumstances proved to be highly unfavorable and, together with natural disasters, prolonged the adjustment process and made it increasingly costly in terms of growth and therefore in terms of the well-being of the population.

Things were not much better in other countries. Unfavorable economic conditions persisted. Mexico disciplined herself internally and, within certain limits, managed to hold on to external financial relations which, nevertheless, became increasingly debilitating and decreasingly productive. Moves to open up the economy led to positive results such as unprecedented dynamism in the export sector and complete stabilization of the balance of payments. Economic recovery, though, remained out of reach. Prospects of a recession in the U.S. economy grew and basic external variables such as interest rates, oil prices, and new waves of protectionism led to greater uncertainty about the immediate future.

During this period, bilateral economic relations have not given Mexico much elbowroom. Outside pressures have come from international financial organizations as well as from creditor banks, with the U.S. government stepping in whenever the situation appears about to cave in. On the trade front, unprecedented growth in Mexican exports has run into a gradual increase in nontariff barriers which in some cases could not be offset by the permanent margin of undervaluation, this sector's primary stimulus. Therefore, and despite "good behavior," Mexico, after five years of adjustment programs, finds herself with little chance of getting back on the road to growth.

Differences with the United States

As far as the United States is concerned, Mexico's economic performance has been satisfactory. Internal adjustment and economic opening have led to more investment opportunities and greater trade penetration. The social cost of the adjustment has not yet shown up on the bottom line. And yet, on the bilateral agenda, pressures have increased.

Rigorous legislation on migratory workers—enacted on the basis of a highly politicized approach that disregarded the economic nature of the phenomenon—has had a pernicious effect on the mood of the relationship. The drug traffic problem took on unparalleled proportions on the bilateral agenda and translated into heavy-handed political pressure. Mexico's position on Central America, maintained and even intensified during the de la Madrid administration, has become a permanent point of disagreement permeating the entire relationship. Differing positions in multilateral organizations, where the United States had shown a wide margin of tolerance, have also become a source of friction and greater estrangement.

Intolerance, intransigence, and communications problems have become recurring components in the bilateral relationship. As meetings between presidents and government missions at all levels multiplied as never before, both differences and efforts to remedy them became more difficult and complex. Minor discrepancies turned into stumbling blocks, and points of agreement slipped through our fingers.

MEXICO IN TRANSITION

The changing scenarios of Mexico's internal structures require a more detailed analysis of her foreign policy. Since the early seventies, Mexico has been undergoing a period of change whose scope and duration are hard to pin down. In the process, the evolution of foreign policy inescapably became more complex.

By definition, foreign policy is an extension and corollary of internal policy. In the midst of internal changes, it is unlikely indeed that foreign policy can remain undisturbed. By its very nature, a country's foreign policy should be coherent with its internal status and make the internal process as suitable as possible to the also-changing international system.

In Mexico's case, the changes that took place during the seventies and eighties have proved to be of greater transcendence. Mexico's international position, however, has been complicated by the fact that, unlike at other moments in its history, the rest of the countries and variables in the international system are also in a process of transformation or adjustment. How, then, are Mexico's internal changes reflected in her foreign policy?

Economic Transformation: Crisis and Structural Change

Over the past fifteen years, Mexico has gone through cyclical periods of economic instability. This has been due to several factors, both internal and external. At the beginning of the seventies, certain problems in the economic development model all over the world had accumulated and turned critical. This was, as mentioned above, precisely the time when the first relatively serious postwar crisis had sprung up in the U.S. economy. This combination of internal and external variables would recur.

After a serious balance of payments crisis in 1979, a vastly ambitious economic plan was undertaken on the basis of oil revenues; when this income dropped off, the mirage vanished and again the combination of internal and external factors produced a new crisis, far more severe than the previous one.

The de la Madrid government, entering office in December of 1982, took off in the eye of the hurricane with a greatly reduced range of action, with errors accumulated from previous administrations, and with more realistic expectations regarding the international situation. The only viable option available to the new administration was that of structural change, i.e., coming up with in-depth solutions to structural problems. In this process, which implied sharp internal economic adjustment, external variables were fully involved. Mexico's developmental challenges were as demanding as were the obstacles to be overcome. Savings and financing were needed for investment, but foreign indebtedness of spectacular dimensions had to be dealt with concurrently.

Foreign exchange was urgently needed, and the nonpetroleum export sector did not seem to have the competitiveness and aggressiveness required to solve the problem. Mexico urgently needed to reorganize public considers finances at a time when the lack of internal and external savings had significantly reduced the range of options.

It was within this dynamic interplay that economic policy decisions would have tremendous influence on foreign policy. Structural adjustment provided for economic opening as a fundamental step. Toward this end, a gradual process of trade liberalization was begun and then stressed with the recurring crises. An aggressive foreign exchange policy promoted the export sector and produced the hoped for results. Significant progress was made in managing foreign debt, one of the most complex aspects faced by the administration, but indebtedness continued to be a serious obstacle to development. Foreign investment was promoted as never before, as was the proliferation of in-bond plants (*maquiladoras*), particularly along the northern border. On the multilateral scene, Mexico signed the protocol to join GATT.

All these decisions on economic policy, involving other countries as they did, had extremely far-reaching consequences on foreign policy. In the first place, the economic crisis in a way gave foreign economic relations priority and new dimensions. The mechanisms for economic and financial matters would adopt a more activist stance abroad. In most cases, this involved circumventing the political apparatus, leading more than once to apparent contradictions. Perhaps the most significant aspect of this was the divergence in sectoral priorities concerning the relationship with the United States. Those who were concerned with the economic situation considered a positive tone for bilateral relations with the United States to be essential and found Mexico's Central American policy an unnecessarily disruptive factor in that regard.

Second, the plan for opening up the economy, implemented so thoroughly and quickly, was to have an exceedingly important impact on Mexico's interaction with most of the economic and financial participants on the international scene. The process of assimilating these new interactions, however, would affect most of Mexico's public and private economic relations abroad and encompass large sectors of society. Accelerated trade liberalization, greater receptiveness to foreign investment, and the promotion of in-bond operations were considered by some sectors as part of a gradual process of integration into the U.S. economy, with serious implications for the sovereignty and independence of national planning and, thus, with substantive effects on the very philosophy of foreign policy.

Finally, there was the nagging concern that an uncompromising process of economic opening would result in increasing internationalization of the external variables. In other words, given the disparity in Mexico's level of development as compared to the major economies, particularly the United States and Japan, external factors and pressures would increasingly influence national planning decisions directly or indirectly. This, in turn, would have a significant effect on national independence and sovereignty.

Be that as it may, what is clear is that the depth and scope of the process begun by de la Madrid to open up the economy have made it an irreversible phenomenon. Its refinement and its implications for foreign policy in the broadest terms, however, are not yet perfectly clear.

The Political System: Deterioration and Transition

Since the late sixties, there has been talk of deterioration in the political system and—in recurring cycles, and above all from foreign observers—speculation on imminent outbreaks of political and social unrest. Representatives of the system, at least in their social rhetoric, repeatedly affirm that the political system's institutions and structures are stronger than ever.

It is true that economic crisis, a subject on which Mexico has had a great deal to say in recent years, carries with it a series of political and social effects whose magnitude and consequences will vary in proportion to the dimensions and length of the crisis and the firmness of the other components of the social apparatus. In the case of Mexico, over the past five years even expectations of improvement have lost a large part of their psychological power—due to the continual process of adjustment without growth that has resulted from the combination of internal and external factors. The defects and inadequacies of the political system have been discussed with increasing vehemence. When the state and, in particular, the government fail to provide what most of the public considers to be a satisfactory response to national problems, there will of necessity be more lively debate and a greater desire to participate.

At this point we must analyze equations such as legitimacy versus political control, "pure democracy" versus "democracy *a la mexicana*," or even authoritarianism versus participation. For the purposes of analysis, however, I shall attempt to situate the present political process in relation to other processes and to its implications for foreign policy. We may take as our point of departure the fact that, given an economic modernization process that includes structural change by way of increased opening to foreign countries and has extremely wide-ranging consequences on society as a whole, remaining structures can hardly stay exactly the same. China's recent crisis and Soviet *perestroika* stand as examples.

Whatever the force driving change—structural paralysis of the system or the need for political adaptation to economic modernization or both—the fact is that the Mexican political system is also in a process of transition. It may not be changing at the rate of the economic modernization and it may still suffer from important deficiencies regarding the definition of its stages and particular characteristics, but what does seem clear is that the political system cannot cling to outmoded forms and traditional principles without becoming highly dysfunctional in the twenty-first century.

The stage of transition and eventual transformation of the Mexican political system of necessity has extremely important implications for foreign policy. When internal policy is closely linked to foreign policy and is simultaneously undergoing important changes, foreign policy is sure to lag behind. It is no coincidence that while the mechanisms in charge of implementing international economic policy act quickly and decisively, the political relations apparatus faces much greater difficulties in definition and implementation. As will be seen below, this makes the Mexican state and government more vulnerable to outside pressure, since the problems of internal legitimacy and coherence are reflected abroad and can be taken advantage of there.

Principles and Foundations of Foreign Policy in the New Scenarios

If we consider the fundamental principles of foreign policy under current scenarios in light of geopolitical conditioning factors, we find that peaceful settlement of controversies, nonuse of force in international relations, self-determination, and nonintervention still hold as basic principles. Even cooperation for development, now more than ever, is justifiable within the Mexican state's international political philosophy. Nonetheless, if we consider the present political and economic scenarios described above, we will uncover new challenges and prospects for Mexico's foreign policy. Although they do not exclude these basic principles, these changes may represent a new dimension in the challenges and scope of foreign policy.

During this decade, Mexican foreign policy has faced an extraordinarily complex scenario in which at least three situations of change converge and interact: regional crisis, economic crisis, and internal political transformation. In the field of geopolitical conditions, the existence of a regional crisis over the Central American conflict has directly impacted Mexico's internal political life (through a growing flow of Central American refugees into Mexican territory) and the country's foreign relations (intensification of border frictions with Guatemala and of diplomatic differences and tensions with the United States, historically an item on the hemispheric agenda). This situation has produced some important changes in the self-definition of Mexican foreign policy and the scope of its activity and presence abroad.

Concepts such as *national interest* and *national security* have entered the public handling of foreign policy. They are used as objective elements that justify and make explicit the way in which implementation of certain external actions not only contributes to upholding the validity of the doctrinal corpus of principles as part of a natural national historic tradition which is a source of internal legitimacy, but also obeys pragmatic reasons and interests both internally and externally. Such interests include: maintaining stable geopolitical surroundings that reduce the potential for conflict on both the northern and southern borders; maintaining internal political equilibrium in the face of developments within the political forces on the left; curbing the potential for greater military involvement in the civil government's priorities; and isolating the Mexican political system from possible Cuban-Soviet influence by recognizing the legitimacy of the processes of change in the region and establishing cordial relations with regimes with diverse political tendencies.

In this area, Mexico is constantly facing the problem, on the one hand, of following a foreign policy line on the Central American region that not only is absolutely consistent with national historic tradition but also responds to objective national interests, and, on the other, of avoiding unnecessary tensions and frictions with the United States that might hinder proper handling and negotiation of the complex network of issues that make up the bilateral agenda. What is in question here is not whether to modify the first part of the equation in an attempt to change the second, but rather how to develop a strategy of bilateral communication that will allow for the appropriate political handling of objective differences.

However, it is not just the external geopolitical environment that has become more complicated. The internal economic and political context within which foreign policy is formulated and shaped shows a panorama of profound transformations at a time when the country is in a position of relative weakness. These factors lead us to propound the thesis that Mexico's foreign policy is now more complex than ever—because of reasons that have as much to do with increasingly close internal/external linkage as with expansion of the spheres of interest and number of participants covered by the foreign policy arena, and with changes in the order of priorities due to the increased weight of economic questions vis-à-vis the political affairs agenda.

Foreign Policy Complexity

Due to both internal and external factors, foreign policy has become increasingly complex. Internal changes, together with processes of transformation abroad, have resulted in the need for a series of sometimes quick-paced adjustments and adaptations that may make inadequate a foreign policy that is based on general principles only. In this sense, it is not a problem of obsolescence of the fundamental principles, but rather of their inability to encompass diverse and altering challenges. Here it seems that the measures which have been implemented in order to adapt to new internal and external scenarios have surpassed the range of action of the basic standards.

Although the complex scenario of changing internal and external realities described above signals a moment of important transition, it does not indicate an in-depth break with the past bases and foundations of Mexican foreign policy. Instead, what these realities bring to the fore is the need for a readaptation of strategies, a clearer definition of the concrete short- and mid-range objectives, better articulation of the various items on the foreign agenda, and the modernization and expansion of the instruments available to foreign policy.

At a time of intense internal transitions, foreign policy will play a central role in providing a wide range of opportunities for internal social forces to have a voice in redefining the national plan that will make it more solid, democratic, and pluralistic.

3

Foundations and Premises of United States Foreign Policy

Lars Schoultz

A few years ago, political scientist Jorge Domínguez wrote that "the defense of the United States depends in part on the cooperation of others such as Mexico, France, and West Germany."[1] When I first read this statement, I was conducting interviews in Washington on the subject of U.S. national security interests in Latin America, and so I incorporated Domínguez's comment into my interview questionnaire. I quickly discovered that this type of statement does not sit well with the many U.S. policymakers who think of Mexico as the land of enchiladas and marijuana. In public comments, these officials will be appropriately diplomatic. Like President Reagan, they will talk about how "we have built a relationship that is mature and mutually respectful," and they will compare Mexico "with any other important country such as the United Kingdom, France, or Japan."[2] But in private conversations, these officials will quickly concede the need for cooperation with the people who invented quiche and perfected the BMW; but it is difficult, they will say, to conceive of U.S. security resting upon cooperation with a people whose major achievement is the tortilla.

The issues that define the relationship between the United States and Mexico test the wisdom and patience of even the best-

---

[1]Jorge I. Domínguez, *U.S. Interests and Policies in the Caribbean and Central America* (Washington, D.C.: American Enterprise Institute, 1982), p. 31.
[2]*Weekly Compilation of Presidential Documents* 22 (January 6, 1986): pp. 6-7.

informed ar.d well-intentioned group of concerned citizens; to add problems of negative cultural stereotypes and prejudices makes all the more difficult any effort to create a relationship that is, in fact, mature and mutually respectful.

The purpose of this paper is to make a modest contribution to the creation of this relationship by examining the beliefs and perceptions that underlie U.S. foreign policy. This paper explores the linkage between U.S. foreign policy interests, on the one hand, and Washington's rapidly changing relationship with Latin America (and especially Mexico), on the other. It begins with an introductory section that focuses upon the global context of postwar U.S. foreign policy, then turns to a more detailed discussion of how Latin America (including Mexico) has been perceived within the general pattern of U.S. foreign policy concerns. After that, a final section examines how these perceptions have changed in the years since World War II, and what consequences these changes might have for the definition and pursuit of new policy alternatives.

THE GLOBAL CONTEXT

Since the end of World War II, the foreign policy of the United States has been dedicated to the containment of communism. The United States pursues this policy because of the belief that Soviet communism is a threat to U.S. peace and security. The 1982 Department of Defense "Assessment of the Global Military Situation" captures perfectly this fundamental premise of postwar U.S. foreign policy: "The Soviet Union poses a greater danger to the American people than any other foreign power in our history. Only the Soviet Union has the power to inflict tens of millions of casualties on our population. Only the Soviet Union has massive and modern conventional and nuclear forces deployed, directly confronting our friends and allies in Europe and Asia. Only the Soviet Union has the forces and geographic proximity to threaten the free world's major source of energy."

In a sense, this statement is endorsed by all U.S. policymakers. The Soviets obviously constitute a credible threat. Moscow's strength dictates that the United States focus its foreign policy upon deterring the use of Soviet power. No one questions the simple historical observation that the survival of any nation requires a prudent regard for the physical strength of any potential adversary.

But most of the officials who have been responsible for U.S. foreign policy during the 1980s believe that the Soviet Union is, in addition to being powerful, possessed by an ideological curse—communism. The result is demonic. President Reagan remarked in 1982 that "the record is clear. Nowhere in its whole sordid history have the promises of communism been redeemed. Everywhere it has exploited and aggravated temporary economic suffering to seize power and then institutionalize economic deprivation and depress human rights." A year later Mr. Reagan characterized Soviet communism as "the focus of evil in the modern world."

To these policymakers, the U.S.-Soviet rivalry is no mere political dispute; it is an issue of fundamental morality. At his first press conference, President Reagan asserted that the Soviets "reserve unto themselves the right to commit any crime, to lie, to cheat"; on the other hand, "we operate on a different set of standards." Two years later, Mr. Reagan argued that "Soviet leaders have openly and publicly declared that the only morality they recognize is that which will further their cause, which is world revolution." To Secretary of State Shultz, "the fundamental difference between East and West is not in economic, or social policy, though those policies differ radically, but in the moral principles on which they are based. It is the difference between tyranny and freedom—an age-old struggle in which the United States never could, and cannot today, remain neutral."

Added to the belief that the Soviet Union is inherently evil is a closely related belief that communism is driven by the dictates of its ideology to relentless expansion. "Let's not delude ourselves," Mr. Reagan told an audience on the campaign trail in 1980, "the Soviet Union underlies all the unrest that is going on. If they weren't engaged in this game of dominoes, there wouldn't be any hot spots in the world." Why do they stir up trouble everywhere? "We know that the ideology of the Soviet leaders does not permit them to leave any western weakness unprobed, any vacuum unfilled," President Reagan told a Los Angeles audience in 1983. In 1984, Secretary of State Shultz reiterated this view of expansionism as a metaphysical imperative of the Soviet character: "The Soviet Union, most importantly and uniquely, is driven not only by Russian history and Soviet state interest but also by what remains of its revolutionary ideology to spread its system by force." Like an untreated cancer, the Soviet menace is compelled by its nature to attempt to spread until it destroys Western civilization.

Yet despite these apparently unchangeable negative images of Soviet communism, the end of the Reagan era seems to be coinciding with the beginning of a new period of détente with the Soviet Union. The leaders of the two superpowers are exchanging visits, and arms reduction treaties are being negotiated and signed. In early 1988, the "focus of evil" language used five years earlier seems oddly anachronistic.

It is possible that the flowering of détente may lead to a change in the hard-line East-West confrontational framework that has dominated U.S.-Latin American relations during the 1980s. Since all regions of the world are interdependent, a significant change in U.S.-Soviet relations will inevitably have some impact on U.S. policy toward Latin America. But not much. This is because the Latin American policy of the United States is governed by a logic of its own that is relatively immune to policy changes elsewhere. This policy is only accidentally (and, history tells us, temporarily) related to the issue of containing communism; indeed, the fundamental logic of U.S. policy toward Latin America antedates the policy of containment by more than a century.

STABILITY IN LATIN AMERICA

"Since the early nineteenth century, the primary interest of the United States in Latin America has been to have the area be a peaceful, secure southern flank."[3] Thus begins the brief discussion of Latin America in the most widely adopted national security textbook of our time. Few U.S. citizens recognize how difficult it is for policymakers to be given these obvious but vague goals— peace and security—and told to convert them into concrete public policy. It is a staggering task.

Because no one in the United States knows how to make Latin America peaceful and secure, U.S. policymakers tend to replace these goals with something that is related but more concrete— something that can be implemented: stability. For more than a century, officials in Washington have determined that stability is the means that would best promote the macrogoals of peace and security, and then they have converted that means into the goal of U.S. policy. This conversion process is not peculiar to inter-

---

[3]Amos A. Jordan and William J. Taylor, Jr., *American National Policy and Process* (Baltimore: Johns Hopkins University Press, 1981), p. 436.

American relations. "Because most important goals (e.g., security, high influence) are too general to provide guidelines for actions," Jervis notes, "actors must establish subgoals (e.g., strong alliances, military preponderance) that are believed to contribute to the higher ones." Subgoals (means) are thereby transformed into ends, and they "often come to be valued for their own sakes, especially when their attainment requires a great deal of time, effort, and attention."[4] Particularly in large bureaucracies, the mere act of doing something (ensuring stability) in time tends to become divorced from the goals (peace and security) that the act was intended to achieve.

In the aftermath of World War II, the United States passed through a brief period during which it felt obliged to commit whatever resources were necessary to ensure stability throughout the non-communist world. We called that policy containment. Billions of dollars and tens of thousands of soldiers' lives were invested in securing the peace in such faraway places as Southeast Asia. After the sobering experience of Vietnam, however, Washington's ambitions moderated. They seemed to rise again in the early Reagan era, but after the debacle in Lebanon they quietly receded, so that by 1987 the administration had considerable difficulty obtaining the imperfect consensus it needed in order to move naval vessels into the Persian Gulf to protect petroleum shipments. For better or for worse, today the "bear any burden, pay any price" language that symbolized the Kennedy commitment to stability has become a curious relic of an overly ambitious era. Now policymakers have more modest goals. Peace, operationalized by a subgoal—the absence of instability in countries ruled by governments friendly toward the United States—is perceived as a requirement of U.S. security in a more limited number of places. For most U.S. policymakers, Latin America remains one such place.

The high value most policymakers place upon stability in Latin America is not a peculiar feature of the Cold War era. The quest for stability has been the basis for U.S. policy toward Latin America for nearly two centuries. The early twentieth century, for example, was not unlike today. Kane tells us that "the constant state of political disorder in the Caribbean was generally regarded by American military strategists with something approaching horror."[5] To Theodore Roosevelt, "the specter of German aggression in the

---

[4]Robert Jervis, *Perception and Misperception in International Politics* (Princeton, N.J.: Princeton University Press, 1976), pp. 411-12.
[5]William Everett Kane, *Civil Strife in Latin America: A Legal U.S. Involvement* (Baltimore: Johns Hopkins University Press, 1972), p. 60.

Caribbean or elsewhere in Latin America became a veritable night-mare with him. He was absolutely convinced that the Kaiser would one day start trouble somewhere in this hemisphere."[6] Over time, the precise *form* of the threat has changed, but the *nature* of the threat has remained fairly constant. This nature was identified in 1904 by President Roosevelt as "a general loosening of the ties of civilized society"—instability.

This basic causal linkage between instability in Latin America and a threat to U.S. security is the cognitive bedrock of U.S. policy toward Latin America. But why should the United States feel threat-ened by instability in Latin America? Unlike most of the other major land divisions of the globe, the United States does not want much from Latin America. Unlike the Middle East, southern Africa, Europe, or Japan, there is very little *in* Latin America that the United States must have in order for U.S. citizens to continue living in the style to which they have become accustomed.

In the area of raw materials, for example, with the notable exception of petroleum from Mexico and bauxite from Jamaica and the Guianas, the United States is not dependent upon access to supplies from Latin America. On other issues of economic access to Latin America, U.S. private investments and bank loans are important—sometimes crucially so—to a number of U.S.-based corporations, but not to the United States as a nation. With the exception of unpaid and unpayable bank loans, which will require some creative bookkeeping, all U.S. investments in Latin America could disappear tomorrow without causing a significant problem for the U.S. economy. Xabier Gorostiaga often notes that the Cen-tral American republics have "dessert economies"—fruits, sugar, non-nutritive beverages—an observation that could be applied to most of the rest of Latin America as well. If necessary, we can skip dessert.

In the areas of military bases and military support, access to Latin America is not of major significance to U.S. security. Hondu-ras aside (as it will be before long), the United States neither needs nor desires additional military bases in Latin America, and the value of existing bases has declined with the development of new technologies such as satellite communications. There is a particu-larly strong agreement among U.S. military officials that the United States does not need the assistance of Latin American militaries,

---

[6]Harold Sprout and Margaret Sprout, *The Rise of American Naval Power, 1776-1918* (Princeton, N.J.: Princeton University Press, 1942), p. 253.

except in cases where a multinational force is appropriate for political reasons.

On Latin American sea lines of communication, only the Caribbean is truly important. Except for an occasional speech that mentions the Panama Canal, no one in Washington worries much about the other sea lines surrounding Latin America. Of the Caribbean, no one disregards the presence of Soviet warships and no one likes the fact that the Cuban navy now includes submarines, but most officials believe that the existence of hostile maritime forces in the Caribbean poses no direct threat that is not already posed by Soviet warships elsewhere.

In short, on the question of access to Latin America, most policymakers believe that the security of the United States would not be adversely affected if Latin America were, say, to sink to the bottom of the sea. In an abstract sense that avoids the calculation of human losses, these officials would be relieved if Latin America did not exist. Given the opportunity to choose between the continued physical presence of our neighboring republics to the south, on the one hand, and a vast ocean broken only by the ice packs of Antarctica, on the other, the probability is quite high that most U.S. policymakers would select the latter option. Why? Because if the region were to disappear, then there would no longer be a need to worry about Latin America's vulnerability to Soviet adventurism. And that is the true significance of Latin America to U.S. security: it is not that policymakers want much of anything from Latin America, but rather that they do not want the Soviet Union to have it.

In 1980, Representative David Obey asked a State Department official the crucial question about the Caribbean region: "Why are we worried? They don't have any weapons to threaten us. There are lots of small countries, as you indicated. Outside of Mexico, there are not very many people. Why should we worry about them?" The response from the State Department's John Bushnell was that "the thing that tends to worry most of your constituents and most of the American people is that they have learned enough geography to know that these places are pretty close to us."[7]

Bushnell's response encapsulates perfectly the belief of many policymakers: geographic proximity dictates not only that the

---

[7]U.S. Congress, House, Committee on Appropriations, Subcommittee on Foreign Operations and Related Agencies, *Foreign Assistance and Related Programs Appropriations for 1981*, 96th Congress, Second Session, 1980, pt. 2, p. 362.

United States should fear instability in the region, but that the Soviet Union should encourage it. Having read in the *Communist Manifesto* that "communists everywhere support every revolutionary movement against the existing social and political order of things," most U.S. policymakers have been particularly wary of Soviet expansion into those areas of the world where the social and political order of things has been favorable to the United States. Latin America is one such area. So it is that for the past forty years, U.S. policy toward Latin America has been a perfect dovetail between a traditional geostrategic belief and postwar anti-communism.

The geostrategic belief is by far the more important of the two. Latin America's significance to U.S. security lies in the fact of its geographic proximity and in the belief that U.S. security requires geographic isolation—the exclusion of other powers from the hemisphere. This belief is as old as U.S. foreign policy. As James Monroe asserted in his famous message to Congress:

> The citizens of the United States cherish sentiments the most friendly in favor of the liberty and happiness of their fellow men on that side of the Atlantic.... We owe it, therefore, to candor and to the amicable relations existing between the United States and those powers, to declare that we should consider any attempt on their part to extend their system to any portion of this hemisphere as dangerous to our peace and safety.

The Monroe Doctrine struck such a responsive chord among U.S. citizens that it quickly became an integral component of the U.S. foreign policy psyche. Of course, the original focus upon incursions by the Holy Alliance in Latin America and by imperial Russia in the Pacific Northwest has, with time, given way to a focus upon European debt collectors, German imperialists, Japanese fishing interests, the Axis powers, and, most recently, Soviet communism. Underlying the specific threat at any particular moment, however, is the belief that U.S. peace and security requires that rival powers be excluded from the Western Hemisphere.

In brief, the fears many policymakers have of instability in Latin America must be understood as a logical adaptation of the Monroe Doctrine to the Cold War conditions that have existed since World War II. Most U.S. citizens have learned about the Monroe Doctrine as part of their socialization into the U.S. political system. They have learned that one reason the United States has been so successful in international relations is that it has excluded rivals from its neighborhood. Thus the threat of Soviet incursions in the hemisphere is a challenge to the nation's 200-year-old heritage of geographic isolation, a unique heritage that allows policymakers the inestimable luxury of not having to defend U.S. borders. It is a challenge to the principle that prudent people keep any potential enemy as far away as possible.

CHANGING REALITIES

Significant changes have occurred in world politics in the years since President Monroe announced his doctrine and since President Truman inaugurated the policy of containment. The examination of these changes is an essential step in understanding the future of U.S. policy toward Latin America, and especially U.S.-Mexican relations. Five changes are of primary significance: one in Latin America, two in the global environment, and two in the United States.

The first change is a remarkable *shift in Latin America's role in world politics*. In the initial era of U.S.-Latin American relations, Washington's neighbors to the south were few in number and almost completely impotent. The basic geostrategic fact governing U.S. policy early in the nineteenth century was that Latin America was not much more than territory; sparsely populated and still largely disorganized, the region had no autonomous weight in international relations. What worried leaders like James Monroe and John Quincy Adams, therefore, is that the territory of Latin America might be used by European powers to threaten U.S. security. The result was the Monroe Doctrine.

For more than a century the United States was able to enforce its policy of excluding other powers from the hemisphere. At first the principal enforcement mechanism was not U.S. power, but rather the rivalries of European powers, which served to reduce somewhat their incursions in Latin America. Later, as the United States developed its military capacities, Washington assumed responsibility for enforcing the Monroe Doctrine. For example, in an effort to keep European creditors (especially the Germans) from intervening militarily in the Caribbean region to collect debts, in 1904 President Roosevelt issued his corollary to the Monroe Doctrine:

If a nation shows that it knows how to act with reasonable efficiency and decency in social and political matters; if it keeps order and pays its obligations, it need fear no interference from the United States. Chronic wrongdoing, or an impotence which results in a general loosening of the ties of civilized society, may in America, as elsewhere, ultimately require intervention by some civilized nation, and in the Western Hemisphere the adherence of the United States to the Monroe Doctrine may force the United States, however reluctantly, in flagrant cases of such wrongdoing or impotence, to the exercise of an international police power.

In 1904 and 1914, the United States carried out brief invasions of the Dominican Republic, and then in 1916, during what the State Department called "a period of chronic and threatened insurrection" (i.e., instability), the Marines landed and occupied the country for more than eight years.

During this same era—in 1912—it appeared as if Japanese fishing interests, with linkages to the Japanese government, were about to purchase a large strip of land on Magdalena Bay, in Mexico's Baja California, from its U.S. owners. Henry Cabot Lodge, chairman of the Senate Committee on Foreign Relations, obtained the overwhelming endorsement (51 to 4) of his colleagues to a resolution proclaiming that

when any harbor or other place in the American continents is so situated that the occupation thereof for naval or military purposes might threaten the communications or the safety of the U.S., the government of the U.S. could not see without grave concern the possession of such harbor or other place by any corporation or association which has such relation to another government, not American, as to give that government practical power of control for naval or military purposes.

This, the Lodge Corollary to the Monroe Doctrine, was a clear infringement upon the sovereignty of the Mexican government. But it also was an obvious extrapolation of the geostrategic tenet that prudent policymakers keep potential adversaries as distant as possible. It applied the thinking of the father of modern U.S. naval strategy, Alfred Thayer Mahan, who wrote in 1890 that "it should be an inviolable resolution of our national policy that no foreign state should henceforth acquire a coaling position within three thousand miles of San Francisco—a distance which includes the Hawaiian and Galapagos Islands and the coast of Central America."[8]

But, as Bernard Brodie once observed, "in the field of modern strategy, time tends to deal severely with concepts as well as facts."[9] The lack of hemispheric solidarity during World War II (and especially Argentina's refusal to declare war on the Axis until about a month before Hitler's suicide) was a sobering experience for many in Washington. The basic lesson U.S. policymakers learned about inter-American relations from World War II was that Washington could not deny an extra-hemispheric adversary access to the hemisphere without the active cooperation of Latin Americans. Unlike the hundred-year period from John Quincy Adams to Alfred Thayer Mahan, by the beginning of the Cold War U.S. officials had come to recognize the existence of about 100 million people in twenty neighboring republics. And so in 1947 U.S. leaders asked the leaders of Latin America's republics to meet with them in Rio de Janeiro, where they all signed the Inter-American Treaty of Reciprocal Assistance. The Rio Treaty was an attempt to formalize what everyone in Washington presumed: that in the rapidly emerging rigid bipolar world, Latin America was going to be on the side of the United States.

The presumption was correct. After U.S. policymakers had straightened out a few kinks in the inter-American system—after they had persuaded Argentina's Peronist government to accept U.S. leadership and after they had helped overthrow Guatemala's Arbenz government in 1954—Latin America played its proper role. The inspection of a number of indicators—perhaps voting patterns in the United Nations is the best—leads to the conclusion that for a number of years most Latin American nations were Washington's toadies in international politics.

In this sense the Cuban revolution was a major watershed. It signalled the breakdown in hemispheric solidarity. Other Latin American nations (Argentina and Mexico in particular) had never

[8]Alfred Thayer Mahan, *The Interest of America in Sea Power: Present and Future*, 12th ed. (Boston: Little, Brown, 1918), p. 26.
[9]Bernard Brodie, *Strategy in the Missile Age* (Princeton, N.J.: Princeton University Press, 1965), p. v.

accepted their assigned role with any enthusiasm, and in the years since the Cuban revolution others have slowly broken away. Today, both the United States and the nations of Latin America are only nominally committed to the Rio Treaty.

There will probably never be a better example of this lack of commitment than the 1982 Falklands/Malvinas War between Argentina and Great Britain. Regardless of who was "right" or "wrong" in this 1982 crisis, the obvious contrast between U.S. behavior in this case, on the one hand, and the type of U.S. reaction that could be expected if a flotilla from any nation were sailing toward one of the United States' NATO allies, on the other, underscores the absence of a true inter-American security community. Public opinion polls indicate that those U.S. citizens who knew anything about the war sided strongly with the British, and not a few U.S. Latin Americanists (especially, in my experience, U.S. human rights activists) were silently pleased by the humiliation of the Argentine military. What the Falklands fiasco demonstrated, then, is that the Rio Treaty is a thin reed. No one could possibly conceive of it as a viable mutual security commitment.

Stated differently, with the exception of Cuba and perhaps El Salvador and Honduras, the region is largely non-aligned in the true sense of the word. One of the best of our recent ambassadors, John Crimmins, captured this non-alignment well when he reported to Congress on his last assignment, Brazil:

> Brazil has shown, certainly publicly, no readiness to enlist in a significant way with us. The current formulators and directors of Brazilian foreign policy are as bent as ever on their standing guidelines that call for the primacy of economic interests, the retention of maximum freedom of action and the avoidance of obligations that are not clearly in Brazil's interests—as that interest is defined solely by Brazil.[10]

Similarly, Mark Falcoff writes that "Argentina has its own cultural traditions and history, its own sense of self, its own aspirations for the future, and it is extremely reluctant to allow others—especially Americans, whom Argentines of all political stripes

---

[10]U.S. Congress, House, Committee on Foreign Affairs, Subcommittee on Inter-American Affairs, *United States-Brazilian Relations*, 97th Congress, Second Session, 1982, p. 39.

do not particularly like or admire—to dictate, or appear to dictate, their course of action."[11] And, of course, there is Mexico, which next to Cuba has been the least complaisant Latin American nation throughout the containment era.

In short, today only policymakers whose intellectual frame of reference remains locked upon the 1940s continue to conceive of Latin America as being on Washington's side of a rigid bipolar world. Certainly it is true that Mexico, like most of Latin America, is on the side of "the West" in an abstract sense. But in a realistic political sense, today Latin America is on its own side, and where the countries of the region sit on any specific issue depends upon how they calculate their own interests, not on how Washington or Moscow calculates the global balance of power.

One major consequence of this "new independence" is that Latin American governments today seem comfortable with an assertive role that was simply unthinkable a short while ago; they no longer follow the leader. Three examples from 1987 underscore this change.

First, of course, is the Central American peace plan. Today, if peace comes to Central America it will come through Latin American diplomacy—through Contadora, the Support Group, and the Arias Plan. It is not so much that Latin Americans have developed their own peace plan, but that the plan flies in the face of the explicitly stated policy of the United States to undermine the government of Nicaragua. Latin Americans act as if they could not care less. One editorial captured the situation perfectly:

> Suddenly it is the United States, not Nicaragua, that is odd man out in Central America. Only a couple of years ago, Washington could count on a fair measure of support from Costa Rica, Guatemala, Honduras and El Salvador in its efforts to contain and eventually overthrow the Sandinista regime in Managua. No more. While these small nations still fear Nicaragua's outsized armed forces and its Marxist-Leninist system, they have evidently had their fill of the overbearing tactics of the Reagan Administration....

---

[11]U.S. Congress, House, Committee on Foreign Affairs, Subcommittee on Western Hemisphere Affairs, *U.S. Policy toward Argentina*, 98th Congress, First Session, 1983, p. 99.

There is nothing new in these sentiments. What is
new is that small, traditionally compliant nations
are daring to defy Washington even in its own back
yard. The perception of the United States as a
mighty power resolute and strong enough to
impose its will is fading.[12]

Guatemalan President Vinicio Cerezo best expressed his colleagues' sentiments: "We want to become the principal actor of our
own history. We Central Americans understand the problems, and
the answers to those problems, better than anyone else." And in
his December 1987 speech accepting the Nobel Peace Prize, Costa
Rica's President Arias told both superpowers to "leave us in peace."

The second example of Latin America's emerging self-
confidence is the eight-nation Latin American summit held in Acapulco, Mexico, in November 1987. "This is history," remarked Brazil's
President José Sarney. "For the first time, we are meeting without
having been convoked by a great power." Not only was the conference actually held without Washington's blessing, but the principal discussions were threatening to positions advanced by the
United States. First, the leaders proposed to invite Cuba to become
once more an active participant in the Organization of American
States.[13] The Acapulco proposal regarding Cuban participation was
made by Uruguayan president Sanguinetti—no radical he—and
strongly endorsed by Brazil, Mexico, and Peru; only Venezuela
expressed reservations about the move. Second, the participants
discussed (but reached no agreement on) ways to address the issue
of Latin America's international debt, most of which is owed to
U.S. banks. And third, the presidents discussed (but again reached
no conclusion on) moving the headquarters of the OAS from
Washington to a city in Latin America. Neither the summit meeting itself nor these specific proposals would have been conceivable
a few short years ago.

---

[12]*The Baltimore Sun,* August 12, 1987, p. 14A.
[13]Although Cuba has always remained a member of the OAS, at the 8th Meeting
of Consultation at Punta del Este, Uruguay, in 1962, the present government of
Cuba was excluded from participation in the inter-American system. At that time,
Mexico alone ignored efforts to isolate Cuba, but by the mid-1970s many OAS
members were offering proposals to reintegrate Cuba. At the 16th Meeting of
Consultation in 1975, OAS members agreed to resume relations with Cuba "at the
levels and in the form that each state deems advisable."

Third, perhaps the most remarkable aspect of this "new independence" is the fact that its current manifestation is most dramatic not in major states like Mexico and Brazil, but in tiny Central America. Since shortly after declaring independence from Spain in the early 1820s, Central America has been dominated by the United States. Central America is where Washington wrote the book on hegemony. Take Nicaragua, for example. With the exception of the United States itself, no other country on earth has ever had a U.S. citizen (William Walker) as its president. No other country on earth has ever been invaded fourteen times by the United States (and this figure does not include the Contra war).[14] No other country has ever been obliged to negotiate an arrangement whereby its national bank was converted into a Connecticut corporation whose stock was largely held by New York bankers. No other country on earth has ever been occupied militarily by the United States for more than nineteen years of a 21-year period, in this case, 1912 to 1933. No other country on earth in peacetime has ever had its harbors mined by the United States. And no other country on earth in peacetime has ever had a government that a U.S. president would openly declare had to say "uncle" in order to restore its good standing in Washington.

The Nicaraguan people have now endured more than seven years of extreme pressure from the most powerful nation in the history of the human race. Yet what has been the result? The economy has become an absolute shambles, with citizens asking their friends traveling from abroad to bring them not Scotch or some new electronic marvel, but toothpaste and toilet paper. Throughout the country, common citizens seem exhausted by the daily pressures of a seven-year war, which came so quickly on the heels of the devastating civil war against the Somoza regime. And yet no Sandinistas are even thinking about saying "uncle." As historian Richard Millett once observed, "the utter bottom line of what it means to be a Sandinista is never to humble yourself in front of the United States. No matter what else it means, that is the bottom

---

[14]The invasions occurred in 1853, 1854, 1857 (twice—April and November), 1867, 1894, 1896, 1898, 1899 (twice—February and March), 1910 (twice—February and May), 1912, and 1926. Although some of these invasions were brief, none has been forgotten by the authors of Nicaraguan textbooks, and some were either especially brutal (the 1854 destruction of San Juan del Norte to avenge an insult to the U.S. minister to Nicaragua, for example); and others (1912 and 1926, for example) have had an indelible impact upon Nicaraguan history. My count for Mexico is twelve U.S. invasions: 1836, 1842, 1844, 1846-48, 1859, 1866, 1870, 1873, 1876, 1913, 1914-17, 1918-19.

line. Any policy which thinks you can scare them, push them or get them to publicly do a mea culpa, is totally misinformed."[15] Jaime Wheelock, Nicaragua's minister of agriculture, captured this attitude best: "For Nicaragua, to be directed by the United States is now unacceptable. The people will fight against this to the end."[16]

At first, this type of talk may seem to be little more than revolutionary bravado, but after seven years of pressure from Washington, the Sandinistas have made believers out of a lot of skeptics. And if a tiny backwater of 2.5 million poverty-stricken Nicaraguans can challenge successfully the hegemonic designs of a neighboring superpower, imagine the new weight of comparative giants such as Argentina, Brazil, and Mexico.

The second change (and the first of two that focus upon the global environment) is *an increase in Soviet power*. Over the course of the past four decades, the Soviet Union has dramatically increased its ability to project power. By the early 1980s, this fact had come to dominate the thinking of many U.S. policymakers, including President Reagan. In his speech to the nation in March 1983 Mr. Reagan began by warning that "for twenty years, the Soviet Union has been accumulating enormous military might"; a year later, the president once more went before the television cameras to tell the public that "the growth of the Soviet military has meant a radical change in the nature of the world we live in."

Today, all well-informed U.S. citizens know that the Soviet Union of 1947 is not the Soviet Union of 1987, but aside from Soviet aid to Cuba and Nicaragua, few seem to recognize how the increase in Soviet power has shifted the geostrategic calculus in Latin America. Moscow is now an active participant in inter-American affairs.

The indicators of this participation are everywhere. Cuba and Nicaragua are most obvious, of course, but other indicators of Soviet activity in Latin America are probably more illustrative of the change that has occurred in recent decades. The Soviet Union's military presence, for example, has grown steadily. It is useful to remember that it was not until 1969 that the Soviet navy first ventured into the Caribbean; at that time, the very fact that they

---

[15]U.S. Congress, House, Committee on Foreign Affairs, Subcommittee on Inter-American Affairs, *Honduras and U.S. Policy: An Emerging Dilemma*, 97th Congress, Second Session, 1982, p. 86.
[16]Interview, Managua, Nicaragua, November 3, 1984.

would sail into the region was remarkable. The fact that they have been doing so regularly for twenty years is no longer remarkable, nor are the Soviet air force flights along the U.S. East Coast to Cuba. What is remarkable is the reaction of the United States. One has only to consider what Theodore Roosevelt's reaction would have been if the German navy were prowling off the U.S. Gulf coast, or what JFK would have done about a Soviet combat brigade in Cuba.

Today, the response from Washington is different, as illustrated by the combat brigade episode. In late August 1979, Democratic Senators Frank Church of Idaho and Richard Stone of Florida were beginning what promised to be difficult reelection campaigns. In an apparent effort to bolster their images among conservative constituents, Church and Stone called separate news conferences to announce that the Senate Foreign Relations Committee had obtained secret documents revealing the existence of a Soviet combat brigade in Cuba. Both demanded the brigade's removal, arguing that its presence violated the 1962 Kennedy-Khrushchev agreement prohibiting an offensive Soviet military capability on the island. Church, chairman of the Committee on Foreign Relations, asserted that his support for ratification of the SALT II treaty was dependent upon the brigade's withdrawal.

After some days of intense media coverage, two facts became evident. First, Soviet troops had been stationed in Cuba since the early 1960s and, second, the Carter administration was having difficulty convincing the Soviets to withdraw the brigade. In a televised speech on September 7, President Carter said that "we consider the presence of a Soviet combat brigade in Cuba to be a very serious matter and that this status quo is not acceptable." In his memoirs, however, the president wrote that three days earlier he had told Senate Majority Leader Robert Byrd that "there was no way to mandate that the Soviets withdraw those troops."[17]

Mr. Carter's apparent ambivalence no doubt stemmed in part from the ambiguity surrounding the brigade's mission. The Soviet position was (and is) that the brigade is a training unit, has no offensive capability, and therefore is not in violation of the 1962 agreement regarding offensive weapons. But U.S. intelligence sources have reported that the unit consists of 2,600 soldiers divided into three infantry battalions and one tank battalion—not a normal training configuration. The brigade is equipped with forty

---

[17]Jimmy Carter, *Keeping Faith: Memoirs of a President* (New York: Bantam Books, 1982), p. 263.

tanks and sixty armored personnel carriers, which is not standard equipment for training units.

Whatever the case, on October 1 President Carter accepted Moscow's assurances that the unit was a training brigade, and that was that. The troops remained in Cuba, Senators Stone and Church lost their bids for reelection, and Washington policymakers came to agree that some types of Soviet force deployments in Cuba will have to be overlooked or, more accurately, defined as "nonoffensive" and therefore outside the confines of the 1962 accord.

For those who believe that the resolution of this problem primarily reflected the fact that Mr. Carter was simply not sufficiently assertive, it is instructive to observe that the most assertive president in recent memory, Ronald Reagan, has also been unable to remove the Cuban troops. In fact, after some initial bombast about "going to the source" of hemispheric instability, he apparently has never tried. The reason for this is extremely clear: the Soviets enjoy considerable strength that they lacked in 1962. There is no longer any assurance that, should we once again stand eyeball-to-eyeball, the Soviets will blink first, as they did in the Cuban missile crisis.

And the military dimension of this new power is not the only important aspect of the change that has occurred in the past generation. The trade-related position of power that the United States has long held in Latin America has also eroded. An excellent example is the U.S. sugar import program, under which the United States has for decades purchased sugar at prices substantially above the world market price. Since all foreign producers want to take advantage of this preferential pricing policy (which has its roots in the Cuban Reciprocal Treaty of 1902 and over time has been expanded to include most Latin American sugar exporters), the United States assigns import quotas to individual countries. In many cases, these quotas spell the difference between prosperity and depression; they thereby provide Washington with considerable political leverage.

But the increase in Soviet power has meant a diminution of this leverage, as the case of Cuba demonstrates. In March 1960, as Cuban-U.S. relations were deteriorating rapidly, a bill was introduced in the House of Representatives to authorize the president to reduce the Cuban sugar quota. Representative Harris McDowell, Jr. expressed the thinking of many of his colleagues when he remarked that "if Cuba's splendid people understand that they must sell their sugar or their economy will be destroyed, they will themselves find a way to deal with the present misleaders and fomenters of hatred." The bill passed the House by a vote of 396 to 0, and in July President Eisenhower slashed the Cuban quota from 779,000 tons to 40,000 tons for the second half of 1960. In December, the Cuban quota was eliminated entirely for the first quarter of 1961.[18]

In response, Cuba arranged to sell elsewhere its 1961 crop: 2.7 million tons of sugar to the Soviet Union, 1.0 million tons to the People's Republic of China, and 300,000 tons to the Eastern bloc countries of Europe. These purchases of four million tons exceeded both the U.S. quota and the amount of sugar Cuba had available for sale. Representative McDowell was both correct and naive. He was correct in noting that Cuba had to sell sugar in order to survive. He was naive in thinking that the United States was the only available purchaser.

And Cuba is no longer an isolated case. The Soviet Union now maintains an active presence throughout Latin America. In Nicaragua, of course, the Soviets have provided sufficient assistance to keep the Nicaraguan revolution from having to capitulate to the United States—they have done for Nicaragua exactly what they did for Cuba two decades earlier. In Peru, the Soviets are the principal suppliers of heavy weapons for the army. In Argentina, the Soviets have become the nation's principal trading partner. In 1960, there were three Soviet embassies in Latin America; today there are nineteen.

All this is not to argue that the Soviet Union has in any way challenged the United States as the overwhelming foreign presence in Latin America. Rather, the point to be made is that, unlike the early period of containment, Washington's major rival is now prepared to play an active role in the region. If the United States refuses to purchase Cuban sugar, Moscow will buy it. If the United States refuses to sell arms to Nicaragua, Moscow will provide them. With limited resources, the Soviet Union cannot replace Washington, but it can (and does) take advantage of special opportunities in Latin America.

---

[18]The United States has imported no Cuban sugar since that time. Since 1963, the Foreign Assistance Act has stipulated that Cuba shall not "be entitled to receive any quota authorizing the importation of Cuban sugar into the United States or to receive any other benefit under any law of the United States."

The third change is *a decline in U.S. resources*. Perhaps the most intelligent single sentence written in recent years about U.S.-Latin American relations is by career ambassador and former assistant secretary of state Viron Vaky: "The problem which most Americans have in thinking about Latin America," he wrote, "is that they have come to consider the dominant position in the world and the overwhelming hegemony the United States exercised in the Hemisphere in the 20 years following World War II as the normal state of affairs."[19]

Of all the lessons that can be drawn from the recent evolution of inter-American relations, the most important by far is that Washington's reach now exceeds its grasp in Latin America. The United States now lacks the resources to realize its aspirations. Quite obviously, the United States retains all the power it will ever need to crush any opposition in the region. But as policymakers discovered long ago in Vietnam, it is in large measure useless power.

Take, for example, the case of El Salvador, a tiny country the size of North Carolina with a population of five million people. Following the 1979 Sandinista victory in nearby Nicaragua, the Carter administration began to pressure the Salvadoran government of General Romero to enact structural reforms, i.e., land redistribution, to defuse growing disaffection. When General Romero balked, in November 1979, a group of reformist civilians and a few reformist military officers, blessed if not encouraged by the United States, engineered a coup and announced plans for a series of sweeping reforms.

But despite strong backing from Washington, the reformists were stymied by their own conservative opposition. After three months of effort, they abandoned the government. The United States then searched frantically for an alternative to (a) the guerrilla left, which by the end of the year would mount its "final offensive," (b) the reformist left, which refused to participate in the government, and (c) the far right, which the U.S. Congress would not support with aid. Washington settled on José Napoleón Duarte, a Christian Democrat who had been living in Venezuela since losing the presidential election (and suffering a vicious attack by the Salvadoran military police) in 1972. Having settled upon

---

[19]Viron P. Vaky, "Hemispheric Relations: 'Everything Is Part of Everything Else,'" *Foreign Affairs* 59 (1981): 639.

Mr. Duarte as its moderate representative, both the Carter and Reagan administrations proceeded to bolster his power with truly extraordinary amounts of military and economic assistance: an average of $438 million per year in the four-year period 1983-1986. Never in the history of inter-American relations has the United States invested so heavily in the stabilization of a Latin American government.

And what are the results? As of 1988, virtually nothing has been resolved. The guerrillas are not as strong as they were in 1980, but they remain an active force capable of prolonging indefinitely their conflict with the Salvadoran military and disrupting indefinitely the Salvadoran economy—approximately $300 million in economic damage in 1986, which about equalled the U.S. economic aid program that year. Perhaps more important, the reforms promised in 1979 have been only partially implemented, and as a consequence the underlying causes of the civil war, which almost everyone agrees are poverty and injustice, have not been addressed.

Meanwhile, like a drug addict, in the 1980s the Salvadoran economy became hooked on U.S. aid, including the aid provided in the form of remittances from over 500,000 Salvadorans now living illegally in the United States. As the U.S. Immigration and Naturalization Service began to implement the fairly stringent provisions of the 1986 Immigration Reform and Control (Simpson-Rodino) Act, President Duarte was forced to ask for an exemption. In a confidential letter to President Reagan in April 1987, Mr. Duarte said that the return of Salvadorans "would reduce drastically the amount of money received by poor Salvadoran people in remittances from relatives now working in the United States. My government estimates that the total value of remittances is some place between $350 million to $600 million annually, and is thus larger than the United States government's assistance to El Salvador." As for the direct provision of U.S. aid, most evaluations in the late 1980s were extremely pessimistic. A report issued in November 1987 by the Congressional Arms Control and Foreign Policy Caucus was titled "Bankrolling Failure." The report concluded that "despite seven years' involvement and $3 billion in aid from U.S. taxpayers, El Salvador remains a nation at war with itself, no closer to peace than when the U.S. began its massive infusions of dollars. Our vast investment in El Salvador has brought neither peace nor political stability nor a sound economy. Instead, we are witnessing a fragmentation—perhaps even a 'Lebanonization'—of Salvadoran society."

In the forty years since the inauguration of the policy of containment, the power of the United States to control (as opposed to influence) events in El Salvador or elsewhere in Latin America all but disappeared. This is not to say that Washington is now impotent. As in the past, the United States can unseat any government in the region. But if today Washington policymakers want to determine who rules in Managua, they will first have to destroy Nicaragua.

That was not the case anywhere in Latin America in the heyday of containment. In early 1953, the National Security Council produced a report, "U.S. Objectives and Courses of Action with Respect to Latin America," for the incoming Eisenhower administration. The report asserted that "our purpose should be to arrest the development of irresponsibility and extreme nationalism and their belief in their immunity from the exercise of U.S. power."[20] A year later a small group of Guatemalans—trained, financed, and supported by the CIA—overthrew the freely elected government of Jacobo Arbenz, demonstrating clearly that Latin America was not immune from the exercise of U.S. power. It was that simple. It no longer is.

If today there is an imbalance between resources and aspirations, then U.S. policymakers can achieve a new balance in one of two ways. They can increase their resources or lower their aspirations. What more can be done, however, to increase Washington's ability to determine outcomes in Central America, yet alone in the major countries of the region? In the 1980s, the United States devoted nearly every reasonably available resource to Central America. What more can be given? Surely future presidents will be unable to devote even more of their time and attention to Central America. Surely no future president, in the salad years of his tenure, will do what Mr. Reagan did in 1983, and devote two of his three speeches on prime time television (one before a joint session of Congress) to talking about Central America. And surely no one can expect Congress to devote more of its energy and attention to Central America. Throughout the 1980s, this tiny region was the single most important foreign policy issue to be addressed by Congress. The U.S. political agenda is not so barren that future leaders can afford to spend even more of their scarce political currency on Central America.

---

[20]National Security Council Report 144, March 6, 1953, p. 11.

And so the United States has to adjust its aspirations. This is a particularly difficult step for a people who have become accustomed to calling themselves the greatest power in the world. U.S. citizens do not like to cut back; instead, they meet challenges, they move ahead. A country involved in reducing its aspirations is antithetical to this image.

Nonetheless, it is instructive to note that the U.S. public and its policymakers are adjusting to the reduced level of U.S. influence elsewhere in the world. Everyone who follows international relations now realizes that the period of U.S. suzerainty in the years immediately following World War II was a transient phenomenon. The U.S. dollar has not been as good as gold for some time, and foreign producers have seized markets that U.S. entrepreneurs once thought were theirs by virtue of victory in World War II. The United States may still be the strongest nation on earth, but not by much. Its citizens are no longer the richest or the best fed. They no longer even pretend to have the best medical care or the longest life expectancy. They have learned to live with the relative diminution of their stature in the world.

But not in Latin America. To begin to discuss the difficulties involved in the adjustment of Washington's aspirations in this region of the world, we must first turn to the fourth change, *the democratization of the U.S. policy-making process.*

Citizens who became interested in U.S. policy toward Latin America in the late 1970s or 1980s often assume that the current high level of public involvement in policy debates is normal. In fact, it is absolutely unprecedented. When the era of containment began in the late 1940s, U.S. policy toward Latin America was made by a small handful of officials and influential outsiders. At the most, they numbered twenty-five. There was no public opinion about Latin America, for during the brief history of public opinion polling in America, the small number of polling organizations had asked no more than a dozen questions about Latin America, and all of them were related to World War II. Moreover, not a single interest group existed with a specific focus on Latin America—not a trade association, not a church group, not even the Latin American Studies Association. In the 1940s and 1950s, few students studied Latin America in U.S. universities. Only one newspaper (the *New York Times*) had a full-time staff correspondent in Latin America, and as a result few citizens read anything about the region.

In Congress, there was no such thing as a "Latin American-ist." Public hearings on Latin America were unknown; instead, the State Department consulted privately with a few key members about U.S. policy. Disagreements between the two branches of government were almost nonexistent, because virtually everyone at both ends of Pennsylvania Avenue shared a common focus upon keeping the Soviet Union and communism out of the hemisphere. Policy disagreements were restricted to debates over important but secondary issues—the appropriate reaction to the expropriation of U.S. investments, for example, and to conflicts over tactics, tim-ing, and budget priorities. Differences of opinion on these secon-dary issues were resolved in the atmosphere of civility that used to characterize the homogeneous U.S. foreign policy establishment. These white, upper-middle-class gentlemen from the Eastern Establishment were pleased to listen with respect to the views of others, to offer alternative perspectives, and then to compromise quickly by splitting the difference, for the difference was always very small. No U.S. citizen with a Hispanic surname got within shouting distance of the policy-making process.

Look at the congressional votes on major containment initia-tives—from the Rio Treaty through the early resolutions on Cuba— and you will find consensus. U.S. participation in the United Nations was approved in 1945 by a 98 percent majority, the Truman Doctrine was accepted in 1947 by 86 percent, the U.S.-Korean Mutual Defense Treaty in 1954 by 93 percent, the Cuban trade embargo in 1961 by 100 percent, and, of course, the Gulf of Tonkin resolution in 1964 by 98 percent in the Senate and 100 percent in the House of Representatives.

This consensus stemmed largely from the narrow spectrum of opinion that participated in the policy-making process. Like all major conflicts, World War II served to consolidate public opinion around the single objective of military victory. Then after the war, when a normal fragmentation of opinion could be expected to reemerge, McCarthyism exerted a stultifying effect on political debates. It was only with Vietnam, which the Cold War interna-tionalists could not resolve satisfactorily, that critics stepped out of the closet and the debates began once again over the content and direction of U.S. foreign policy.

With the benefit of hindsight, it is now clear that the postwar period has been characterized by an absolute explosion of politi-cal participation in the creation of U.S. policy toward Latin America.

The public's emergence from its intellectual cocoon coincided with the explosive growth of colleges and universities across the country, with the Cuban revolution, with the Alliance for Progress, and with a general interest in the subject of Third World development. Thousands of citizens began to study Latin America and previously ignored subjects such as social change and instability. At the same time, large numbers of U.S. citizens went to live and work in Latin America, not as relatively wealthy businesspeople, but as Peace Corps volunteers and as church workers. They spent their time with the poor, and they developed new interpretations of Latin America's reality.

These citizens also developed an intense interest in U.S. policy toward Latin America. And their interest led them to take the quintessentially gringo step of forming interest groups, dozens and dozens of them, with representatives prowling the halls of power in Washington. In Congress itself, not only has there been a remarkable increase in the number of members with a major interest in Latin America—an interest that in many cases has been forced upon them by their constituents—but also there has been a stunning destruction of the cozy relationship that Congress once had with administration makers of foreign policy. For better or for worse, broad currents of U.S. opinion now participate in the policy-influencing (and, increasingly, the policy-making) process.

The reason why this democratization of the policy process has led to conflict is—and here is the fifth and final change—that *these new participants have startlingly different beliefs about what is actually happening in Latin America.* This, of course, is not surprising, for the new participants come from startlingly different backgrounds. Senator Christopher Dodd, chairman of the Senate Foreign Relations Subcommittee on Western Hemisphere Affairs, spent two years of his life as a Peace Corps volunteer in a rural village in the Dominican Republic. The Rev. Joseph Eldridge, founder of the Washington Office on Latin America, was expelled from his post as a Methodist minister in Chile in 1973. Betsy Crites and Gail Phares, national directors of Witness for Peace, are former Catholic layworkers who spent years working with base communities in Central America.

These people believe passionately that communism is not a problem to be addressed in Latin America. The problem, in their view, is poverty and injustice. These people believe that instability in Latin America is the manifestation of a broadly human phenomenon: rebellion growing out of a "natural" opposition to a situation that is fundamentally unfair. These citizens agree with Barrington Moore that "there are indications of a widespread feeling that people, even the most humble members of society, ought to have enough resources or facilities to do their job in the social order, and that there is something morally wrong or even outrageous when these resources are unavailable." And so these citizens also agree with Moore's conclusion: "personal and private retention *without use* of resources that are in short supply and needed by others is somehow immoral and a violation of the higher rights of the community."[21]

Ironically, Jeane Kirkpatrick has most effectively summarized the impact of this belief on U.S. citizens and their policymakers: "The extremes of wealth and poverty characteristic of traditional societies ... offends us," she wrote in 1979. "Moreover, the relative lack of concern of rich, comfortable rulers for the poverty, ignorance, and disease of 'their' people is likely to be interpreted by Americans as moral dereliction pure and simple. The truth is that Americans can hardly bear such societies and such rulers."[22]

These perceptions of stark poverty and an uncaring selfish elite are what most inflame many U.S. citizens. In some cases, it is the driving force in their lives. Crusaders for the poor of Latin America, they have chosen Washington as the field of battle. When these people hear President Reagan say that "the Soviet Union underlies all the trouble that is going on" in Latin America, they become absolutely livid.

But when President Reagan, Ambassador Kirkpatrick, or Assistant Secretary Abrams hear these dewy-eyed liberals talking about poverty and injustice, they wonder about their common sense. Don't they know that, when instability flares, often the only alternative to an admittedly unpleasant authoritarianism is communist totalitarianism? Don't they know that the United States can work to democratize authoritarian regimes in Latin America, but that, once in power, totalitarian communists are all but impossible to unseat? Aren't they willing "to face the unpleasant fact that, if victorious, violent insurgency headed by Marxist revolutionaries is unlikely to lead to anything but totalitarian tyranny"?[23]

---

[21]Barrington Moore, Jr., *Injustice: The Social Bases of Obedience and Revolt* (White Plains, N.Y.: M.E. Sharpe, 1978), pp. 38, 47.
[22]Jeane J. Kirkpatrick, "Dictators and Double Standards," *Commentary* 68 (November 1979): 42.
[23]Kirkpatrick, "Dictators and Double Standards," p. 45.

It is difficult to overestimate the profound divisions that have come to characterize the contemporary policy-making process. This is the post-Vietnam loss of consensus, a much-discussed topic in the contemporary literature on U.S. foreign policy. The expanded policy-making process is dominated by equally matched groups of individuals who have fundamentally different beliefs about what is actually occurring in Latin America. Unwilling to compromise over basic principles, these officials have checked one another.

CONCLUSION

This is where we are today: five major changes have occurred in the years since the United States adopted the policy of containment: in Latin America's role in world politics; in the Soviet Union's ability to project power; in the balance between our resources and our aspirations; in the democratization of the U.S. policy-making process; and in the beliefs of U.S. policymakers. These are profoundly important changes that will determine the trajectory of U.S.-Latin American relations well into the twenty-first century.

In charting a viable relationship between the United States and Mexico, policymakers on both sides of the border will have to take these changes into consideration. They will need first to recognize that, barring another revolution somewhere in the region, the inability thus far of the United States to adjust to these five changes—an inability highlighted by U.S. policy toward Central America—means that the United States is about to decrease dramatically the amount of attention it allocates to Latin America. We have probably seen during the Reagan administration the largest expenditure of U.S. political and financial resources on Latin America that we will see during the twentieth century. The administration tried hard but did not succeed, and its successors will react to the failure in precisely the way Washington reacted to defeat in Vietnam: first by processing the refugees (this time from Central America), and then by withdrawing its attention.

For U.S.-Mexican relations, I suspect that this is a change for the better. Eugene Douglas, U.S. coordinator for refugee affairs and an analyst with whom I normally find little to agree, correctly observes that the United States and Mexico "seem to get along best when Washington is preoccupied with a global, not just a hemispheric, agenda." Given the very different interpretations the two governments have of instability in Latin America, conflict between the United States and Mexico is almost certain whenever

Washington's eyes are focused upon the region, for they only focus there when large-scale instability erupts.

And even if the decrease in U.S. involvement is not interpreted as a change for the better, it is still probably inevitable. The conflicting beliefs about U.S. policy and the democratization of the U.S. policy-making process virtually guarantee a vacillating, incoherent policy in the years immediately ahead. It must be recognized that we have just witnessed the end of the strongest administration the United States is likely to see for some time. Yet in its policy toward Latin America, this administration resolved absolutely nothing. Facing a much stronger Latin America in a global environment characterized by a much stronger Soviet Union and a domestic environment characterized by dissension, the Reagan administration left office without having achieved anything positive of significance in its policy toward Latin America.

In short, in its policy toward Latin America the United States will be forced by existing circumstances to muddle through the coming years. This should be interpreted as a major opportunity for Mexico and the other nations of the region, for a nation whose goal is to muddle through will probably lack an agenda. U.S. policy will be reactive. If instability can be kept below the threshold that sounds alarms in Washington, then there is no reason to believe that the agenda cannot be determined by Latin Americans.

SECTION

II

INSTRUMENTS

4

The Making of Mexican Policy toward the United States

Jorge Chabat

Studies on decision-making processes in Mexican foreign policy are not very abundant. This is due primarily to the fact that available information is not very comprehensive, on the one hand, and that there has been a tendency to consider the president as the determining factor in decision-making, on the other, the result being that there is no way to identify patterns of conduct. In addition, in those cases where there is information, it is not clear that it always refers to cases from which generalizations may be drawn. One may even wonder whether it is possible to establish general guidelines of behavior throughout a succession of concrete cases with varying importance and representativeness. While these problems will be considered below, this essay is primarily an exercise in classifying overall tendencies in the decision-making process as a result of certain transformations which have taken place in Mexican foreign policy during de la Madrid's *sexenio*. We shall review those transformations and then analyze the formal functions of the agencies dealing with other countries in order to appreciate the degree of splintering in the Mexican bureaucracy. Finally we will review the direction that the decision-making process toward the United States may take in future.

MEXICAN FOREIGN POLICY: WHAT HAS CHANGED
DURING THE DE LA MADRID TERM OF OFFICE

Any overall review of the changes in Mexican foreign policy
during de la Madrid's term in office would first highlight the
government's explicit intention to change its pattern of economic
development. This change, which involved dropping the develop-
ment-stabilizing model for one which emphasizes promoting
exports and which was characterized by de la Madrid as "the most
outstanding structural change in the past half century,"[1] has clear
repercussions for Mexican foreign policy. It implies greater contact with other countries and naturally presupposes more economic
substance in this contact. In this sense, the difference with the
foreign policies of Echeverría and López Portillo shows up much
more clearly. While Echeverría saw the model of stabilizing development coming to an end and attempted to respond with an active
Third World policy—which did not imply an in-depth reform of
the productive apparatus—López Portillo developed a very short-
lived policy of "regional power" supported by the oil boom and
foreign indebtedness. Thus, during the de la Madrid administration there was a very clear economic transformation effort which
definitely set the limits and scope of foreign policy.

A second element closely tied to the previous feature was the
importance of the foreign debt for the Mexican government under
de la Madrid. The level of Mexican indebtedness, which was three
times larger by the beginning of the de la Madrid's administration than it had been in 1976 and represented a serious financial
problem for Mexico, distinguished a large part of de la Madrid
foreign policy. Many financial resources and much of the
government's diplomatic attention poured into this problem. This,
in turn, was reflected in an important increase in the negotiating
capacity of the bureaucratic agencies dealing with this matter, to
the detriment of the traditional diplomatic agencies.[2] It also led the
Mexican government to consider payment of the foreign debt—so
as not to cancel economic development—as another of its foreign
policy priorities.

A third element which guided de la Madrid's foreign policy
was the definition of a very clear concept of national security in
the face of the internal political instability threatened by the Central

---

[1] *El Sol de México* (Mexico City), August 29, 1987.
[2] This will be reflected in the bureaucratic infighting mentioned below.

American conflicts. This concept appeared toward the end of the López Portillo term of office, beginning with the mass presence of Guatemalan refugees in Mexico in 1981, and is, without doubt, a novelty in Mexican foreign policy. This concern for the effects of the Central American crisis in Mexico has spurred Mexico's participation in the Contadora Group and explains in good measure the Mexican insistence on maintaining this mechanism despite U.S. pressures against it.

This concern for the Central American crisis, the interest in paying off the foreign debt, and the consolidation of an economic model to promote Mexican exports constituted the three great priorities of the foreign policy of the de la Madrid administration. These elements and others discussed below formed a decision-making framework for foreign issues which differed substantially from past approaches.

Fourth, as a result of foreign policy priorities, open interbureaucratic squabbles erupted in the field of foreign policy. These focused basically on two subjects: foreign debt and Guatemalan refugees. In the former case, the divergence lay between the Ministry of Foreign Relations' position—and initially that of the Bank of Mexico—of seeking political agreement with Latin America, and the Ministry of Finance's position of seeking a direct arrangement with the creditor banks. This two-track policy seems to have been defined in favor of the Ministry of Finance position, although one could hardly say the matter has yet been settled definitively.[3] In the case of the Guatemalan refugees, the differing positions between the Ministry of Foreign Relations and the Ministry of Gobernación

---

[3]In this regard, see Hermann Aschentrupp, "La crisis de endeudamiento y las negociaciones en América Latina," *Carta de Política Exterior Mexicana* 4:3 (July-September 1984); idem, "La tercera ronda de negociaciones sobre deuda externa; las percepciones de México y Estados Unidos," ibid. 6:2 (April-June 1986); idem, "Deuda y diplomacia financiera en la estrategia de negociación de México para 1986," ibid. 6:1 (January-March 1986). As a significant detail concerning the way in which this dispute was settled, we have the disappearance of the Underministry of Economic Affairs within the Ministry of Foreign Relations in 1985. The underminister, Jorge Eduardo Navarrete, had advocated approaching Latin America through the Cartagena Consensus. The disappearance of the underministry took place within the framework of general budget cutbacks in Mexican public administration. Nonetheless, the fact that this agency in particular was affected—in spite of there being other, newer offices at the same level dealing with questions that shortly before had been assigned to lower-ranking bureaucratic levels—seems to stand out. Mexico's tendency not to organize a Latin American debtors' front was clearly evident in the meeting of eight Latin American presidents held in Mexico City at the end of November 1987.

also crossed the line of bureaucratic discretion.[4] In this case, while the Foreign Ministry's position was to preserve the right of asylum and Mexico's diplomatic prestige, the Ministry of Gobernación was more concerned with maintaining control of the southern border and with repercussions on political stability in southern Mexico. This discrepancy over Guatemalan refugees also reflected a difference in the concept of national security. Whereas Foreign Relations is concerned more about U.S. military intervention in the area, the Ministry of Gobernación feared the repercussions of guerrilla activities in Central America on Mexican political stability.[5] The 1984 relocation of Guatemalan refugees in the state of Quintana Roo, a step which appeared to attend more to the Ministry of Gobernación point of view, preserved Mexico's diplomatic image abroad. The same may be said of the "Contadora solution." Contadora's insistence on the need to avoid any kind of armed conflict in the area took up the Ministry of Foreign Relations' concern for maintaining the principles of nonintervention, self-determination of the people, and peaceful solution of controversies. At the same time, it appeared to be an effective mechanism for avoiding the side effects (refugees, for example) of an armed conflict and tended to reduce the strength of revolutionary movements in several Central American countries by legitimizing established governments and forcing the armed opposition to the negotiating table.

In both cases, what stands out is that these conflicts within the bureaucracy come up precisely on subjects which involved two of the government's priorities, that is, avoiding a confrontation with the international banks, and preserving the stability of the southern zone. Moreover, the way both conflicts were channeled does not contradict either of these priorities.

On this point, we should note the discussion promoted by de la Madrid on Mexico's entry into GATT in 1985, in which diverse government and non-governmental opinions were expressed. This could hardly be considered an interbureaucratic dispute, however.

---

[4]For the differences in position in the case of the Guatemalan refugees, see Mario Arriola, "México y el problema de los refugiados guatemaltecos," *Cuadernos de Política Exterior Mexicana* 1:1 (Mexico City: Centro de Investigación y Docencia Económicas, A.C. [CIDE], 1984). Also see Elizabeth G. Ferris, "The Politics of Asylum, Mexico and the Central American Refugees," *Journal of Inter-American Studies and World Affairs* 26:3 (August 1984): 357-384.
[5]The *Economist*, July 23-29, 1983, p. 28.

Besides the fact that the decision to join GATT was unanimous within the foreign trade cabinet, the president's encouragement of the discussions was intended to legitimize the decision.[6]

A fifth element which should be emphasized is the low profile which de la Madrid maintained in matters of foreign policy. When comparing de la Madrid's style to that of his two predecessors, the difference becomes quite clear. President Echeverría developed his foreign policy in response to adverse economic conditions abroad, but he nonetheless gave it a personal style reflected in several unusual decisions; although their consequences were unimportant, they gave rise to various interpretations on the element of personality in foreign policy.[7] López Portillo's personal influence became obvious beginning with his second year in office, when he carried on a series of verbal confrontations with the U.S. government. This led some observers to characterize his foreign policy, primarily in Central America, as "*machismo.*"[8] Without attempting to attribute Echeverría's and López Portillo's foreign policies basically to the element of personality, the contrast with de la Madrid is clear. De la Madrid preferred to leave the elements of conflict in foreign policy to his collaborators and to make sporadic declarations which did not, in general, provoke open friction.[9]

---

[6]María Amparo Casar and Guadalupe González, "Proceso de toma de decisiones y política exterior en México: el ingreso al GATT," paper read at the Ninth Meeting of Centers Belonging to the RIAL, Brasilia, November 29-December 2, 1987.
[7]Yoram Shapira, "La política exterior de México bajo el régimen de Echeverría: retrospectiva," *Foro Internacional* 19:1 (July-September 1978).
[8]Daniel James, "Mexico: America's Newest Problem?" *The Washington Quarterly,* 1980, no. 3; Bruce Bagley, "Mexico in the 1980's, A New Regional Power," *Current History* 90 (1981); Jorge Chabat, "Condicionantes del activismo de la política exterior mexicana (1960-1985)," in *Fundamentos y prioridades de la política exterior de México,* ed. Humberto Garza (Mexico City: El Colegio de México, 1986).
[9]This characteristic can be clearly seen in the Central American issue since the 1983 de la Madrid-Reagan meeting, at which, in spite of clear differences, the tone was cordial and the Mexican president made only veiled, indirect references to the United States. This position was later maintained; in 1984, while the Mexican foreign minister was openly criticizing U.S. policy in the region, de la Madrid was subtly chiding the Kissinger Plan. In the meeting of the two presidents in January of 1986, the Central American question was minimized at the presidential level, although Bernardo Sepúlveda, at the foreign minister level, expressed Mexican opposition to the Contras and requested greater U.S. cooperation for the Contadora process. Jorge Chabat, "La entrevista de la Madrid-Reagan: logros y desacuerdos," *Carta de Política Exterior Mexicana* 3:4 (July-August 1983); idem, "Las relaciones México-Estados Unidos en 1983: un compás de espera," ibid. 4:1 (January-March 1984). Also Bruce Michael Bagley, "La interdependencia entre Estados Unidos y México a finales de los ochenta," *Cuadernos Semestrales,* no. 20 (Mexico City: CIDE, 1986).

A sixth element to be emphasized in Miguel de la Madrid's foreign policy was his use, incipient in some cases, of new instruments. Even though some of these instruments were not new in the panorama of Mexican foreign policy, their use and their importance did increase. First, within bilateral diplomacy, although no special emphasis can be noted in the use of embassies, consulates, in particular those in the United States, took on a more important role. This importance—reflected in the explicit intention of the Mexican chancellery to strengthen and facilitate its action in various meetings held in 1987[10]—no doubt had to do with the putting into practice of the Simpson-Rodino law. Without predicting that the work of consulates will necessarily take on political tones,[11] it is clear that many of the day-to-day interests of Mexican foreign policy, including the promotion of tourism and exports, will be advanced through this mechanism. However, future development of these instruments will hinge on the principle of nonintervention, a cornerstone of Mexican foreign policy, and the legal limitations set forth in the Organic Law of the Mexican Foreign Service, which forbids foreign service personnel to "intervene in internal or political affairs of the country to which they are assigned or in the country's international affairs not having to do with Mexico."[12]

On the other hand, we have multilateral diplomacy, which naturally goes back as far as Mexico's foreign policy does. During Miguel de la Madrid's term, however, this instrument was appreciably encouraged, in contrast to López Portillo's bilateral policy. This emphasis on the multilateral side can be found beginning from the early period of the de la Madrid administration with the creation of the Contadora Group and the Group of Six concerning disarmament, as well as in various multilateral forums of an economic nature.[13] The emphasis on the use of this instrument was

---

[10]Jorge Chabat, "Algunas reflexiones sobre el papel de los consulados en la coyuntura actual," *Carta de Política Exterior Mexicana* 7:2 (April-June 1987); María Rosa García and David R. Maciel, "El México de afuera: políticas mexicanas de protección en Estados Unidos," *Revista Mexicana de Política Exterior* 3:12 (July-September 1986).
[11]Jorge C. Castañeda, in "Más allá de los principios," *Nexos* 110 (February 1987), proposes politicizing the consulates.
[12]"Ley Orgánica del Servicio Exterior Mexicana," *Diario Oficial*, January 8, 1982, Article 48. For a discussion of the activities of the consulates, see Castañeda, "Más allá de los principios," and Chabat, "Algunas reflexiones."
[13]Mario Ojeda, *México: el surgimiento de una política exterior activa* (Mexico City: Secretaría de Educación Pública, 1986), pp. 199-200; and Ricardo Macouzet Noriega, "La diplomacia multilateral de México en la coyuntura actual: La II Reunión

in part a response to the priorities in foreign policy, as well as an attempt to diminish the degree of direct confrontation with the United States.

Another instrument which seems to have grown under de la Madrid is the utilization of lobbying the U.S. Congress. On this subject, the information is fragmentary and hard to pin down. However, there is evidence that the Mexican government hired Michael Deaver—a collaborator of James Baker when the latter was White House chief of personnel—to handle public relations with Mexico by means of a specialized lobby.[14] One cannot help but notice the secrecy with which the Mexican government handled the matter of Deaver's work, which suggests a concern on his part about the possible consequences that the use of this instrument might have in terms of the principle of nonintervention.

Nevertheless, given the growing number of subjects of conflicts in Mexican-U.S. relations, it is reasonable to expect an increase in the use of this instrument, although it is probable that a similar level of discretion will be maintained, or that the Mexican government will encourage the private sector to take the initiative in the employment of lobbies.

Along this line, we can also point to a discrete increase in propaganda efforts directed toward U.S. public opinion by the Mexican government. This effort, a classic instrument of promotion of the "national interest" of a country, was not new. The governments of Echeverría and López Portillo had made sporadic efforts to influence foreign communication media, characteristically orienting their message toward the U.S. broadcasting media. This policy, developed during recent years with a certain awkwardness on the part of the Mexican government,[15] can no doubt be a

---

del Grupo de los Seis." At the end of 1986, the Ministry of Foreign Relations' interest in fostering the use of multilateral diplomacy was plainly evident. See "Ante amenazas a la soberanía, política multilateral: SRE," *Excélsior* (Mexico City), December 12, 1986, front page.

[14]Carlos Ramírez, *Operación Gavin* (Mexico City: El Día en Libros), p. 220.

[15]As a result of Jack Anderson's article published in the *Washington Post* on May 15, 1984, the Mexican government—primarily through the Public Information Agency of the Presidency of the Republic—has insistently tried to influence U.S. public opinion. It should be pointed out that said article gave rise to a diplomatic protest note to the U.S. government. Along this line, the 1985 tour of the United States by the head of the Public Information Agency, Manuel Alonso, to give information on the campaign against drug trafficking in Mexico should be mentioned. Recently, the U.S. magazine *Leaders* devoted a special supplement to de la Madrid and several members of his cabinet. See *Proceso* 396 (June 4, 1984) and *Proceso* 565 (September 1, 1987).

fundamental element of foreign policy in the future. In any case, it should be noted that a factor limiting the success of this instrument is the independence generally maintained by the media in the United States and their insusceptibility to this type of campaign.

To this description of current foreign policy instruments we should add the role which mechanisms outside the executive branch are beginning to play. Although it is the executive branch that is legally authorized to conduct foreign policy, as we shall see later, Mexican private enterprise, governors, and mayors play a part as well. As for the first group, it seems clear that an economic model which aims to promote exports and which increasingly depends on private enterprise will have a great need of this sector in the shaping of foreign relations. In this sense, de la Madrid's statements during his trip to China and Japan at the end of 1986, in the company of the main representatives of Mexican private enterprise, are significant: he made an express appeal that "each sector of Mexican society should assume its role in international relations, not permitting these to remain solely the responsibility of the executive branch."[16]

On the other hand, based on the growing rate of border transactions between Mexico and the United States, it is reasonable to expect increasing decision-making autonomy for governors and mayors in border areas. So far, however, the truth is that governors' "foreign policy" has not differed substantially from the guidelines set by the executive branch. As a matter of fact, there is a feeling among Mexican governors that formal agreements should be made at the foreign ministry level.[17] Thus, although it is reasonable to expect greater autonomy in these activities—especially should an opposition party candidate become the governor of a border state—policies followed by governors and mayors constitute more an element of support for executive branch decisions than a source of conflict. This suggests the existence of an instrument which, like private enterprise efforts, can help promote Mexican foreign policy if properly coordinated.

A final characteristic of de la Madrid's foreign policy has been the presence of strong pressures by the U.S. government on sub-

---

[16]*Excélsior* (Mexico City), December 11, 1986, front page.
[17]This is inferred from the meeting of border state governors from Mexico and the United States held in New Mexico in December of 1987. *Excélsior*, December 12, 1987, front page.

jects which were, until recently, untouchable, such as the Mexican political system and foreign policy. Without attempting to make a detailed study of these pressures, it would be worthwhile to note that upon turning to areas that had not been disputed before in bilateral relations, they confronted a Mexican government that was incapable of expressing an adequate response. In regard to the problem of drug smuggling and concretely concerning the pressures arising from the kidnapping and murder of DEA agent Enrique Camarena, the bureaucratic apparatus established in Mexico was unable from the outset to respond satisfactorily, despite the fact that it was a police matter. The difficulty the Mexican bureaucracy experienced in the struggle against drug trafficking is explained by the Mexican agents' susceptibility to pressures from drug traffickers. In fact, it took an interview between U.S. Ambassador Gavin and President de la Madrid to address the issue of cleaning up the Mexican agencies involved in drug control, since many of their members were involved in drug trafficking.[18] When the Mexican political system became one of the main points of discussion during the Helms hearings,[19] the Mexican response was even less articulate. The minister of foreign relations issued a few statements protesting what was said in the hearings. The next day, the Mexican ambassador presented a note of protest, which the State Department answered in a conciliatory tone. The Mexican government later sponsored a massive mobilization rejecting the Helms hearings. The Mexican government's concern about the judgments on the Mexican political system did not succeed in keeping the U.S. press from resurrecting the subject again from time to time, or in keeping Ambassador Charles Pilliod (following the line of his predecessor, Gavin) or Assistant Secretary of State Elliot Abrams from criticizing Mexican foreign policy.[20]

The direct pressure of the U.S. government on the Mexican president succeeded in extracting a response from the bureaucracy associated with the fight against drug trafficking which would satisfy U.S. interests, at least for the moment; but the more general criticisms of the Mexican political system did not provoke

---

[18]Ramírez, *Operación Gavin*, pp. 173ff.

[19]The hearings were held in May of 1986. See Juan González M. et al., "El impacto de las audiencias Helms en la relación bilateral," *Carta de Política Exterior Mexicana* 6:2 (April-June 1986).

[20]For a good list of these criticisms, see Priscila Sosa, "El contexto de las nuevas percepciones norteamericanas sobre México," *Cuadernos Semestrales*, no. 2 (Mexico City: CIDE, 1986).

immediate changes. This is especially important if one remembers that, in the case of the policy of Mexico in Central America, Ambassador Gavin himself had an interview with President de la Madrid in 1985 to convince Mexico to reverse its decision to participate in the Contadora Group, but no important change was brought about in this policy. This suggests that in those subjects in which the Mexican government feels its national security is at stake, there is a very great capacity to resist external pressures. But on drug trafficking, which the Mexican government itself considers to be a potential danger for its own stability (in the obstruction of formal bureaucratic channels), there is intervention from the presidential level, even against the pressures of traditional groups.

On the other hand, Mexico's inarticulate response over the cleanliness of its elections suggests that on this subject there was no consensus within the Mexican government concerning its importance for internal stability. To the extent that this factor is considered a threat to stability, as candidate Salinas de Gortari suggested, the concern of the Mexican government probably coincides with that of the U.S. government.

Thus, we have a situation where unusual pressures exerted by the United States on certain subjects in Mexico allow us to delineate a pattern of conduct within the Mexican government which suggests that formal bureaucratic agencies tend to make decisions when these are compatible with present priorities of Mexican foreign policy. On the other hand, when these bureaucratic mechanisms are blocked by pressure from traditional sectors of Mexican society (such as in the drug trafficking problem), presidential intervention is the result.

As we can see, changes during de la Madrid's term of office make it possible to outline several distinctive features of the foreign policy decision-making process. On one hand, the existence of national priorities provides for the establishment of the parameters within which these decisions will operate. Likewise, the decreasing weight of presidential personality, together with the rise of open bureaucratic infighting, suggests a greater weight for formal bureaucratic mechanisms in the decision-making process—as long as they do not clash with the established priorities. At the same time, the existence of bureaucratic squabbles, together with the growing complexity of foreign policy issues, suggests insufficient coordination by the executive branch, as reflected in the clumsy use of several of the instruments of Mexican foreign policy. In this sense, it would be worthwhile to review the formal bureaucracy related to foreign affairs, to illustrate some of the coordination problems presently facing Mexican foreign policy.

THE FORMAL BUREAUCRATIC STRUCTURE

According to the Mexican Constitution, the president of the republic is in charge of "directing diplomatic negotiations and signing treaties with foreign powers, submitting them for ratification by the federal Congress."[21] This presidential authorization—complemented by the Constitution's silence on the acts covered by this phrase—is what leads some authors to affirm that "the officeholder's foreign relations powers are his alone, not shared under internal law with any other authority."[22] On this point, it is interesting to note that the growing interaction of Mexico with the rest of the world on issues which go far beyond mere diplomatic negotiations led President de la Madrid to propose an amendment to this article of the Constitution in which the concept of "diplomatic negotiations" would be replaced by the much broader concept of "foreign policy." This amendment also proposed that the traditional principles of foreign policy be included. These principles are self-determination by the people, nonintervention, peaceful settlement of controversies, a prohibition against threat or use of force in international relations, judicial equality among nations, international cooperation for development, and the achievement of international peace and security.[23]

In addition to directing foreign policy, the president also holds the authority to nominate and freely remove cabinet ministers (including the minister of foreign relations) and diplomatic representatives, as well as to appoint, with Senate approval, ministers, diplomatic representatives, and consuls general. Also subject to this same approval, he is authorized to name colonels and other higher-ranking officers of the national army, navy, and air force; to name other officers of these services under the terms of law; to have all

---

[21]*Constitución Política de los Estados Unidos Mexicanos* (Mexico City: Porrúa, 1986), Article 89, Section X. See Jorge Chabat, "El marco jurídico de la política exterior: tendencias y perspectivas," *Cuadernos de Política Exterior Mexicana*, no. 2 (Mexico City: CIDE, 1986).
[22]Statement by Felipe Tena Ramírez, quoted in Jorge Carpizo, *El presidencialismo mexicano* (Mexico City: Siglo XXI, 1978), p. 130.
[23]*Excélsior*, November 7, 1987.

permanent armed forces available for internal security and external defense of the federation; to declare war on behalf of the country, under prior congressional enactment; to approve all types of
ports; and to establish land and sea custom houses and designate
their locations.[24]

On the other hand, it must be pointed out that the legislative
branch participation in foreign policy is extremely limited. Congress has some authority to control the executive branch's ability
to take on public debt commitments. It can also enact laws on
several aspects of foreign policy, emigration and immigration,
organization of the diplomatic and consular corps, contributions
to foreign trade, and regulation of foreign investment. For its part,
the Senate is responsible for "analyzing the foreign policy" carried
out by the president, as well as for approving treaties signed by
the executive branch, ratifying presidential appointments to the
armed forces and the diplomatic corps, and authorizing the president to mobilize troops within the country and to allow the passage of foreign troops.[25]

What stands out in this description of the president's foreign
policy powers is the ample authority that the president has in that
respect, with very limited formal controls by the legislative branch
although these controls have a certain importance in economic
aspects. In practice, the existence of a legislative branch dominated
by the official party has provided a very limited counterbalance
to presidential decisions in general. This suggests that, unless some
change occurs in the correlation of party forces in Congress or an
important split occurs within the official party, this tendency will
be maintained for the medium term.

On analyzing the distribution of functions within the bureaucracy which supports the president and to which many foreign
policy functions are delegated, the panorama appears to be more
complex. First of all, we have the Organic Law of Public Administration which grants the Ministry of Foreign Relations the authority to "conduct foreign policy," for which " it will intervene in all
kinds of treaties, agreements, and conventions in which the country will be a part," as well as the authority to "promote, favor, and
insure coordination of actions on foreign matters, of agencies and
entities of the Federal Public Administration."[26] It should also

---

[24]*Constitución Política*, Art. 89; Chabat, "El marco jurídico."
[25]Chabat, "El marco jurídico," p. 18.
[26]Ibid., p. 23.

manage the Mexican Foreign Service and, by means of same, defend Mexico's good name abroad; grant protection to Mexicans; collect consular fees and other taxes; exercise notary functions; act as an office of public records or vital statistics and legal aid; and acquire, administer, and conserve the nation's property abroad. It should also participate in international commissions, congresses, conferences, and expositions and in international bodies and institutes to which the Mexican government belongs, and take part in questions related to territorial boundaries of the country and international waters. On the other hand, it has the authority to grant foreigners permits to acquire control of lands and waters in the republic in order to exploit natural resources, and to participate in Mexican profit or nonprofit corporations. Finally, the Ministry of Foreign Relations should take part in questions related to nationality and naturalization, keep and use the Great Seal of the Nation, archive signed originals of diplomatic documents with effects abroad and foreign documents with effects in Mexico, as well as take part, through the attorney general of the republic, in extradition according to the law and international letters rogatory, to make them arrive at their destination.[27]

Notwithstanding the broad gamut of attributes possessed by the Ministry of Foreign Relations, some of the subjects that have come to form part of present-day foreign policy, as understood in the broadest sense, do not fall on this ministry. The Ministry of National Defense deals with matters relative to mobilizing the country in case of war, controls foreign arms trade, and takes part in granting permits for international scientific expeditions within Mexican territory. The Ministry of the Navy exercises sovereignty over territorial waters and takes part in granting permits to international scientific expeditions in Mexican waters. The Ministry of Gobernación, in turn, has responsibility for applying Article 33 of the Constitution, which provides for the expulsion of those foreigners whose presence in the country is deemed detrimental by the executive branch and prohibits foreigners from participating in national politics. In addition, it is in charge of administering the islands under federal jurisdiction in both oceans, exercising the right of expropriation, formulating and carrying out population policy, and, of course, conducting internal policy under the responsibility of the executive branch but not assigned to other agencies.[28]

---

[27]Ibid., pp. 23-24.
[28]Ibid., p. 24.

For its part, the Ministry of Finance and Public Credit should direct custom services and inspection and the Fiscal Police of the Federation, manage the public debt of the federation and of the Department of the Federal District, and direct monetary and credit policy. The Ministry of Energy, Mines and Government-controlled Industry should control the tax registry of petroleum and mining, as well as regulate the petroleum, basic petrochemical, mining, electric, and nuclear industries. The Ministry of Commerce and Industrial Development has the authority to formulate and carry out general foreign trade policies, as well as to promote said trade and regulate and orient foreign investment and the transfer of technology.[29]

The Ministry of Tourism, in addition to formulating and carrying out policy for developing domestic tourist activity, must issue opinions to the Ministry of Commerce and Industrial Development in those cases in which foreign investment is involved in tourism development projects or in establishing tourist services. It also promotes and facilitates tourism and tourist development from abroad, in coordination with the Ministry of Foreign Relations.[30]

For its part, the Office of the Attorney General of the Republic should issue its opinion as judicial adviser to the federal government, take part as public ministry of the federation on all matters in which the latter is part, as well as prosecute and investigate crimes of a federal nature—among them drug trafficking—and exercise in court the corresponding criminal action. It likewise has the authority to propose to the president instruments which are international in scope in questions of prosecution and enforcement and police or judicial cooperation.[31]

In addition to the above-mentioned attributes of the various ministries which have to do with foreign policy, there are others which carry out specific activities related to international treaties of different types, such as the Ministries of Agriculture and Hydraulic Resources, Communication and Transportation, Public Education, Labor and Social Welfare, and Fishing.[32]

As can be appreciated from this overview, various executive branch agencies are involved in formulating foreign policy. We can

---

[29]Ibid.
[30]Ibid.
[31]"Reglamento Interior de la Procuraduría General de la República," *Diario Oficial*, August 9, 1985.
[32]Chabat, "El marco jurídico," p. 25.

even see that of the current administration's foreign policy priorities (promoting exports, managing the public debt, and maintaining internal stability in the face of the Central American conflict) two fall directly under the responsibility of the Ministry of Commerce and Industrial Development[33] and the Ministry of Finance and Public Credit, while the third is shared by Foreign Relations, Gobernación, Defense, and Navy. It is also interesting to note that, despite the fact that the Ministry of Commerce and Industrial Development has the authority to formulate and conduct foreign trade policies and the obligation to promote such trade, the Organic Law of the Mexican Foreign Service assigns the heads of consular offices authority to "promote trade and tourism with Mexico in their respective consular districts and to regularly report on same to the Ministry of Foreign Relations."[34] This authority evidently implies coordination between the Ministry of Foreign Relations and the Ministry of Commerce, as well as with the Ministry of Tourism, whose authority to promote and facilitate tourist activity and development from abroad should be coordinated, as indicated in the Law of Public Administration, with Foreign Relations.

A review of the structure of the various cabinet ministries with attributes that involve them with other countries reveals the existence of a great number of agencies, some at bureau level, that are in charge of subjects vital to foreign policy; this in turn suggests splintering in decision-making. The appendix to this paper details the principal attributes of agencies which link them to the foreign affairs arena.

One clear implication in this diverse array of institutional functions possessed by various agencies is the emphasis on the *coordination* of their activities by the Ministry of Foreign Relations. However, some overlap can be perceived, especially with the Ministry of Commerce and Industrial Development and the Ministry of Finance and Public Credit.

Another element which should be emphasized is that several of the functions that are becoming important for Mexican foreign policy and will be more so in the future (in addition to the priorities

---

[33]The fact stands out, for example, that foreign trade promotion had been assigned to the Ministry of Foreign Relations—in conjunction with the Ministry of Commerce and Industrial Development—in the 1958 Law on Cabinet Ministries and Departments, prior to the 1976 law now in effect.

[34]"Ley Orgánica del Servicio Exterior Mexicano," *Diario Oficial*, January 8, 1987, Art. 47, Sec. b.

that the government has clearly outlined)—such as promoting the image of the country (the Ministry of Tourism) and developing cultural programs on the border and in Mexican communities abroad (the Ministry of Public Education)—come under ministries *other than Foreign Relations.* Likewise, as already indicated, it is clear that the attributions in priority foreign policy areas—such as promoting foreign trade and investment, negotiating the foreign debt, and migration policies—also come under ministries other than Foreign Relations.

On the other hand, a certain *splintering of functions* emerges in relation to agencies which have to do with the United States, especially in economic matters. In political matters—although it is true that the Ministry of Foreign Relations retains a greater control of formal relations, through embassies, consulates, the Protection and Consular Services Bureau, and the North America Bureau—some of these, such as the difficult problem of drug traffic, have been moved to the Attorney General of the Republic, and those dealing with the image of the country, to the Ministry of Tourism.

It is obvious, after the interbureaucratic conflicts of the de la Madrid years, that the formal bureaucratic framework is too complex, and that the Ministry of Foreign Relations' coordination efforts in bilateral and multilateral areas of economic negotiation are only partly successful. The problem, of course, is not simple, because in addition to these problems of coordination there are problems such as the foreign debt, which falls under the responsibility of the Ministry of Finance and Public Credit.

A quick analysis of the budgets of the various agencies also reflects inequalities in power among them. For example, the Public Credit Bureau of the Ministry of Finance and Public Credit, which handles the foreign debt, had a 1986 budget ten times greater than the sum of the budgets of the Bilateral Economic Relations and Multilateral Economic Relations Bureaus of the Ministry of Foreign Relations.[35] And the International Trade Negotiations Bureau of the Ministry of Commerce and Industrial Development had a 1986 budget which was double the sum of the two Foreign Relations bureaus just mentioned.[36]

---

[35]Miguel de la Madrid, *Quinto Informe de Gobierno*, Appendices (Mexico City: Secretaría de la Presidencia, September 1987).
[36]Ibid.

As for agencies of the Ministry of Foreign Relations which are linked more directly to the United States, the North America Bureau had a 1986 budget which was 1.7 percent of the total budget for the ministry, a greater percentage than the Eastern Europe and USSR Bureau (1 percent) but less than that of the Latin America and Caribbean Bureau (2.9 percent) and of the Africa, Asia, and Oceania Bureau (2.3 percent). The budget for the North America Bureau is relatively high when we consider that each of the bureaus with which it is compared covers several countries, and even entire continents. It is also interesting to point out that the Protection and Consular Services Bureau, dedicated largely to the problems of undocumented Mexicans in the United States, had in 1986 a budget equivalent to 4.3 percent of the total budget of the ministry, which is the highest of any single agency except the Foreign Service Bureau, upon which Mexican diplomatic personnel abroad depend, which in 1986 accounted for 43.5 percent of the budget of the ministry.[37]

An example of the importance which the Office of the Attorney General gives to combatting drug trafficking—work which draws a good part of U.S. political pressure—is the high percentage of this agency's budget which went to the campaign against drug trafficking and abuse in 1986 (27.6 percent), even though in comparative terms the percentage has decreased appreciably if compared to 1983's 38 percent, the highest level during the de la Madrid administration. Nevertheless, in absolute terms this allocation in 1986, for instance, was two-and-a-half times that of the important Public Credit Bureau of the Ministry of Finance and Public Credit.

To conclude this section, let us delve further into the problem of coordination among the various agencies that deal with other countries. Two hypotheses are feasible. The first would assume that this lack of coordination has come about spontaneously in response to abrupt Mexican government contact with other countries. If this were the case, the problem might be solved with the passage of time, as the various agencies take on their formally assigned duties and begin to respond to the coordination efforts which regulations delegate to the Ministry of Foreign Relations. This hypothesis would leave unresolved the problem of formal responsibilities for foreign trade, foreign debt, and control of migrants which fall upon

---

[37]Ibid.

by the Ministries of Commerce, Finance, and Gobernación, respectively.

Under a second hypothesis, the lack of coordination would be the calculated creation of a president who does not want a technically unqualified Ministry of Foreign Relations to handle priority foreign policy issues. Since the political cost of formally withdrawing the Foreign Ministry's authority to coordinate foreign policy is obviously very high, under this hypothesis the president would let things take their course and would intervene only when the handling of the priority issues were upset precisely by the Ministry of Foreign Relations—as in the case of the foreign debt negotiation and, in part, with the Guatemalan refugees.

Whichever hypothesis should prove true, it seems obvious that the problem of coordination will persist unless coordination is achieved through comprehensive action at the level of the specialized cabinets. On this point, even though this option of bureaucratic coordination formally exists—having been instituted by President de la Madrid through the Federal Public Administration Law at the beginning of his administration—it has not been implemented in the area of foreign policy. In fact, there are only four specialized cabinets: Agriculture and Livestock, Foreign Trade, Economics, and Health. Of these, the Ministry of Foreign Relations participates in only the specialized cabinet on the economy, together with eminently economic ministries, those of Commerce and Industrial Development; Energy, Mines, and Government-controlled Industry; Finance and Public Credit; Planning and Budget; and Controllership.[38] In this regard, it should be mentioned that several of the important foreign policy decisions made under de la Madrid (entry into GATT, debt policy) were defined in those cabinets, making them an important future element in the analysis of decision-making.

PERSPECTIVES

This description of the characteristic features of Miguel de la Madrid's foreign policy and of the formal framework of the bureaucracy dealing with other countries allows us to outline a

---

[38]"Acuerdo por el que se crea la Dirección General del Secretariado Técnico de Gabinetes de la Presidencia de la República," *Diario Oficial,* January 19, 1983.

panorama characterized by a trend toward greater importance and autonomy for executive branch agencies. The outline suggests that these agencies act with relative autonomy so long as they do not stray from the foreign policy priorities set by the Mexican government. Moreover, the work of these bureaucratic agencies is obstructed less the more that they operate in areas that are relatively insusceptible to pressure from traditional groups inside Mexico. On the other hand, the Mexican government does not appear very interested in providing these agencies with a greater degree of coordination since this feature does not seem to particularly affect fulfillment of the established priorities.

This general situation seems to extend to the relationship with the United States, despite the fact that during recent years the relationship has experienced a series of unusual pressures. In any case, this conflictive relationship has revealed a certain inability on the part of the Mexican government to respond effectively through its bureaucratic agencies. This ineffectiveness, however, does not appear to have blocked the achievement of the established priorities. It is therefore feasible to expect that attempts to articulate responses to the United States through novel means will continue.

The future outlook therefore appears to be characterized by the following features:

- A decision-making process that tends to center more on the cabinet ministers and less on the president.

- An increasing trend toward greater legislative branch involvement in foreign policy, although it is hard to say when this involvement might become a real counterbalance to executive branch decisions. That would be possible with a more autonomous legislative branch as a result of greater presence in the legislature of opposition legislators or of important factions within the PRI majority.[39]

---

[39]Some statements by the official party's presidential candidate, Carlos Salinas de Gortari, revealed serious concern over the low level of credibility of election results. It is therefore reasonable to expect these results to reflect some opposition party victories that might affect the official party's monopoly in Congress. A radical change in this regard does not seem feasible in the near future, however.

- Mexican government insistence on sticking to priorities— possibly differing from present insistence on doing so[40]—such that foreign pressure cannot achieve many concessions.

- A decrease in the number of Mexican government agencies which respond to pressures exerted by nongovernmental groups, which made these agencies ineffective in the past. If they are to become efficient, they may well do so under the umbrella of presidential authority.

- Increasing use of diverse foreign policy instruments by bureaucratic agencies, with which not only the decision-making process, but also the implementation of those decisions, will tend toward deconcentration.

- Increasing risk that the splintering among the agencies in charge of decisions with foreign ramifications will contradict foreign policy priorities, which makes it feasible to expect the eventual creation of a mechanism for comprehensive coordination.

- If the splintering does affect the degree of foreign policy effectiveness but the coordination mechanism is not set up, the risk will be run that many decisions and actions by these agencies will conflict with the decisions of other agencies, making their real ability to influence events unpredictable.

- In case of conflict among Mexican foreign policy priorities, we might expect priorities associated with internal stability to prevail and those associated with the promotion of economic development to be given secondary importance. In this sense, should repayment of the foreign debt threaten internal stability, a moratorium is possible.

---

[40]These priorities have been confirmed by Salinas de Gortari. Regarding foreign debt negotiation, however, he has left open the possibility of a change in the policy followed to date. Replying to a question from the *New York Times* correspondent on the possibility that Mexico might change her generally conciliatory tone concerning the payment of her foreign debt, Salinas said, "What is considered impossible today might be considered possible tomorrow," *Excélsior*, January 18, 1988, front page.

APPENDIX — AGENCIES ENGAGED IN FOREIGN POLICY OF MEXICO[41]

MINISTRY OF COMMERCE AND INDUSTRIAL DEVELOPMENT

Economic Negotiations and International Affairs Bureau:

— Studies and proposes measures to improve international trade dealings.

— Coordinates negotiation and economic cooperation activities at a national and international level in different forums for multilateral or bilateral negotiations.

— Coordinates measures to defend Mexican exports against restrictive actions or unfair practices.

— Proposes to international organizations strategies and plans for negotiation on tariff and non-tariff barriers so as to optimize Mexico's participation in economic negotiations and international affairs.

— Collects and develops information on international trade for negotiating purposes.

— Participates with specialists on international, industrial, and technological cooperation and on joint venture agreements.

Foreign Investment Bureau:

— Implements foreign investment policies according to criteria from the National Foreign Investment Commission and analyzes the performance of investments.

— Operates the National Registry of Foreign Investments as provided for in the Law to Promote Mexican Investment and Regulate Foreign Investment and issues the respective certificates.

— Issues foreign investment authorizations as per resolutions of the National Foreign Investment Commission and oversees compliance with said authorizations.

---

[41]The description of functions is based on the internal regulations of the various ministries.

— Oversees and verifies compliance with the Law to Promote Mexican Investment and Regulate Foreign Investment and imposes penalties for noncompliance.

— Participates with the Technology Transfer Bureau in determining policies and decisions on technology transfer.

Foreign Trade Services Bureau:

— Studies, analyzes, and evaluates foreign trade controls.

— Analyzes, processes, and rules on requests for import and export licenses.

— Proposes and assigns maximum quotas for products subject to import or export programs.

— Determines, having heard the opinion of the Border Affairs Bureau, import quotas for the country's border areas and free zones.

— Coordinates with other units of the Ministry of Commerce and of the federal government that provide input regarding requests for product import or export licenses.

Tariff Bureau:

— Proposes the establishment, amendment, or repeal of customs classifications and analyzes and evaluates the effects of the duties.

— Proposes official prices for export and import goods as well as import subsidies.

Border Affairs Bureau:

— Proposes guidelines for the program to develop border areas and free zones.

— Participates in setting import quotas for the border area.

— Participates in analyzing the development of international border trade and industrial relations.

— Assists in establishing in-bond plants (*maquiladoras*) in border areas and free zones.

MINISTRY OF FINANCE AND PUBLIC CREDIT

International Fiscal Affairs Bureau:

— Formulates Ministry of Finance fiscal policies in its dealings abroad.

— Acts as the technical body for coordinating the domestic financial sector in implementing bilateral fiscal policy abroad.

— Coordinates fiscal policy related to foreign trade.

— Formulates fiscal policy related to foreign investment.

— Promotes programs to assist in attracting technical and economic resources from abroad.

— Participates, in coordination with the Public Credit Bureau, in formulating Ministry of Finance policy regarding international economic and financial organizations.

— Evaluates and proposes reciprocal foreign economic aid mechanisms in coordination with other agencies of the federal government and carries out specific activities in this regard.

— Takes part, in coordination with the Public Credit Bureau, in the formulation and evaluation of public credit policy.

— Analyzes and evaluates the effect of the international economic situation on the domestic economy and the foreign exchange program.

Public Credit Bureau:

— Proposes federal government public credit policy in coordination with the Fiscal Planning Bureau.

— Proposes public credit budget allocations.

— Formulates and follows up on the credit program for handling the federal government's foreign exchange requirements.

— Formulates and implements policies regarding international financial organizations.

— Formulates policies and programs for attracting resources from international markets.

— Proposes, with the participation of the central bank (Banco de México), the National Foreign Trade Bank, and the corresponding authorities, foreign trade financing policy.

— Coordinates, implements, and evaluates financing obtained from the International Reconstruction and Development Bank and the Inter-American Development Bank.

— Collects, documents, and disseminates information on the international money and capital market.

— Evaluates projects to be financed with resources from outside the public sector.

— Defines and evaluates policies for the negotiation of bilateral financing.

— Promotes and supports the use of bilateral agencies' overall lines of credit.

MINISTRY OF PUBLIC EDUCATION

International Relations Bureau:

— Promotes and expands cooperative activities and scientific, educational, cultural, technical, and artistic exchange with other countries and international organizations, in coordination with the Ministry of Foreign Relations and other responsible agencies.

— Represents the Ministry of Public Education in commitments derived from the above international agreements.

— Coordinates Ministry of Public Education units in the fulfillment of international agreements.

— Assists the minister of public education in coordinating with the international organizations that carry out educational and cultural activities in Mexico.

— Encourages and organizes Ministry of Public Education participation in international scientific, educational, cultural, technical, and artistic events.

— Promotes and disseminates Mexican culture abroad, primarily through programs designed for groups of Mexican origin residing abroad.

— Studies the cultural needs of the residents of the border areas and proposes suitable activities.

— Hosts foreign officials visiting the country on official business related to the Ministry of Public Education.

— Assists the minister of public education, within the bureau's sphere of responsibility, in the tasks assigned by the Organic Law of Federal Public Administration; the Federal Budget, Accounting, and Public Expense Law; the General Law on Public Indebtedness; and other applicable provisions.

MINISTRY OF AGRICULTURE AND WATER RESOURCES

International Affairs Bureau:

— Coordinates the relations of the agricultural, livestock, and forestry sector with international organizations, institutions, and other countries, under standards issued by the Ministry of Foreign Relations.

— Proposes to the Ministries of Foreign Relations and Commerce and Industrial Development the establishment of policies concerning international affairs and foreign trade of interest to the Ministry of Agriculture and implements programs derived from these policies.

— Identifies and analyzes the needs and possibilities for international technical, economic, commercial, and financial cooperation within the sphere of responsibility of the Ministry of Agriculture and promotes arrangements for the appropriate agreements.

— Represents the Ministry of Agriculture at and coordinates its participation in international meetings.

— Participates in defining and implementing the policies of the Ministry of Agriculture's Import and Export Program.

— Analyzes expected supply and demand in international markets in order to orient Ministry of Agriculture import/export programs.

— Acts as liaison between the Ministry of Agriculture and other executive branch agencies in dealings with foreign governments and international organizations.

— Monitors implementation of international agreements and trade agreements which fall under the purview of the Ministry of Agriculture.

— Coordinates agencies of the agricultural sector in order to reinforce and open foreign markets for agricultural, livestock, and forestry products.

— Participates in the Ministry of Commerce and Industrial Development's processing of import and export licenses for agricultural, livestock, and forestry products.

— Sets up quality standards programs for domestic agricultural, livestock, and forestry products sold on the international market and furnishes the standards to the Ministry of Commerce and Industrial Development.

— Proposes policies for international promotion of technological development and training.

— Sets standards for, supervises, and evaluates Agricultural, Livestock, and Forestry Consulting Offices abroad as per Ministry of Foreign Relations guidelines for foreign service personnel.

— Sets the overall import/export quotas derived from the Ministry of Agriculture's international commitments.

— Records current Ministry of Agriculture international agreements and regulations so as to facilitate their enforcement.

— Requests that the Ministry of Commerce and Industrial Development give imports by the Ministry of Agriculture and government-controlled firms in the agricultural sector favorable tax treatment.

— Advises government-controlled firms from the agricultural sector on international matters.

— Promotes international relations programs to support the development of border areas and free zones in matters falling under the responsibility of the Ministry of Agriculture.

— Gathers foreign market information on agricultural, livestock, and forestry products.

— Promotes increased foreign marketing for products from the agricultural and livestock sector and proposes import substitution policies to the Ministry of Commerce and Industrial Development.

— Participates in meetings related to agricultural-sector foreign trade.

— Promotes negotiations to obtain the foreign financing needed by the Ministry of Agriculture and monitors and records the agreements under standards of the Ministries of Programming and Budget and Finance and Public Credit.

MINISTRY OF TOURISM

International Promotion Bureau:

— Designs and implements tourism promotion, advertising, and public relations campaigns abroad.

— Schedules promotion and advertising so as to encourage the flow of foreign tourists toward domestic tourist destinations.

— Designs and implements promotional activities abroad for Priority Tourism Development Zones.

— Supports the international tourism promotion and advertising activities carried out by federal agencies and advises private parties that request assistance in developing this type of activities.

— Evaluates and measures the impact abroad of Ministry of Tourism promotional and advertising campaigns and carries out opinion surveys and diagnostic studies regarding the country's tourism image abroad.

— Designs and develops promotional and informative material on tourism for foreign advertising campaigns.

— Represents the Ministry of Tourism at events held abroad and in which the country's tourist image is promoted.

— Promotes and develops familiarization tours to domestic tourist destinations for travel industry professionals and international press representatives.

Foreign Offices Bureau:

— Proposes standards and guidelines for the operation of Ministry of Tourism offices abroad and coordinates their operation.

— Processes, controls, and updates tourist information available in Ministry of Tourism offices abroad.

— Establishes bases for the dissemination of tourist information and advertising handled by the foreign offices.

— Develops studies on the influx of foreign tourists and the competitiveness of domestic tourist services.

MINISTRY OF ENERGY, MINES, AND GOVERNMENT-CONTROLLED INDUSTRY

Bureau of International Transactions involving Energy and Government-controlled Industry:

— Proposes strategic guidelines to be followed by the Ministry of Energy and Mines and the coordinated government-controlled entities under general foreign policy approaches.

— Proposes policies and mechanisms to replace imports and to promote and market abroad the goods and services of the coordinated government-controlled entities.

— Draws up the foreign trade opinions and resolutions requested of the Ministry of Energy and Mines.

— Coordinates the participation of the ministry's administrative units and the coordinated government-controlled entities in international meetings which they attend and monitors their consistency with sectoral policy and the country's foreign policy principles.

— Comments on drafts of contracts and transactions of a bilateral or multilateral nature involving the energy sector.

— Coordinates, through the ministry's administrative units, the development of the foreign trade program of the coordinated government-controlled entities.

— Supports and advises the minister of energy, mines, and government-controlled industries and the ministry's administrative units on handling international matters.

MINISTRY OF FISHING

International Fishing Affairs Bureau:

— Proposes to the Ministry of Foreign Relations the signing of international fishing treaties and agreements.

— Analyzes the international agreements that involve functions of the Ministry of Fishing and the fisheries sector and notifies the responsible units about them.

— Promotes the signing and implementation of multilateral and bilateral fisheries production programs, monitors their implementation, and oversees the payment of dues to international organizations related to fishing.

— Promotes, through the Ministry of Finance and Public Credit, foreign financing for the development of fishing in Mexico.

— Promotes, through the Ministry of Commerce and Industrial Development, foreign trade in Mexican fish products and describes and evaluates export potential.

— Comments on the chartering of fishing companies through joint ventures with foreigners, supervises fulfillment of their commitments, and instructs investors regarding the necessary procedures.

— Takes cognizance of penalties against and detentions of foreign vessels for violation of legal provisions which the Ministry of Fishing is responsible for enforcing.

— Receives, rules on, and forwards to the appropriate administrative unit applications from foreigners for licenses to carry out fishing activities.

— Promotes international meetings on fishing and, as needed, takes part in them.

— Carries out studies on the structure, operation, and evolution of the economic and social situation abroad that might impact the development of domestic fishing.

— Assists in gathering information on fishing at an international level and forwards it to the respective administrative units.

— Coordinates the activities of Ministry of Fishing delegates abroad.

MINISTRY OF COMMUNICATION AND TRANSPORTATION

Civil Aeronautics Bureau:

— Plans, coordinates, and controls public and private domestic and international air transportation services.

— Processes requests for concessions or licenses to provide domestic and international air transportation services and takes part in negotiating agreements on the operation of international air carriers.

— Authorizes, within the framework of its statutory powers, aircraft import licenses.

— Rules on the applicability of aeronautical standards and methods recommended by international organizations.

Merchant Marine Bureau:

— Takes part in negotiating international agreements on maritime transportation and contamination and human safety at sea.

— Designs, studies, and proposes improvements for signals installed according to domestic and international standards and requirements.

Post Office Bureau:

— Plans, operates, and controls the postal services referred to in the Law on General Communication Channels and those established by international agreements.

— Proposes the regulations required for compliance with international postal agreements.

Telecommunications Bureau:

— Takes part in developing technical standards and Mexico's proposals in international meetings.

MINISTRY OF GOBERNACIÓN

Immigration Services Bureau:

— Processes and rules on the entry into, stay in, and exit from the country by foreigners and the cancellation, when called for, of the immigration statuses granted.

— Grants to foreigners who meet legal requirements permits to acquire real estate or rights to same or stock in companies involved in buying, selling, or holding real estate.

— Processes, orders, and carries out the expulsion of foreigners who need to be deported and distributes to the Foreign Service and the local Immigration Services Offices circulars to prevent entry.

— Proposes appropriate standards for migratory movements and determines the most suitable purpose to be served by immigration.

— Keeps the National Register of Foreigners.

— Investigates if foreigners comply with established immigration requirements and, in case of violation of the legal provisions, turns the violator over to the proper authorities.

— Files immigration documentation.

MINISTRY OF HEALTH

International Affairs Coordinating Commission:

— Acts as liaison with the Ministry of Foreign Relations for Ministry of Health administrative units on international issues related to the health sector.

— Coordinates activities for implementing international agreements on health and takes part in the development of the respective projects.

— Supplies international organizations with domestic health information and coordinates Ministry of Health participation in those organizations.

— Provides information supplied by international organizations to domestic public and private institutions that need it.

— Supports and advises Ministry of Health officials on official business abroad and foreigners visiting Mexico for professional reasons related to health.

— Comments on the process of importing and exporting drugs in collaboration with the International Drug Control Board, the Health Product Input Control Bureau, and the Biological Agent and Reagent Administration.

— Takes cognizance of, discusses, and, if called for, approves international health matters in which Mexico participates.

MINISTRY OF NATIONAL DEFENSE

National Defense Chiefs of Staff:

— Plans and coordinates matters related to national defense.

— Maintains liaison with government agencies in order to fulfill joint tasks and organizes, coordinates, supervises, and manages the ministry's public relations.

— Channels liaison with the armed forces of other countries and monitors good relations with accredited foreign military personnel in Mexico.

MINISTRY OF THE NAVY

— Exercises the high command of the Mexican navy and, as needed, plans and directs the nation's maritime and naval power for the purposes of internal security and foreign defense.

— Coordinates with the Ministry of National Defense in developing national security plans.

OFFICE OF THE ATTORNEY GENERAL OF THE REPUBLIC

Drug Control Agency:

— Plans and directs the programs of the campaign against the production and distribution of drugs, psychotropics, and other harmful or hazardous substances, as set forth in penal and health legislation.

— Coordinates, supervises, and controls the destruction of fields and laboratories producing drugs, psychotropics, and other harmful and hazardous substances and the destruction or turning over to proper authorities of the substances and other objects that are confiscated.

— Approves the herbicides, aids, and operating and safety equipment used in the campaign.

— Rules on district attorney requests for determination of the legal status of defendants accused of health crimes and coordinates with the judicial police investigations carried out in this regard.

— Guides Attorney General's Office air services for the location, fumigation, and verification of the areas covered by the campaign against drug production and distribution.

GOVERNMENT OF THE FEDERAL DISTRICT

Public Information and Relations Bureau:

— Organizes and supervises interviews and press conferences with domestic and international journalists.

— Handles arrangements for invitations which the government of the Federal District must extend in carrying out its functions.

MINISTRY OF FOREIGN RELATIONS

Regional Bureaus (North America, Latin America and Caribbean, Western Europe, Eastern Europe and USSR, Africa, Asia, and Oceania):

— Submit foreign policy options and participate in designing short-, medium-, or long-term international action programs for a country in the region or for the entire region, based on general foreign policy guidelines.

— Develop the political reports and analyses required for formulating bilateral foreign policy.

— Gather information on the political aspect of the internal situation and international position of the countries of the region.

— Act as an institutional conduit for transmitting instructions on bilateral political matters to the heads of the foreign service offices.

— Propose the opening or closing of diplomatic missions and consular offices.

— Systematically evaluate application of the guidelines and instructions sent to the diplomatic missions regarding foreign policy and action programs.

— Gather, in coordination with the respective administrative units, information on bilateral economic, cultural, and scientific/ technological cooperation programs carried out by the federal government with the countries of the region as well as information on the work done in Mexican diplomatic missions by representatives of other agencies of the Mexican government.

— Handle bilateral political matters with the embassies accredited by the government of Mexico and be the channel between them and other agencies of the federal government.

— Apply for in-transit or visitation permits from federal government agencies for foreign navy vessels as well as permits for overflights and landings by foreign military aircraft.

— Apply for similar authorizations from foreign governments for Mexican navy ships and Mexican military aircraft.

— Process foreign military scholarships granted by the federal government.

— Request from other federal government agencies the permits which foreign governments ask for in order to carry out research in Mexican territory or jurisdictional waters.

Foreign Service Bureau:

— Keeps the register of Mexican foreign service personnel assigned to diplomatic missions, consular offices, and international organizations.

— Coordinates with other responsible administrative units everything related to personnel assigned abroad.

Bilateral Economic Relations Bureau:

— Plans, schedules, develops, and evaluates the activities of preparing, signing, implementing, coordinating, and following up on the bilateral agreements and commissions for economic cooperation and high level visits in coordination with the proper federal government agencies.

— Participates in the bilateral foreign policy activities of the financial sector.

— Makes sure that the different bilateral collaborative economic activities fall within an coherent plan that satisfies the country's economic and social development requirements.

— Collaborates with federal government organizations that handle bilateral international financial questions and participates in the interministerial economic mechanisms that deal with bilateral affairs.

— Coordinates Mexico's participation in and takes part in bilateral international economic meetings and events.

— Supports the promotion of foreign trade through embassies and consulates, through the gathering, dissemination, follow-up, and evaluation of information.

International Boundaries and Rivers Bureau:

— Monitors implementation of and compliance with treaties on boundaries and the use of the waters of international rivers.

— Provides technical expertise in the negotiation of all types of international agreements related to the country's territorial limits and international river waters.

— Assures coordination and liaison between the ministry and other federal government agencies, within the bureau's sphere of responsibility.

— Formulates guidelines and standards for Mexico's participation in the International Boundaries and Water Commission.

— Supervises the work of the Mexican sections of the International Boundaries and Water Commission.

Protection and Consular Services Bureau:

— Instructs foreign service offices as to how to handle cases in which protection is to be provided Mexican nationals abroad.

— Takes part, with other federal government agencies, in negotiating, executing, and supervising programs for Mexican workers abroad.

— Notifies the bilateral or multilateral ministry bureaus of cases of violation of basic human rights or breaches of international agreements or treaties which are detrimental to Mexican nationals.

— Supervises compliance with the Organic Law of the Mexican Foreign Service by consular offices and ministry delegations.

— Issues passports and identification and travel documents.

— Issues visas in foreign passports.

— Acts as liaison between the Ministry of National Defense and Mexican foreign service offices in applying the National Military Service Law and the Federal Firearms and Explosives Law.

— Proposes the opening or closing of honorary Mexican consulates and the naming and functions of Mexico's honorary consuls and vice consuls.

— Processes with the proper authorities complaints or accusations made by tourists in Mexican consular offices regarding services received or commercial transactions carried out during their stay in Mexico.

Legal Affairs Bureau:

— Rules on questions of nationality and naturalization.

— Grants foreigners licenses to acquire control of land and water and to acquire concessions for exploiting mines, waters, or mineral fuels; for acquiring real estate; for taking part in the exploitation of natural resources; for investing in commercial and industrial companies; and for forming part of Mexican profit and nonprofit corporations.

— Takes part in extradition proceedings.

United Nations Bureau:

— Contributes points of view for Mexico's participation regarding political, legal, and social issues in the various United Nations bodies.

— Contributes points of view for Mexico's participation in worldwide or regional, but not inter-American, non-United Nations international governmental or nongovernmental organizations.

— Supports and facilitates the participation of federal government agencies in the United Nations and in the organizations mentioned above.

— Coordinates with Ministry of Foreign Relations administrative units and other federal government agencies participation as Mexico's representative to the United Nations and other organizations under its responsibility.

— Supervises and coordinates the work of the missions to United Nations bodies and other governmental organizations under the bureau's responsibility as well as the activities of the delegations that represent Mexico in each case.

International Organizations Bureau:

— Contributes points of view for Mexico's participation in the Organization of American States and the conferences and organizations of the inter-American system.

— Contributes points of view for Mexico's participation in the specialized organizations of the United Nations system related to education, science, culture, labor, tourism, health, housing, copyrights, and meteorology.

— Contributes points of view for Mexico's participation in autonomous international bodies connected with the above-mentioned organizations and in which the federal government has an interest.

— Supports participation by Ministry of Foreign Relations administrative units and federal government agencies in the specialized organizations in their sphere of responsibility.

— Coordinates with Ministry of Foreign Relations administrative units and other federal government agencies participation as Mexico's representative to the organizations mentioned above.

— Supervises and coordinates the work of the permanent missions to the international organizations under the bureau's responsibility as well as the activities of the Mexican delegations.

Multilateral Economic Relations Bureau:

— Formulates guidelines and standards for Mexico's participation in international forums on economic questions.

— Coordinates the activities of Mexican delegations participating in meetings of international economic organizations.

— Coordinates, through the holding of interministerial meetings or other mechanisms, the definition of guidelines and proposals for Mexico's actions on multilateral economic questions.

— Compiles and appropriately disseminates among interested offices of the Ministry of Foreign Relations and other federal government offices information on multilateral economic negotiations.

— Assists in the proper follow-up on commitments undertaken in multilateral economic forums.

— Facilitates the effective fulfillment of the functions of multilateral economic organizations represented in Mexico.

International Technical Cooperation Bureau:

— Draws up and monitors compliance with the National Program for International Technical Cooperation in coordination with the responsible federal government agencies.

— Participates in negotiating and implementing the basic and supplementary agreements for establishing bilateral and multilateral international technical cooperation programs.

— Coordinates the meetings of bilateral technical cooperation commissions held in fulfillment of current agreements.

— Participates in the formulation of guidelines and standards for Mexico's participation in bilateral and multilateral international technical cooperation forums.

Cultural Affairs Bureau:

— Contributes points of view for formulating general guidelines for Mexico's foreign policy regarding cultural exchanges, with the collaboration of Ministry of Foreign Relations administrative units and the responsible federal government agencies.

— Collaborates with the Ministry of Public Education in disseminating Mexico's culture abroad and promotes Mexico's cultural and educational relations with other countries.

— Promotes, encourages, and assures coordination for the cultural activities carried out abroad by federal government agencies.

— Coordinates Mexico's participation in international cultural organizations.

— Implements, in coordination with the responsible national institutions, binational exchange programs approved by the mixed commissions established by the cultural exchange agreements in which Mexico takes part.

— Nominates cultural attachés and counselors for diplomatic missions and directs, coordinates, and monitors their work.

Protocol Bureau:

— Acts as liaison between the accredited diplomatic corps in Mexico and Mexico's federal government agencies and states.

— Acts as liaison between the Ministry of Foreign Relations and the foreign consular corps accredited in Mexico.

— Handles arrangements for trips abroad by the president of the republic and the minister of foreign relations.

— Handles arrangements for and participates in official visits to Mexico by heads of state, foreign ministers, or other foreign dignitaries.

— Monitors compliance with provisions regarding immunity and prerogatives for the diplomatic and consular corps as well as personnel of international organizations stationed in Mexico.

— Keeps the register of the accredited diplomatic and consular corps as well as of the personnel of international organizations stationed in Mexico and of the international experts assigned to technical cooperation projects and programs carried out in Mexico.

5

The Making of U.S. Policy toward Mexico: Should We Expect Coherence?

Carlos Rico F.

From at least the end of the Second World War until the very late sixties, Mexican-U.S. relations enjoyed a sense of stability. Among the most relevant characteristics of this period were a very low level of attention paid to Mexico and Mexican issues in the United Sates in general and a consistently low priority of those same issues in the agenda of U.S. foreign relations. The first "Operation Intercept" in 1969 and the measures introduced by the Nixon administration in U.S. international economic policy inaugurated a process of profound redefinition in the basic terms of the bilateral relationship which continues to this day. During this decade and a half, reference has frequently been made to a given year (1975-76, 1979, etc.) as the "worst year" for Mexican-U.S. relations in recent history. Relations between the two countries have, in fact, ridden a roller coaster on which, with extreme speed in historical terms, periods of rapprochement have alternated with phases of extreme mutual recrimination. Profound changes in the politics and the economics of both countries, as well as in the international context of the relationship, made such a process almost inevitable.[1]

---

[1]These ideas are more fully developed in Carlos Rico, "Terms of Endearment: The Search for New Basic Understandings in Mexican-U.S. Relations," paper prepared for the Project on Mexican-U.S. Interdependence, School of Advanced International Studies, Washington D.C., 1988.

The de la Madrid administration represents a particularly interesting example of the "roller coaster" dynamics. During its early
years it seemed able simultaneously to ingratiate itself with U.S.
authorities in a significant number of spheres—particularly economic and financial—and maintain a fairly independent stance in
other areas, basically foreign policy and security, causing irritation
in different sectors of the U.S. government. In 1985-86, however,
that tightrope act seemed to end as a new period of acrimony and
mutual recrimination set in—with a vengeance. That low point in
the relationship had a series of paradoxical results. Far from
defining the new tone of the relationship, as many feared on both
sides of the border, it marked the high-water mark in the process
of deterioration. At least one point was made increasingly clear:
attention was being paid to Mexico in the United States—even if
the kind of attention paid was very far from what those Mexican
sectors which had long sought such attention had in mind.

This produced rapid results on both sides of the border. In the
United States the extremes reached by some radical critics, as well
as the mostly negative reaction in Mexico to the charges made,
brought an increased awareness of the potentially negative effects
of "Mexico-bashing," in particular given the intricate web of connections linking the two countries. Paradoxically—as if to prove
the complexity of Mexican-U.S. interactions—things were moving
ahead in specific issue areas even in the worst moments of that
difficult period.

On the Mexican side of the border, concern grew as a result of
the apparent low level of influence or even ability of Mexico to
convey its case to relevant audiences. Combined with the increasingly consensual assumption that attention to Mexican issues in
Washington could not be expected to diminish significantly in the
future, the need to "do something" became increasingly clear.

A whole series of activities began—initiated not only by the
Mexican government, but by several non-governmental actors as
well. Cabinet and sub-cabinet level officials stepped up their visits
to and contacts in the United States, the legislative branch undertook new "public relations" activities, Mexican officials and
"influential" North American opinion makers tried new kinds of
interactions, etc. Most of these efforts were implicitly (and sometimes explicitly) directed at the same question which has provided
the point of departure for this essay: is it possible, and if so how,
to increase Mexican influence in the United States?

This paper presents some elements that may help clarify such issues. Taking its clue from the general topic of the workshop for which it was prepared, it starts from a more restricted version of the same query: can the Mexican *government* increase its influence in *Washington*, and what are the costs and benefits of the policies aimed in that direction? Its objective is to help clarify not only the ways in which influence may be increased, but also the parameters within which such influence may be exercised and the choices (based on the costs and benefits mentioned above) to be made before any option can be followed.

The first section of the paper provides some essential background—the roots of conflict in Mexican-U.S. relations and the place and role that intergovernmental relations have in their wider context. Following this overview of the basic context in which intergovernmental relations take place is a summary of the ways in which both governments are organized to deal with each other. When discussing the basic dynamics of their decision-making processes, a distinction is made between (a) more permanent aspects related to political culture and the basic traits of their political systems and (b) other factors which may determine changes in those "ways of doing things" over time. A good part of this section and, in fact, of the paper as a whole is dedicated to a conceptual framework which may help clarify the distinctions between the two types of factors.

Lastly, some of the main implications of the analytical framework for bilateral relations are spelled out in order to give the basic background of policy recommendations regarding: (1) the potential identification of points of access to the U.S. policy-making mechanisms (both domestic and foreign policy) which concern Mexico, (2) changes in the structure of the Mexican government (in Mexico and its foreign posts) which may maximize the potential of those points of access, (3) most adequate negotiating styles and strategies, and (4) mechanisms to improve Mexico's ability to understanding the limits and constraints of U.S. governmental behavior in specific policy areas.

ESSENTIAL BACKGROUND ELEMENTS

Two introductory background elements merit at least a brief description before proceeding. The first is related to the *roots of conflict in Mexican-U.S. relations.* If we are to distinguish between those disagreements which may be solved in the short, medium, or long run and those which both governments can only learn to manage or even live with, we must explore the basic roots of those conflicts.[2] It is impossible to spell out the basic "realities" of U.S.-Mexican relations in this paper. Unless one wants to create unrealistic expectations, however, it is necessary to reiterate that many factors—from different international roles and perspectives to the fact that political debate in each of these countries is organized on fairly consensual grounds and that there is a limited overlap between the terms of consensus in Mexico and the United States—create built-in tendencies toward conflict and disagreement, almost regardless of governmental intentions. It is also true that there are obvious factors—such as the fact that both countries share the same kind of socioeconomic system—that generate parallel tendencies toward convergence and shared interests. However, we must not expect too much of any measures proposed in the realm of intergovernmental relations to deal with "structural" problems or, for that matter, with disagreements which may well be deeply rooted in other spheres of this extremely complex relationship.

The second essential background element relates to *the place of intergovernmental relations in the array of actors and actions which constitute the complex web of Mexican-U.S. "asymmetric interdependence."*[3] We must recognize the basic constraints which this web of interactions creates and which could potentially limit the real scope of even the most coherent and rational governmental policy.

Relations between Mexico and the United States provide an extremely rich example of what authors such as Keohane and Nye[4] have called "transnational" and "transgovernmental" politics. The basic elements to which the first of those concepts refers to include:

- The presence of a very large number of nongovernmental actors. These actors may have a direct impact on intergovernmental relations (those that take place between the top officials of two countries or between those agencies formally in charge of foreign affairs) through their efforts to influence the positions of either one of those governments. They may also heavily influence

---

[2]For a treatment of those "roots" see Rico, "Terms of Endearment."
[3]These issues, as well as the conceptual framework of "complex asymmetric interdependence" have been dealt with at greater length in Carlos Rico, "The Limits of the Rhetoric of 'Interdependence' and the Future of U.S.-Mexican Relations," in *U.S.-Mexican Relations: Conflict or Convergence*, edited by Manuel García y Griego and Carlos Vázquez (Los Angeles: University of California, Los Angeles, 1981).
[4]Robert Keohane and Joseph Nye, Jr., eds., *Transnational Relations and World Politics* (Cambridge: Harvard University Press, 1971).

the context in which those interactions take place by pursuing "foreign policies" of their own. Thus, bilateral relations may be deeply affected by the activities of a myriad of such actors: drug dealers, commercial banks, Florida orange producers, political parties, etc. The open loss of the monopoly on communications with the U.S. side which the Mexican government and a few intellectuals maintained until not too many years ago may be considered a good example for other developments associated with this aspect of the bilateral relationship.

• Since the interests (political, economic, ideological, symbolic, etc.) of these different nongovernmental actors do not necessarily coincide, there may be situations in which "foreign policy" and "domestic politics" will be extremely difficult to separate. There will be domestic winners and losers, and the clear identification of the "national interest" will become increasingly difficult. In fact, there will be cases in which issues considered as domestic in one country will have a direct impact on the other— even if the politics of the decision-making process in some of those instances have not included any consideration of the basic concerns of the second country. The decade and a half of domestic debate which preceded the passing of the Simpson-Rodino immigration bill in late 1986 provides plenty of examples in this regard. Until recently this second characteristic, when applied to Mexican-U.S. relations, seemed to accrue primarily to the United States. However, it has now started to have a clear impact on the Mexican side. As the "relative autonomy" of the Mexican state continues to erode in the near future, as Mexican civil society mobilizes in an increasingly autonomous way, and as the conduct of foreign relations increasingly impinges on concrete interests of Mexican nongovernmental actors, we can expect this tendency to become stronger.

• It is possible to identify instances in which specific interest groups on opposite sides of the border will have more in common with each other than with their respective "co-nationals." The result will be the emergence of transnational alliances such as the one between Mexican fresh vegetable producers and North American food distributors. We see this alliance in action whenever U.S. growers try to limit the importation of Mexican produce.[5] But such alliances are not restricted to the activities of

---

[5]David Mares, "La política norteamericana en el comercio de hortalizas: Washington frente a México en las 'Guerras del Tomate,'" typescript (Mexico: El Colegio de México, 1980).

nongovernmental actors. They also affect the relations between sub-units of the two governments. This brings us to the second concept introduced above: "transgovernmental relations."

An exercise similar to the one just presented can be conducted in relation to the role of those units of both governments which, despite not being charged with the conduct of foreign relations, have not only their own "foreign policies" but also active bilateral contacts and activities. Almost all units of *both* governments have some kind of activity which is or may be related to relations between the two countries. This also forms part of the increasing interconnection between foreign policy and domestic politics discussed above. In this case "bureaucratic politics" and "transgovernmental alliances" are the expression of the logic described above in relation to the role of nongovernmental actors.

This discussion would be incomplete without a mention, even if in abbreviated form, of two additional complications in the management of the bilateral relationship, which are more relevant to the North American than to the Mexican case. The first one is related to the role of Congress in U.S.-Mexican relations. Those trends that have been highlighted above are also relevant to understanding the role of the legislative branch in U.S.-Mexican relations. The second element is the judiciary, to be discussed shortly.

My basic contention would be that this bilateral relationship provides a good example of the process through which not only has Congress, in a sense, "reached for" foreign policy, but foreign policy has also reached Congress. That is, many issue areas that have traditionally fallen within the turf of the legislative branch have tended to take on increasing "foreign policy" dimensions in recent years. Thus the U.S. legislative branch has not only increased the level of attention it pays to Mexican affairs, but, maybe even more importantly, decisions that it has made (in many issue areas that have been traditionally considered "domestic") without consideration of their potential impact on Mexico as part of legislative deliberations have had profound consequences for bilateral relations.[6]

---

[6]See in this regard the seminal piece by Donald Wyman, "The United States Congress and the Formulation of United States Policy toward Mexico," paper presented at the Seminar on Latin America and Decisionmaking Processes in the United States," Instituto de Estudios de Estados Unidos-CIDE, July 1980.

It is not surprising that most legislative activities in this regard have taken place in committees and subcommittees *other than* those formally charged with foreign affairs responsibilities. A final point is the consideration that if power is diffuse in the U.S. executive branch, it is much more so in the legislative. The increase in the number of actors is thus much greater than the term "Congress" would imply.

At least in the U.S. case, the other relatively autonomous public actor in the bilateral relationship is the judiciary. There is almost no literature on this subject but it has become increasingly clear that the role of the courts in adjudicating disputes in issue areas that have an increasing "foreign policy" dimension (drugs, trade, immigration, etc.) will add to the extremely complex web of autonomous and semi-autonomous actors and actions in which intergovernmental relations are immersed. These are the crucial contextual factors to be considered in any analysis of the logic of decision-making in either country.

DECISION-MAKING PROCESSES IN MEXICO AND THE UNITED STATES

When one looks at the intergovernmental level of Mexican-U.S. relations, it would seem that there is a greater degree of internal coherence on the Mexican side. It has even been argued, for example, that when Mexican political actors and observers project on the United States the image of a "unitary rational actor," to use Allison's descriptive phrase,[7] they do it not only because of their lack of familiarity with U.S. political structures, but primarily because they are more comfortable using as a point of reference their own political system. As anyone who has participated in even a single Mexican foreign policy decision knows (secondary sources are almost non-existent in this matter), things do not work quite that way on the Mexican side of the border. However, in relative terms and despite changes in recent years, the Mexican *governmental* side is usually able to present more of a common front than its U.S. counterpart. Conventional wisdom attributes such a situation to differences between the political systems of Mexico and the United States. Given the specific subject matter of this paper, I will deal in more detail with the North American political system.

---

[7]Graham T. Allison, *Essence of Decision; Explaining the Cuban Missile Crisis* (Boston: Little, Brown, 1971).

Without pretending to do justice to the complexities of the U.S. political system, two elements seem particularly relevant. The first would be the existence of "a constitutional system that shares formal powers among institutions,"[8] and in which "government power is functionalized within the executive branch, within Congress, and between the two."[9] The second would be the "redundant" and "overlapping" characteristics not only of the political system as a whole but of the executive branch in particular.[10] The subject of our analysis is, thus, hardly the output of a single formal organization. The Mexican political system, in turn, may be characterized by reference to a few key elements: "an ample degree of state autonomy, a high level of concentration of power, the absence of a real division of powers, a dominant party and a corporatist scheme of organization for the main social classes."[11]

These differences are clearly important, for example, as regards relations between the executive and the legislative branches or between the federal and state and even local governments. In the case of Mexico, those agencies would face severe constraints in any attempt to develop more or less autonomous relations with their counterparts which could be considered to be threatening to the central executive organs of the federal government. However, this is only half the story.

The other half relates more directly to issue-area constraints that affect both governments. To summarize: Mexican actions are more coherent because the key players in Mexico's political system (those able to impose a certain amount of coherence into the game) consider bilateral relations to have a much greater priority for them and their country than is the case with their North American counterparts. At the same time, until recently Mexico's central authorities had faced fewer domestic political constraints when dealing with most issues of the bilateral relationship than did their opposite numbers. This relation between what I have elsewhere called "state priority" ("governmental priority" may

---

[8]Richard E. Neustadt, *Presidential Power: The Politics of Power With Reflections on Johnson and Nixon* (New York: John Wiley & Sons, 1971), p. 12.

[9]Hugh Heclo, *A Government of Strangers: Executive Politics in Washington* (Washington, D.C.: Brookings Institution, 1977), p. 154.

[10]Martin Landau, "Redundancy, Rationality, and the Problem of Duplication and Overlap," in *Bureaucratic Power in National Politics*, ed. Francis E. Rourke (Boston: Little, Brown, 1978), pp. 422-436.

[11]María Amparo Casar and Guadalupe González, "Proceso de toma de decisiones y política exterior en México: el ingreso al GATT," paper presented at the IX Reunión de Centros Miembros del RIAL, Brasilia, November 29-December 2, 1987, p. 4.

sound less alien to most North American ears) and "domestic impact"[12] constitutes the gist of a conceptual framework which, in spite of having been developed with the specific aim of understanding U.S. foreign policy processes, may help clarify some of the basic characteristics of *both* governmental structures.

The following paragraphs will examine some issue area-related factors which may explain a higher degree of "unitary rational" action on the Mexican part. The point of departure of any attempt to understand foreign policy-making is the fairly obvious contention that there is not a single decision-making process, but rather processes whose characteristics are conditioned by the specific issue area one is interested in analyzing. The degree of coherence that the definition and implementation of foreign policy assumes— which will be our main concern when developing our analysis— changes from one issue area to another. In other words, in some issue areas and even in the handling of some bilateral relations, one can expect that the "traditional conception" of international relations (according to which states behave like "unitary rational actors") may be more relevant than in others.

If one wants to go beyond the obvious, however, it is necessary to spell out the main variables one could use in constructing a typology of issue areas which could clarify these possibilities. It is at this point that the two variables introduced at the end of the previous section become directly relevant.

By using that "traditional conception" and such alternative paradigms as the "bureaucratic politics" one, two extremes (policy as "outcome," on the one hand, and policy as the product of perfectly rational calculation, on the other) constitute the limits of our typology. Our central contention would be that, even after assuming the fragmentation of the policy process and the multiplicity of participants, in some issue areas the decision-making process would tend to resemble the characteristics of the unitary rational actor more than in others. This does not mean that elements such as the organizational dimensions of the process would not be extremely relevant even in those cases that are closer to the "rational ideal," but it certainly qualifies the *kinds* of domestic conflict which can be expected in the different cases.

---

[12]Carlos Rico, *Method and Madness: Looking for a Typology of Issue Areas in U.S. Foreign Policy Making* (Mexico: Instituto de Estudios de Estados Unidos [CIDE], 1981). The following paragraphs draw heavily from this piece.

My basic assumption follows—with some reservations[13]—from Hilsman's notion of the existence of a series of "concentric rings of power" in the North American case. It holds that a greater degree of coherence and "rationality" (in the restricted and instrumental conception of the term used in this essay) can be expected in those issues that reach the "inner circles," just as an increasing degree of fragmentation and confusion would appear as we move to the outer ones. The basic reason for this is the existence of what Amos Perlmutter calls the "presidential political center."[14] Supporting this view is Wildavsky's assertion in relation to a different set of problems: other participants "would rarely resist a direct presidential command."[15] The crucial element, at times disregarded, is the degree of presidential involvement in a given issue, a crucial element even if "presidential leadership is like a spotlight that can sweep across the range of executive activities but can concentrate on only a few at a time."[16] Mexican or North American presidents' days, after all, are also limited to a mere twenty-four hours.

What factors, then, would bring a given policy to the attention of one of those circles? Our first criterion for the construction of a typology attempts to provide some clues in this regard.

"Crisis" and "Routine" Situations

To establish our point of departure we can draw on a distinction frequently made in the literature on both international relations and the study of organizations: that which differentiates the way "crisis" situations are handled vis-à-vis the management of

---

[13]These reservations are directly related to the following implicit assumptions of his model: (a) In the field of foreign policy it is possible to limit the participating actors to those related to the federal government and not in any sense to the different states of the union. (b) Foreign policy is an area mainly, almost exclusively, related to the activities of the executive branch. It seems clear that the model is derived from what could be considered "classical dimensions" of foreign policy: military, strategic, and political. In this sense it does not account in a proper way either for the "intermestic" issues or for the agenda of international relations which came to dominate the seventies, in which the clear hierarchy of issues and the predominance of the politico-military dimensions was to a point questioned. See Roger Hilsman, *To Move a Nation* (New York: Dell, 1967), pp. 541-544.

[14]Amos Perlmutter, "The Presidential Political Center and Foreign Policy: A Critique of the Revisionist and Bureaucratic-Political Orientations," *World Politics* 32:1 (October 1974).

[15]Aaron Wildavsky, *The Politics of the Budgetary Process*, 3d ed. (Boston: Little, Brown, 1979), p. 36.

[16]Hugh Heclo, *A Government of Strangers*, p. 12.

"routine" day-to-day problems.[17] Crisis situations, we are told, are "a powerful stimulus to action"[18] which "tend to jump the bounds of regular channels above all because of the involvement of top officials who seek to handle things their own way."[19]

A decision taken in response to a crisis situation will be one that *all participants regard as fateful in the extreme.*[20] This points to the presence of a wide consensus as regards the existence of a challenge to interests common to all actors participating in the decision-making process. The "national interest" could be more easily identified in such a situation. The goals to be pursued are in a sense widely shared by all who participate in such basic consensus.

As regards the agreement on the existence of a "common threat," if one excludes those extremely rare cases related to the sheer physical survival of the nation (I stress the term physical because in some nations one can find examples not only of individuals but of considerably large social groups for whom the cultural, social, or even political survival of the national identity does not constitute a high-priority goal), a threat would seem to be defined largely by the values which dominate the political life of the society, or at least the belief systems of those actors which participate in the relevant decision-making process. This underlines the importance of the *images* that relevant actors share during a given historical period.

In a formulation which is particularly useful for the next point of our argument, Charles Hermann identifies three properties of a crisis situation. A crisis (1) threatens high-priority goals of the decision-making unit; (2) restricts the amount of time available for response; and (3) surprises the members of the decision-making unit by its occurrence.[21]

By now it must be clear that crisis and routine are only the extreme points of a continuum. On the basis of his three properties

---

[17]See, for example, Philip Selznick, *Leadership in Administration: A Sociological Interpretation* (New York: Harper & Row, 1957), pp. 29-38.

[18]Herbert Kaufman, *Administrative Feedback: Monitoring Subordinates' Behavior* (Washington, D.C.: Brookings Institution, 1973), p. 79.

[19]I. M. Destler, *Presidents, Bureaucrats and Foreign Policy: The Politics of Organizational Reform* (Princeton: Princeton University Press, 1974), pp. 62-63.

[20]Hilsman, *To Move a Nation*, p. 18, emphasis added.

[21]Charles F. Hermann, "International Crisis as a Situational Variable," in *International Politics and Foreign Policy: A Reader in Research and Theory*, ed. James N. Rosenau, rev. ed. (New York: Free Press, 1969), p. 414.

of the "crisis situation," Hermann develops eight basic potential situations that derive from the combination of only the binary extremes of each of them. This type of distinction could in a sense be the basis for a sort of *continuum*, which would have the "crisis situation" as one of its final points, and would descend toward the other end according to the level of priority that a given issue area would have on the scale of the central decision-makers in the political system.

The amount of attention that the central decision-makers would be willing to pay both to the definition and to the implementation aspects of a given policy could be considered as an indicator of the level of "governmental priority" involved. The "governmental priority" needed for achieving a high degree of coherence in a given instance would seem to depend on at least two considerations: the first would be the degree to which other issues would approach the "critical" end of the continuum, thus competing for the attention of the central decision-makers. The second would be directly related to our second criterion for the construction of a typology and could be expressed as the degree of both intergovernmental and nongovernmental complexity of the issue, that is, the number of institutional actors participating, directly or indirectly, in the decision, and the kinds of conflicts of interest present. A final point is that the level of priority assigned to a given issue can and does vary from agency to agency depending on its specific "turf," which is an important element to consider when trying to define the kind of bureaucratic politics that can be expected.

With this in mind, let us turn to a brief discussion of the decision-making processes that take place at the other end of our continuum—"routine" relations (low threat, extended response time, anticipated occurrence). These might be thought to comprise the great majority of the specific foreign policies of the U.S. government which shape its relations with most nations. Policy, after all, is made at all levels of the organization, not just at the top.

As regards the sort of decision-making processes that can be expected as we approach the "routine" end of the continuum, a number of different hypotheses can be offered. On the one hand it could be that in the "ideal type" routine situation there would be some elements that could lead the relevant government to act in a predictable and, to a point, "rational" manner. It would be important to behave in accordance with the rules of the game as summed up in the various "international regimes," especially in situations where there was little to be gained from not respecting them. The predictability in the behavior of other international actors would seem to be worth the price.

Political and bureaucratic factors would also seem to lead toward predictability: routine relations would seem the realm of standard operating procedures more than of bureaucratic politics and infighting. And even in cases where other non-executive branch and nongovernmental actors participated, the extremely low element of "newness" or "surprise" in a given situation would lead to more or less institutionalized and established patterns of influence and processes of decision-making, be it in the form of "iron triangles" or of "issue networks."

In cases which do not fall at either the "routine" or "crisis" extreme of the continuum, the number of participants might increase, contradictory goals and means could surface in the discussion, etc. We would find ourselves in almost perfect terrain for a domestic politics-foreign policy linkage type of analysis. That the "domestic politics" would be mainly bureaucratic, or would also involve the legislative branch, seems to depend again largely on the kind of factors raised by our second criterion for the construction of a typology, to which we now turn.

Domestic Impact of Policy Issues

Our first criterion has emphasized the governmental dimensions of the conflicts which can take place within the limits of our crisis-routine continuum. In the argument developed above, the "national politics" with which "foreign policy" was presumed to be linked remained mainly bureaucratic in nature. To a point this is an expression of the basic elements used in defining "crisis," which are more closely related to problems of peace and war where presidential supremacy seems to be greater.

We turn now to a different and wider set of "domestic politics," in which winners and/or losers can be identified at the national, nongovernmental level. The dynamics of conflict are not limited in this case to sources such as those related to the existence of competing organizational tasks, missions, and perception; rather they can be perceived as "restraints" on policymakers no longer isolated from the direct impact of national political life in its widest sense.

Our main contention here is that in recent years foreign policy and domestic politics thus defined have become increasingly linked, heightening the potential complexity of the setting in which foreign policy decisions are made. This is due to an increase in the number of actions for which, even though they fall in the foreign policy field, the nation as a whole is not the only potential winner or loser.

Not only the degree but also the kind of domestic impact that a given "foreign" policy has, and especially the scope and intensity of conflict associated with it, become the main data needed to develop our second criterion for the construction of a typology. An adequate treatment of these questions would require a well grounded discussion of the relative merits and potentially complementary areas of the main "paradigms of American politics." Such discussion is beyond the scope of this paper.

A first approximation to the kind of typology that could be developed, however, can be gained from some major efforts in the sphere of domestic politics. The distribution of perceived costs and benefits to the different participants seems to be the key element in this regard. For the purposes of this paper, it is useful to postulate two basic kinds of possible non-crisis patterns of domestic politics which would characterize given foreign policy issue areas:

- situations in which the predominance of a single kind of non-governmental interest can be easily ascertained (distributive-client); and

- situations in which the domestic impact of a given foreign policy assumes the form of a real conflict among nongovernmental interests which can take several forms (regulatory-interest groups, entrepreneurial, or, if such a theoretical possibility could exist in the United States, redistributive).

Governmental Priority and Domestic Impact

On the basis of this very crude classification, it would now seem possible to posit some of the potential relations of our two criteria. The basic logic of each one of the two represents different "pulls" in the decision-making process.

The first, reflecting a peculiar form of situation analysis, centers on those factors *which impel the central decision-makers of the political system* to assign a high degree of priority to the given issue area in their own agendas. On this basis I defined a crisis-routine continuum and stressed the central role that dominant values and goals have in the characterization as well as in the definition of those "operational goals" that the foreign *policies* of the United States may try to attain.

In contrast, the second criterion emphasized those other elements that *could impede or at the least make difficult such coherent behavior* even in a case of relatively high priority, by bringing new participants into the decision-making process. In this respect the distribution of *perceived costs and benefits* to different nongovernmental interests was the main element guiding our discussion.

It seems fairly clear that some of the most interesting combinations of the two criteria would be found in the "middle ground" of our continuum of governmental priority. There, for example, one could find instances where an increase in the relative priority of a given issue or area would lead, not to a reduction, but to an increase in the number of participants, as would be the case with the mass media. Increasing priority accruing to a country would also cause an issue previously dealt with in a stable, "routinized" way, to be brought into the realm of bureaucratic politics. This would produce an increase in the level of coordination when "the left hand must know what the right one is doing." (A possible example is the PRM-41 process described by Thorup in this volume.) That would be the case, for example, in an instance of linkage politics at the intergovernmental level.[22] These very simple examples can point out the not so obvious combinations that one could discover if the different issue areas in foreign policy were properly identified.

IMPLICATIONS FOR U.S.-MEXICAN RELATIONS

A first important element to keep in mind is that the main elements which have guided our analysis change over time. Thus, not only the relative levels of priority of different issues or countries can change, but so can the written and unwritten rules which structure the decision-making process. Of special interest in this regard would be changes both in the foreign policy consensus and in the wider dominant values of society.

---

[22]Keohane and Nye, *Transnational Relations and World Politics*, pp. 30-31.

A second general implication of the framework presented becomes apparent when one looks not at the foreign policy of a single government but at intergovernmental relations. Here the application of the ideas developed in this paper could serve to identify a relative advantage of the weaker side in a negotiation if the level of priority it assigned to the outcome was higher and the impact of domestic politics lower than those of the dominant partner. There are, however, particularly relevant implications for understanding the decision-making processes of each one of the countries involved in our analysis. Again, given the subject matter of this paper, I will focus on the North American case.

There are, of course, great differences in the overall foreign policy context in which priority is in fact assigned to a given issue or bilateral relation. In this connection, two elements are particularly relevant. The first relates to the specific international role of each country and, in particular, to the geographic range of U.S. commitments. U.S. decision-makers have many other concerns in addition to Mexico.

The second element is related to the "potentially very broad" nature of U.S. foreign policy and international relations.[23] This becomes an important factor in the Mexican case which makes it almost impossible for any given "foreign policy" to fall within the "turf" of a single governmental agency or pertain to only one of the several institutions which share power in the U.S. political system. One of the clearest examples of such complexity is the "arsenal of instruments" which the Herter Committee thought— more than twenty years ago—to be available to the "new diplomacy" of the Kennedy administration, and which included not only "traditional diplomacy," but also "international law, intelligence, political action, technical assistance and informational and psychology programs, monetary policies, trade development programs, educational exchange, cultural programs, and, more recently, measures to counter-insurgency movements."[24]

On the Mexican side, of course, the geographic span of attention is much smaller and the range of foreign policy instruments very limited. Priority assigned to relations with the United States faces almost no competition.

---

[23]I. M. Destler, *Presidents, Bureaucrats and Foreign Policy*, p. 161.
[24]Ibid, p. 168.

The bureaucratic complexity of governmental structures which plays a role in bilateral relations has at least two relevant consequences for our analysis. One is the great number of governmental actors which have a say in the conduct of policy. If for U.S. foreign policy as a whole it is true that "no less than forty government agencies have a hand in foreign relations,"[25] in the case of relations with Mexico we must add a good number of additional "domestic" agencies. The result is even more complexity in any U.S. government attempt to formulate a single, coherent Mexican policy.

Second, the various aspects of such a broad field are frequently closely related. And this de facto linkage is not limited to different "faces" of foreign policy but presents itself also in the relationship between foreign policy and domestic politics. One result of the emergence of a new "intermestic"[26] agenda is the proliferation of participants, not only within the executive branch but also in the executive-legislative interplay and the nongovernmental sphere.

Additional complexities for the Mexican case lie in other aspects of the decision-making process in the United States. For example, at least in some instances the cast of characters could expand to include the state level, as in the case of negotiations on border issues such as the management of shared resources. An even clearer example could be the need to alter profoundly the role which studies of foreign policy-making usually assign both to Congress and to those "domestic" agencies for which "foreign" affairs are not the main sphere of action and which do not participate in coordinating bodies such as the National Security Council.

A final point relates to the key reason why it will be very difficult for Mexico to achieve a consistent degree of attention and priority in U.S. foreign policy-making. I have posited that such attention is more likely in the case of perceived threats to consensual values. In the case of the United States, one can easily find both broad values widely shared throughout society (the belief in the superiority of a free-market economy and liberal democracy), and, at least during the postwar period, more specific images, also

---

[25]F. S. Northedge, "Elements of United States Policy," in *The Foreign Policy of Powers*, ed. F. S. Northedge (New York: Free Press, 1975), p. 44.
[26]Bayless Manning, "The Congress, the Executive and Intermestic Affairs: Three Proposals," *Foreign Affairs* 55:1-2 (January 1977).

widely shared, in this case by the policymakers (and agreed to by the public at large). The central features of this foreign policy consensus have been enumerated by Morton H. Halperin,[27] and described by James Chace as dominated, at least after the Korean War, by a "broadly based anti-communism rather than by the original theme of containing perceived Soviet expansion."[28] Based on both kinds of belief systems, it would not be hard to propose (1) as examples of a crisis situation, broad and direct challenges of a strategic-military nature, and (2) as situations which would fall very near that extreme of the continuum, those social and political changes in other countries which—when looked at through the lens of consensus described by Halperin and Chace, among others— could be interpreted as "losses to communism."

If this analysis is correct, more "rationality" and attention could be expected in dealings with "enemies" (where threat is defined by the foreign policy consideration) than with "friends." In the same vein, "rationality" would increase when U.S. governmental action was necessary to prevent a "friend" from becoming an "enemy," etc.

Mexico seems thus to be a particularly clear example of a country whose relative priority has increased, but in relation to which the constraints of domestic politics have also grown. As a result of the interplay of these two factors, it may not be realistic in the near future to expect a significant improvement in the level of coherence and rationality that characterizes the management of Mexican-U.S. intergovernmental relations. It will be imperative for the Mexican government, if it wishes to increase its influence in Washington, to undertake what it has refused (or been unable) to do: to use the legitimate margins that U.S. domestic politics open up for promoting Mexican positions through the maze of the U.S. decision-making processes. Needless to say, this is an area in which Mexican experience and capabilities are, at present, rather limited. Important changes will have to be made in both the mechanisms and the assumptions on the basis of which our authorities have approached these issues. It is to be hoped that we will have the political will to try.

---

[27]Morton H. Halperin, *Bureaucratic Politics and Foreign Policy* (Washington, D.C.: Brookings Institution, 1974), pp. 11-12.
[28]James Chace, "Is a Foreign Policy Consensus Possible?" *Foreign Affairs*, 57:1-3 (Fall 1978): 3.

6

U.S. Policy-making toward Mexico: Prospects for Administrative Reform

Cathryn L. Thorup

Incoming U.S. administrations routinely pledge their efforts to the improvement of U.S.-Mexican relations, an endeavor that frequently involves some revamping of the relevant policy-making structure. The pressure for major new bureaucratic initiatives is especially strong every twelve years when the U.S. and Mexican presidential election cycles coincide—a moment considered particularly auspicious for reflection, renewal, and reform. This was the case in 1976 when Presidents Jimmy Carter and José López Portillo took office, and it is the case today.

Announcement by Mexico of the discovery of major oil reserves in 1976 shifted Washington's strategic view of that country and changed the way policies toward Mexico were conceptualized, organized, and implemented by the Carter administration. Both the subsequent dramatic decline in Mexico's economic position and reassertion of U.S. hegemony in the international arena provided the backdrop for a quite different bureaucratic approach by the U.S. government during the Reagan administration. This paper will explore the process of policy development, coordination, and conflict management that comprises U.S. policy-making toward

The author would like to thank the Overseas Development Council and the Center for U.S.-Mexican Studies, UCSD, for their support in the preparation of this study; and Robert L. Ayres, Guy F. Erb, and Richard E. Feinberg for comments on an early draft.

Mexico by examining in detail the Carter administration's approach to U.S.-Mexican relations and briefly contrasting it with the experiences of the Reagan administration.

Both administrations were pledged generally to improving the bilateral relationship, but the specific goals and strategies employed were very different. Each had their share of success stories, but in both cases there were periods of significant deterioration in U.S.-Mexican relations and a lingering sense that the relationship could have progressed more smoothly, with less need for episodic crisis management, if events had been handled differently.

In policy terms, the objective here is to contribute to recommendations leading not necessarily to a more *harmonious* bilateral relationship, but rather to a good *working* relationship, where conflicts and differences are dealt with effectively and efficiently. Ad hoc crisis management seems to guarantee an erratic and fragile interaction. One alternative is to clarify national priorities and coordinate policy-making and implementation in an attempt to temper the capacity of special interest groups and relatively minor bureaucratic actors and/or events to overshadow broader U.S. interests in Mexico. Examination of the Office of the U.S. Coordinator for Mexican Affairs established under Carter and comparison with the ad hoc management style characteristic of the Reagan administration will clarify the problems and possibilities associated with such an undertaking. The central questions for analysis are: Is it desirable for the U.S. government to pull together a coherent machinery for dealing with Mexico and, if so, what would it look like?

THE "DANGERS" OF ADMINISTRATIVE REFORM

Academics and, to a lesser extent, politicians have a tendency to advocate massive, overarching changes when they examine bureaucratic procedures, ending up either "reinventing the wheel" or pushing for reforms so far-reaching that they stand little chance of implementation. Bureaucrats, on the other hand, tend to exhibit an inherent bias against the adoption of new standard operating procedures, and thus to rationalize the failings of the status quo and overstate the dangers associated with change. The objective of the analysis presented here is to steer a course somewhere between the bureaucratic Cassandras and the academic and political Quixotes. With this is mind, several caveats are in order.

First, good process is no substitute for good policy. There is no inherent value in a "coordinated" policy *per se*—it depends on *what* one is coordinating. If poor policies are pursued through exceptionally well-coordinated procedures, the results will be even more disastrous than if they had been pursued through disorganized, ad hoc mechanisms. For this reason, it is vital that any new U.S. administration clearly define what it wants out of the bilateral relationship before moving to design the process by which to obtain its objectives. By the same token, a good system for subsequent policy evaluation can enhance the prospects for accurate feedback and informed tinkering with both procedure and policy. While emphasizing that process cannot—and should not—be separated from content, this paper will concentrate on the procedural side of the equation. It must assume enlightened policies.

Second, it is argued that policy coordination entails the hopeless task of selecting among a wide variety of domestic concerns. While true that such choices are difficult, trade-offs among competing interests are made each day in every realm of the U.S. government, from the Senate Budget Committee to the Supreme Court. A democratic system, of course, needs to take into account the needs and wishes of its citizens, but this is different than allowing foreign policy-making to be held hostage to special interests. In the case of U.S.-Mexican relations, there are overarching, long-term U.S. national interests that constitute a first priority.

Third, one danger of administrative reform concerns raised expectations. Nowhere is this more evident than in the case of the United States and Mexico. All too often pronouncements by new U.S. administrations signaling a sincere desire to improve U.S.-Mexican relations have been followed by inattention and deterioration.[1] Even so, the decision that the dangers of failure outweigh the potential benefits of success must be made on a case-by-case basis. To reject new initiatives simply because they might be overly

---

[1]Presidents Carter and Reagan were certainly not the first U.S. leaders to consider Mexico a priority concern and to want to put their personal stamp on the bilateral relationship. In a letter to John Foster Dulles, dated June 14, 1955, President Eisenhower wrote, "I probably have written you more often on the subject of Mexico than any other single matter.... I am so earnestly of the opinion that the soundness and friendliness of our relationship with Mexico must be a first and continuing concern of ours." Eisenhower designated his brother, Milton Eisenhower, as a special travelling intermediary to represent him in discussions with Mexican President López Mateos. See Dwight D. Eisenhower, *Waging Peace, 1956-1961: The White House Years* (Garden City, N. Y.: Doubleday, 1965), pp. 517-518, 344.

ambitious, potentially raising false expectations for improvement in the bilateral relationship, is both shortsighted and overly pessimistic.[2]

Fourth, while the paper will by design focus on the objectives of U.S. policymakers, it is important not to lose sight of their bilateral counterparts. Clearly Mexico's relative strengths and weaknesses will enhance or diminish that country's responsiveness to U.S. initiatives and that, in turn, will affect the ability of U.S. policymakers to implement their policies. A weakened Mexico would in most cases have a more limited margin of maneuver vis-à-vis the United States.[3]

Finally, to suggest no new initiatives and continuation of the status quo would be an endorsement of current policy-making as state of the art, implying that the mechanisms now in place work well or, at least, cannot be improved upon. This is not the case.

THE DISMEMBERED BUREAUCRACY

The erratic nature of U.S-Mexican relations during 1985 and 1986 underscores the dangers of a fragmented U.S. policy-making process, bouncing between brinkmanship and damage control. As domestic and foreign policy issues in U.S.-Mexican relations have become increasingly interwoven and acquired higher stakes, more issues have crowded the bilateral agenda and more actors have demanded a say in policy formulation. As each government agency pursues its own program with regard to Mexico, certain domestic constituent interests may be well served but the body of U.S. national interests is not. As a result, the overall bilateral relationship is damaged as the urgent consistently supersedes the important and policymakers fall prisoner to the vacillations of public pressure. This was the case both during the Camarena episode in early 1985 and the Helms Senate hearings in mid-1986, when relatively minor actors within the U.S. government were able to

---

[2]For an alternative view, see: Susan Kaufman Purcell, "Mexico-U.S. Relations: Big Initiatives Can Cause Big Problems," *Foreign Affairs*, 60:1-3 (winter 1981-82): 379-392.
[3]There are situations in which weakness might paradoxically afford Mexico strength—the threat of political turmoil, debt repudiation, and so forth. Further, just the perception of weakness (either by U.S. policymakers who then take a harder line or by Mexican policymakers who then overestimate the constraints to action) can also limit Mexico's margin of maneuver.

draw a large portion of the U.S. bureaucracy behind them in support of "get tough" policies toward Mexico.[4]

Without central management of U.S. policy toward Mexico, there is no entity to evaluate problems as they arise, anticipate difficulties further ahead, assign priorities, or regulate the flow of demands that Washington places on the Mexican system. There is no capacity to assess and coordinate the trade-offs that must be made among the demands of a multitude of U.S. actors. The cumulative impact on Mexico of this ad hoc pressure is tremendous, frequently unanticipated, and potentially harmful to long-term U.S. interests.

At times of crisis in the bilateral relationship, momentum is generated for the establishment of formal mechanisms to coordinate U.S. policy toward Mexico. Talk of a "special relationship" resurfaces, and less concern is expressed about "favoritism" setting precedents that could bedevil U.S. ties with other developing countries. It was in such a setting that a major review of U.S. policy toward Mexico was undertaken in August 1979. But prior to evaluating that process, it is important to note two significant changes that altered the nature of the bilateral relationship during the period under study and that significantly affect the outlook for future administrative reform.

DISCONTINUITIES IN U.S.-MEXICAN RELATIONS

To downplay the need for changes in U.S. policy-making toward Mexico, some analysts have argued that U.S.-Mexican relations have always had their ups and downs, and that tensions in government-to-government relations are only one part of the complex exchange of people, goods, and services between the two countries. This is of course true, but such thinking may obscure more than it illuminates. While certainly there are many constants in the bilateral relationship, excessive focus on what has remained

---

[4]Enrique Camarena was a U.S. Drug Enforcement agent who was tortured and killed in February 1985 while operating in Mexico. His death was followed by a strong public condemnation in the United States of Mexican law enforcement and a series of reprisals that negatively affected other aspects of the bilateral relationship. Senator Jesse Helms held a series of three subcommittee hearings on Mexico in May and June 1986. The overall tone was highly critical and the Mexican reaction was swift and heated. The result was a marked deterioration in the bilateral relationship.

the same may blind us to the massive shifts that have taken place over the past decade. These shifts can be grouped into two broad categories:

- the growing strategic importance of Mexico to the United States; and

- the spiralling complexity of the relationship, resulting from the rising interaction of domestic and foreign policy, the addition of new bilateral actors and issues, and more vigorous U.S. involvement in areas previously in the exclusive domain of the Mexican government.

From the point of view of the two administrations, Mexico's strategic importance was based, very generally, on what Mexico could do *for* the United States during the Carter administration and what it could do *to* the United States under Reagan. Mexico's strategic importance began to shift dramatically in 1976 with announcement of the discovery of vast oil reserves. This disclosure came on the heels of the oil price shock of 1973-74, and just prior to the second shock of mid-1979. By July 1979, the Carter administration was feeling the full brunt of public dissatisfaction with oil-induced inflation, and the moral equivalent of war had been announced as a spur to energy conservation in the United States.

On the part of the administration, the sense of U.S. vulnerability to external shocks was high, and Mexico's new role as a medium-sized regional power was debated. The expectation was that Mexico would now be a tougher negotiator with the United States, and that the stakes—both in terms of access to Mexico's oil and the economic opportunities that oil-driven development might engender—would be higher than ever. Suddenly a newly strengthened Mexico was on the map again.

During the first year of the Reagan administration, there was a similar sense that Mexico had much to offer the United States. Not only were the economic opportunities bountiful, but more importantly—for an adminstration consumed with the desire to reassert both its global and hemispheric influence—Mexico was viewed as a potential ally, or at least a useful mediator, in U.S. relations with Latin America and, in particular, with Central America. The debt crisis of 1982—and the subsequent crash of the Mexican economy—and Mexico's unwillingness to toe the line on U.S. policy toward Central America constituted a rude awakening. A newly weakened Mexico was still on the map, but increasingly it was because of areas of disagreement with the United States: over the pace and content of economic liberalization, the depth of political opening, and policies toward Central America, migration, drug trafficking, and corruption.

In the late 1970s, some observers believed that when U.S. energy concerns subsided the spotlight would shift and Mexico would once again fade from the policy horizon. But preoccupation with the U.S. energy crisis was replaced in the United States with concern over Mexico's economic dilemma. During this entire period—from 1976 to the present—the message was brought home to both the U.S. public and private sectors that, like it or not, their future was inextricably enmeshed with that of their neighbor. The United States no longer had the luxury of choosing whether or not to pay attention to Mexico.

What is noteworthy is that the discontinuity in the nature of the strategic relationship entails not only a higher relative ranking for Mexico among U.S. foreign policy priorities but, more significantly, a modification of the traditional concept of national security as applied to Mexico. In the past, the chief preoccupation was Mexican political stability per se. Now added to that is a more nuanced and complex concern regarding the nature and direction of Mexico's economic and political development and its foreign policy, and their potential impact on the United States. This shift may produce policies that operate at cross-purposes. Pressure from the United States regarding Mexican foreign or economic policies, for example, might in some circumstances be counterproductive to the pursuit of Mexican political stability.

The second major discontinuity in U.S.-Mexican relations is their rising complexity, contributing to and highlighting the lack of any centralized control over the conduct of bilateral interaction. The linkage between domestic and foreign policy is perhaps nowhere more palpable than in this particular bilateral relationship. As the domestic/foreign policy interface (the now-famous "intermestic connection") has expanded,[5] so too have the number of actors involved in the relationship and the variety of issues considered.

On both sides of the border, domestic interest groups have assumed an increasingly important role in U.S.-Mexican relations.

---

[5]Bayless Manning, "The Congress, The Executive and Intermestic Affairs: Three Proposals," *Foreign Affairs* 55:2 (January 1977): 309.

In the United States, in particular, an astonishing number of domestic actors from all parts of the country regularly voice their concerns—through a wide variety of channels—on an expanding number of issues directly or indirectly affecting Mexico. The diversity of views expressed in Mexico is also rapidly increasing as new political actors, such as Cuauhtémoc Cárdenas and the Party of the Democratic Revolution (PRD), push for political opening.[6] The rising strength of these new social forces was underscored by the strong showing by opposition parties in the July 1988 elections.

At the level of regional politics, it has long been recognized that there are special "border" issues, but increasing regional autonomy and strength is forcing national policymakers in both countries to pay more attention to local and state actors. Frequently, as evidenced by the debates over the *maquila* industry, the interests of the border area conflict with those of other regions of the United States.

The variety of domestic interests and the absence in either country of a clear national policy consensus on the bilateral relationship open up possibilities for cross-national coalitions and cooperation. Although there may be a great deal of infighting among the various domestic interest groups on each side of the border, future cooperation *across the border* will frequently originate outside government-to-government channels—reflecting growing recognition of a commonality of interests among some of these groups.

At the federal level, the expanding number of executive branch agencies involved in U.S.-Mexican relations mirrors the increase in societal involvement. The first meeting of the working group that handled the formal review of U.S. policy toward Mexico during the Carter administration, for example, was attended by over 100 participants.[7] Similarly, the U.S. Congress reflects increased constituent concern for U.S. policy toward Mexico and the expansion of "intermestic" concerns.[8] At times Congress acts as a useful

---

[6]Cuauhtémoc Cárdenas, a former member of Mexico's Institutional Revolutionary party (PRI), was the candidate of the National Democratic Front (FDN)—a coalition of left-leaning political parties—for the presidency of Mexico in July 1988. He was officially credited with having won 31 percent of the vote compared with 50 percent for Carlos Salinas de Gortari, the candidate of the PRI. In October 1988, Cárdenas helped to found the Party of the Democratic Revolution (PRD). Salinas de Gortari took office as president of Mexico in December 1988.
[7]Personal interview with Viron P. Vaky, December 12, 1985.
[8]For more on the role of Congress, see Donald L. Wyman, "The United States Congress and the Making of U.S. Policy toward Mexico," Working Papers in U.S.-

counterweight to executive branch action (or inaction) on Mexico, but frequently, for lack of a well-informed, broad perspective, it acts as a parochial spoiler. This was the case, for example, with the Helms Senate hearings in mid-1986.

The rise in U.S. public interest in Mexico has been paired with a growing awareness on the part of both the government and the private sector of the variety of opportunities and risks that Mexico holds for the United States. The U.S. government has attempted at times to respond to the demands of various domestic interests, at other times to mold or use those interests to bolster its own policies. The result is that more public attention—well informed or not—is being paid to Mexico today in the United States than at any time in recent history.

A final factor contributing to the increased complexity of the bilateral relationship has been the escalating involvement by the United States—particularly during the Reagan administration—in a variety of Mexican domestic affairs. This includes issues traditionally regarded as "off limits" to the United States (such as the Mexican political process) and areas where there was "agreement to disagree" (for example, in the United Nations). Further, some areas that were previously considered examples of bilateral cooperation have been redefined as bilateral problems (e.g., the narcotics issue), thus requiring a different sort of attention.

These two major discontinuities—the shift in the nature of the strategic relationship and the increased complexity of U.S.-Mexican relations—profoundly altered the underpinnings of U.S. policy-making toward Mexico even as it evolved under the Carter and Reagan administrations. These changes challenge accepted notions regarding the texture, context, and content of U.S.-Mexican ties and alter the constraints to innovative administrative reform.

THE CASE FOR ADMINISTRATIVE REFORM

Careful analysis of the efforts of both the Carter and Reagan administrations to remold U.S. policy-making toward Mexico highlights the importance of centralized policy management and clarifies the relative merits of these two approaches.

Mexican Studies, no. 13 (La Jolla, Calif.: Program in U.S.-Mexican Studies, University of California, San Diego, 1981).

The Carter Years: Formal Coordination

The Carter administration launched the most ambitious project to date to reevaluate policy and revamp process in U.S. policy-
making toward Mexico. In October 1979, following an exhaustive
review of U.S. policy toward Mexico and in response to a perceived
need to develop a more cohesive strategy for dealing with an
increasingly important neighbor, the Office of the U.S. Coordinator for Mexican Affairs was formally established. Despite the
controversy that surrounded this precedent-shattering bureaucratic
mechanism—and broad disagreement regarding its efficacy—
there has been virtually no in-depth, scholarly analysis of this
important endeavor.

The backdrop to the Carter administration's reassessment of
the state of U.S.-Mexican relations was unique. It was a time in
which U.S. global hegemony was visibly in decline and there was
a marked sense of national vulnerability to external political and
economic pressure. Rising inflation added to domestic discontent.
The Carter administration was by mid-1979 under siege at home
and abroad.[9]

Coming to terms with the downside of global interdependence
in the wake of the first round of OPEC oil price increases, the Carter
administration recognized that there was a pressing need for the
United States to engage in a series of complex negotiations with a
variety of countries in both the economic and political arenas. It
was just at this time that astounding levels of oil and gas reserves
were confirmed in Mexico. A newly strengthened Mexico challenged traditional U.S. thinking regarding its southern neighbor.[10]
If the early Carter administration had been anxious to bolster
Mexico's self-confidence, now there was concern about the concessions an oil-rich Mexico could exact from the United States.[11]
At the same time, it was hoped that somehow Mexico would help

---

[9]This was not mitigated by the foreign policy triumphs of the Panama Canal Treaty
of September 1977 and the Camp David Accords of March 1979, and was exacerbated by the taking of U.S. hostages in Iran in November 1979 and the Soviet
invasion of Afghanistan in December 1979.
[10]According to participants in a special congressional study mission sent to Mexico City in mid-1979, "the nature of the relationship is changing, and the reason
can be summed up in one word: oil." See "United States-Mexican Relations and
the Energy Crisis," Report of a Special Study Mission to Mexico City, July 1-4, 1979
(Washington, D.C.: U.S. Government Printing Office, June 1980), p. 1.
[11]"[I]nfluence, leverage, and bargaining potential—once overwhelmingly in favor
of the United States—are shifting somewhat in Mexico's direction." (From a leaked

"solve" the U.S. energy problem. Thus, at a time when the United States was obsessed with oil and gas prices and supplies, Mexico's energy finds and its potential as an emerging economic power were of rising strategic importance.[12]

This was also a period of great friction between the two countries, exacerbated by bouts of ineffectiveness on the part of the U.S. ambassador to Mexico, Patrick Lucey.[13] Although Jimmy Carter and José López Portillo had each expressed their intention to improve both the content and style of U.S.-Mexican relations early in their administrations (and López Portillo had been Carter's first official foreign visitor), the results were disappointing. Tensions heightened following the U.S. veto in 1977 of an agreement to purchase Mexican gas, a move that publicly embarrassed López Portillo. In a speech in Washington, D.C. on October 30, 1978, Jorge Castañeda stated:

> I discount—and don't give any credit to—any sudden newly discovered or rediscovered good will, sympathy or moral considerations on the part of the United States that could change its basic attitude towards Mexico. Its past history with us, its present-day arrogance, selfishness and conservative mood will not allow for a change. Great powers will act as great powers. The nature of our mutual relationship depends essentially on Mexico's attitude and conduct.[14]

National Security Council review of Mexico policy—"Response to Presidential Review Memorandum-41"—reported in J. P. Smith, "U.S. Study Eyes Oil in Mexico, Outlines Options," *Washington Post*, December 15, 1978, p. A26.) The "Response to Presidential Review Memorandum-41" will be referred to here as PRM-41.

[12]This produced concern in Mexico that an energy-starved United States might forcibly attempt to control Mexican oil exports.

[13]Lucey's predecessor, John Jova, served as U.S. ambassador to Mexico from January 1974 to February 1977 and is regarded in both countries as one of the most outstanding U.S. ambassadors ever to serve in Mexico. Lucey, a former governor of Wisconsin, was U.S. ambassador to Mexico from July 1977 through October 1979. Following his departure, the post was vacant until May 1980 when Julian Nava became U.S. ambassador to Mexico. The appointment of Nava was criticized by some as a political move to win Hispanic votes for Carter's reelection bid. Neither Nava nor Lucey received high marks in either country for their work. Nava left his post in April 1981 and was replaced by John Gavin.

[14]Jorge Castañeda, "Mexico and the World," speech delivered in Washington, D.C., October 30, 1978, p. 3. Included as a declassified annex to PRM-41. Castañeda, a professor at El Colegio de México, became Mexico's minister of foreign affairs the following year.

And at a lunch with President Carter in Mexico City on February 14, 1979, in apparent reference to the gas fiasco, López Portillo said that:

> between permanent rather than casual neighbors, surprise moves and sudden deceit and abuse are poisonous fruit which sooner or later will have an adverse effect.[15]

Given the deteriorating atmosphere to which these strong words attest and the fact that many of the "basic truths" about U.S.-Mexican relations had been stood on their heads with the discovery of oil, it is not surprising that the Carter administration initiated a major review of U.S. policy toward Mexico.[16] Nor was it unexpected, given Carter's penchant for administrative reform, that significant restructuring of the bureaucracy was undertaken as a result of that process.

On August 14, 1978, National Security Advisor Zbigniew Brzezinski—in a memo directed to the vice president, the secretary of state, and fourteen other cabinet-level officials and heads of agencies—requested that the Policy Review Committee of the National Security Council (NSC) review U.S.-Mexican relations.[17] "The central objective of the review is to develop a coordinated and

---

[15]In *Keesing's Contemporary Archives* (London: Keesings Publication Longman Group, Ltd.) vol. 25, April 13, 1979, p. 29549.

[16]"[T]he cumulative impact of unmanaged tension could end the conditions that have enabled the United States to discount Mexico's nearness." (From PRM-41 as reported by Smith, "U.S. Study Eyes Oil," p. A26.)

[17]The PRM-41 endeavor had many intellectual precursors. As early as 1977, in a study commissioned by the U.S. Department of State, David Ronfeldt and Caesar Sereseres pointed to "the lack of a central policy concept and of an organizational interface that can motivate dialogue and provide overall direction in bilateral relations." See David Ronfeldt and Caesar Sereseres, "The Management of U.S.-Mexico Interdependence: Drift Toward Failure?" in *Mexico-U.S. Relations: Conflict and Convergence*, ed. Carlos Vásquez and Manuel García y Griego (Los Angeles: Chicano Studies Research Center Publications Latin American Center, University of California, Los Angeles, 1983), p. 45.

Senator Sarbanes stressed the need for interdepartmental consultation on U.S. policy toward Latin America and for special attention to Mexico in hearings held in October 1978. See Hearings before the Subcommittee on Western Hemisphere Affairs of the Committee on Foreign Relations, United States Senate, 95th Congress, Second Session, on "Major Trends and Issues in the United States' Relations with the Nations of Latin America and the Caribbean," October 4, 5, and 6, 1978, pp. 143, 155.

See also Sidney Weintraub, "Organizing the U.S.-Mexican Relationship," in *United States Relations with Mexico: Context and Content*, ed. Richard D. Erb and Stanley R. Ross (Washington, D.C. and London: American Enterprise Institute for Public Policy Research, 1981), pp. 64-72.

well-integrated approach to our relations with Mexico. To do so, we need to improve our understanding of the interrelationships of the issues which concern our two countries."[18]

The "Response to Presidential Review Memorandum-41" (PRM-41) was to focus on the longer-term prospects for cooperation on the central issues in U.S.-Mexican relations. Attention was to be paid to the impact of different bilateral and multilateral policies on patterns of Mexican economic development, on domestic U.S. policies, on specific interest groups in the United States, and on U.S. regional concerns.[19] The various issues in U.S.-Mexican relations were to be related to one another, potential trade-offs identified, policy packages suggested, and comprehensive strategies for dealing with the relationship elaborated.

During the next few months numerous drafts of PRM-41 were reviewed by many different parts of the U.S. bureaucracy. A number of newspapers published articles based on statements leaked by individuals apparently hoping to influence the process, testifying to the high degree of bureaucratic infighting that accompanied the endeavor.[20]

The document was completed in late 1978 and has still not been fully declassified.[21] PRM-41 was divided into five principal sections: analysis of the stakes in U.S.-Mexican relations (including discussion of U.S. and Mexican interests and the dynamics of the relationship); alternative, overarching policy directions; the major

---

Several individuals played a prominent role in the actual PRM-41 exercise in terms of conceptualizing the process, moving it through the bureaucracy and/or actually drafting the document. Included here are Viron P. Vaky, Robert Pastor, Luigi Einaudi, Richard E. Feinberg, Everett Briggs, and David Ronfeldt.

[18]National Security Council memorandum, from Zbigniew Brzezinski, "Review of U.S. Policies Toward Mexico," Presidential Review Memorandum/NSC-41, Washington, D.C., August 14, 1978, p. 1.

[19]In addition to the conceptual importance of studying the linkage of foreign and domestic issues, there was a pragmatic concern that Carter's policy toward Mexico could become a campaign issue.

[20]Smith, "U.S. Study Eyes Oil," pp. Al, A26; Neal R. Peirce and Jerry Hagstrom, "Unique Problems, Joint Solutions along the Mexican Border," *National Journal* 27 (July 7, 1979): 1122-1126; Jack Nelson, "Carter to Replace Envoy to Mexico to Improve Ties," *Los Angeles Times*, March 23, 1979, pp. 1, 10; "What's News," *Wall Street Journal*, March 26, 1979, p. 1.

[21]The author succeeded in having a portion of the main text of PRM-41 declassified in November 1985, in addition to two of its fourteen annexes. A follow-up appeal (NSC case number F85-852) resulted in the declassification of all but a few lines of the document in October 1988. The additional twelve annexes (with the exception of a few lines) were also declassified at that time.

issues (energy, trade, migration, and the border); optional frame-works for managing U.S.-Mexican relations; and administrative organization. While the document emphasized Mexico's role as an emerging energy power,[22] it stressed that U.S. interests in Mexico included a wide array of both domestic and foreign policy issues. PRM-41 predicted that, while oil would improve Mexico's bargaining position, there seemed to be little danger that Mexico would become openly hostile to the United States unless attempts were made to close the border. The underlying concern expressed was that while ad hoc, case-by-case decision-making facilitated the pinpointing of special interests, it complicated the identification of national interests. As a result, U.S. policy was viewed as shapeless and contradictory. A different concept of the relationship was therefore deemed necessary by the authors of the document.

PRM-41 suggested that there were two overall policy directions in which the relationship could move: (1) for the United States to regard Mexico in global terms as an upper-tier developing country without special status; and (2) to view Mexico as a potential full partner of the United States, meriting special attention. Since these were such stark alternatives, the document went on to analyze each major issue area and provided a variety of policy options for each.

The memorandum stated that while there was no consensus on the relative importance of the different issues, it was increasingly clear that they were interrelated and that genuine adjustment by both countries would be necessary in order to deal with them. The report went on to describe the four major issue areas in U.S.-Mexican relations and examined the pros and cons of the two or three policy options suggested for dealing with each of them.

PRM-41 argued that greater bilateral coordination was a sine qua non for improving U.S.-Mexican relations. It stated, however, that intensified consultation is only a stop-gap measure, and it was

---

The information here is based upon this declassified material, a leaked version of an earlier draft of PRM-41 which appeared in the *Washington Post* on December 15, 1978, a speech by Luigi Einaudi—one of the principal drafters of PRM-41—which has been indicated to embody the general spirit of the policy review memorandum, discussions with many participants in the review process, and extensive interviews with a variety of other public and private sector actors.

[22]This is of course the direct result of the overriding concern for energy which characterized the U.S. government during the months in which the PRM-41 document was elaborated. It is interesting that a review document prepared during the latter part of the Reagan administration makes almost no mention of energy.

first necessary that U.S. policymakers know what they want from the relationship. The three main alternatives were: (1) to continue current policies with some modest changes so as to avoid major friction and to increase consultation; (2) to move toward separate development, with each country going its own way; and (3) to promote a partnership based on the premise that a common destiny requires a new relationship characterized by leadership and commitment on both sides. The document addressed the relative merits of the different alternatives, linking each to a package of options for the individual issue areas. Implementation of the chosen alternative should not be developed unilaterally but rather in consultation with Mexico, according to PRM-41. One possibility would be to seek a package agreement, but this would be difficult in that it could appear to sacrifice some interests at the cost of others. A second course would be a sequential strategy involving a series of loosely linked negotiations.

The final section postulated that the prevailing organizational styles—of compartmentalization on the U.S. side and centralization in Mexico—were ill-suited to the management of the complex problems of U.S.-Mexican relations. One approach likely to produce a successful outcome would include three measures: a process to engage both governments at a high level on a continuing basis; a strengthened interagency process like that used to elaborate PRM-41 itself; and a special U.S. representative for Mexican or North American affairs to give general direction on specific issues, provide a comprehensive framework for the relationship, and act as a central reference point on border matters.[23] The other alternative was simply to upgrade the existing consultative mechanism. Either option could be supplemented by a binational public and private advisory group with an independent professional staff to evaluate joint proposals.

The document was both insightful and substantively sophisticated, and it underscored a belief in the importance of Mexico to the United States. It reflected a clear underlying recognition of the need for a reassessment of U.S. policies toward Mexico and the procedures by which to pursue U.S. objectives. Concern for the domestic impact of U.S.-Mexican relations was evident, as was the desire for a comprehensive bilateral strategy.

---

[23]These three suggestions later formed the basis for Carter's memorandum of April 26, 1979, in which he detailed new procedures for dealing with the bilateral relationship.

It is significant that the document did not—as was the fear on the part of some in both countries—pretend to devise a strategy for U.S. access to or control over Mexican energy reserves. On the contrary, great care was taken to state that the principal U.S. energy objective was the maximum level of oil exports compatible with Mexican political stability and economic absorptive capacity.[24] In essence, this document put the brakes on those in the administration who might have viewed Mexico as a giant oil well right in the backyard of the United States. PRM-41 stated that a stable, progressive, and friendly Mexico was in the U.S. interest, emphasizing that no one issue should be allowed to overwhelm the overall objectives of U.S. policy toward Mexico.[25] Given Mexico's future economic potential, it was viewed as more important that the United States develop a cooperative relationship with Mexico in the hope of influencing its overall development strategy in a way consistent with U.S. interests.

On April 26, 1979, following completion of PRM-41, President Carter sent a memo to eighteen cabinet officers, heads of agencies, and advisers to the president on the subject of the coordination of U.S. policy toward Mexico. He highlighted the increasing domestic and international importance of U.S. relations with Mexico and the intensity and complexity of that relationship in the future. The president noted his decision to take steps "to improve our ability to address effectively all issues which affect U.S. relations with Mexico." Dual objectives were identified: "to ensure that all U.S. policies toward Mexico ... promote basic U.S. national interests and are consistent with our overall policy toward Mexico."

Toward this end, the president asked the above-mentioned agencies to give high priority to all issues in their jurisdiction affecting Mexico. Secondly, they were asked that all proposed actions that would affect Mexico be carefully coordinated to be consistent with overall U.S. policy toward the area and to be based on

---

[24]This same point was made, at about the same time and in language similar to that of PRM-41, in a study prepared for the U.S. Department of Energy: "Experts on Mexico aside, too few have noticed that a strong emphasis on near-term U.S. energy problems may lead to policies that conflict with, or at least diverge from, the traditional U.S. objective that Mexico be a stable, cooperative and productive neighbor.... [T]oo rapid [petroleum] development could quickly change Mexico from a secure to an insecure source of petroleum." David Ronfeldt, Richard Nehring, and Arturo Gándara, "Mexico's Petroleum and U.S. Policy: Implications for the 1980s," Executive Summary, R-2510/DOE (Santa Monica, Calif.: Rand Corporation, 1980), pp. 2, 8.
[25]Presidential Memorandum, "Coordination of United States Policy Toward Mexico," The White House, Washington, D.C., April 26, 1979.

the "fullest possible prior consultations with the Government of Mexico."

To achieve the "fundamental Administration-wide objective of establishing a sound, long-term relationship with Mexico," the president directed three measures:

• Nomination of Robert Krueger as ambassador-at-large and United States coordinator for Mexican affairs;[26]

• Establishment of a Senior Interagency Group on U.S. Policy toward Mexico; and

• Strengthening of the U.S.-Mexico Consultative Mechanism.

Krueger's role was conceptualized as being broader than that of simply "coordinating" policy; under the first measure, he was directed to assist the president and the secretary of state in the development, coordination, and implementation of effective national policies toward Mexico. The U.S. coordinator for Mexican affairs was responsible for ensuring that all U.S. activities directly or indirectly affecting Mexico be developed and carried out in a coherent, flexible manner. Specifically, Krueger's tasks as outlined by President Carter were:

— Development and formulation of United States policy toward Mexico;

— Review and coordination of any and all U.S. Government programs and activities that affect U.S.-Mexican relations, whether directly or indirectly;

— Management of U.S. participation in the working groups established under the U.S.-Mexico Consultative Mechanism, ensuring also that any existing overlapping entities are integrated into the process or altered as may be necessary to avoid duplication;

---

[26]Robert Krueger served as U.S. representative from Texas from 1975 until his electoral defeat in 1979. With a doctorate from Oxford University, Krueger—a specialist in Shakespeare—had served as professor and dean of the College of Arts and Sciences at Duke University from 1961 to 1973. At the time of his nomination, he was a businessman and rancher residing in New Braunfels, Texas. Krueger's nomination was strongly endorsed by Robert Strauss, then U.S. special trade representative, who thought it would win the president votes in Texas.

— Advice to myself, the Secretary of State and other
Cabinet officers and Agency Heads and the U.S.
Ambassador to Mexico on the effects of contem-
plated actions by any agency of the Government
on our relations with Mexico; and,

— Initiation of reports and recommendations for
appropriate courses of action, including periodic
reports to me on major developments and
issues.[27]

Further, Krueger was to serve as chairman of the new Senior
Interagency Group on U.S. Policy toward Mexico and U.S. executive director for the U.S.-Mexico Consultative Mechanism. His office
was to be located in the U.S. Department of State; Everett Briggs,
the director of the Office of Mexican Affairs at the Department of
State, would serve as deputy coordinator.

Subsequent to Carter's memorandum, Krueger began to serve
informally as the coordinator designate. His nomination was sent
to the Senate for confirmation in June 1979, and two confirmation
hearings were held the following September.[28] Krueger was finally
confirmed by the Senate, following another long debate on October 22, 1979, by a vote of 48 in favor, 35 against, and 17 not voting.
The long delay between his nomination and confirmation was the
result of rancorous disagreement regarding the new position and
resentment over the lack of prior consultation with Congress.[29]
Krueger's nomination received more extensive consideration than
that of any other ambassadorial nominee of that time.

---

[27]Presidential Memorandum, "Coordination of United States Policy," p. 2.
[28]Krueger himself was questioned in exhaustive detail on September 17, and Deputy
Secretary of State Warren Christopher was asked to respond to questions on
September 24, 1979.
   The confirmation hearings were also influenced by leaked material. During the
hearings, Senator Lugar quoted from a *Los Angeles Times* article but included information which had not actually appeared in that article. Compare Jack Nelson,
"Carter to Replace Envoy to Mexico to Improve Ties," *Los Angeles Times*, March
23, 1979, pp. 1, 10, with Hearings before the Committee on Foreign Relations, United
States Senate, 96th Congress, First Session, on "The Nomination of Robert Krueger
to Be Ambassador-at-Large and Coordinator for Mexican Affairs," September 17
and 24, 1979 (Washington, D.C.: U.S. Government Printing Office, 1979), p. 22.
[29]In this regard, Senator Zorinsky's letter to Zbigniew Brzezinski requesting congressional access to PRM-41 is instructive: its "availability will serve the mutually shared goal of better communication and enhanced cooperation between the
legislative and executive branches of our government with respect to this major
foreign policy issue." It is unclear why the administration remained adamant in
its decision not to share PRM-41 with the Senate since it would have put to rest
much of the criticism leveled at the new position. Hearings on "The Nomination
of Robert Krueger," pp. 34-35.

The acrimonious debate in the Senate was not directed at Krueger himself; rather it reflected wide-ranging disagreement regarding the wisdom and feasibility of establishing a special coordinator for Mexico, and whether or not that individual should be given the title of ambassador-at-large. Some senators felt that relations with Mexico were no more complex or important than ties with other countries and therefore did not merit special treatment. There was concern that the arrangement constituted a stark break with the past and established a precedent that was neither desirable nor replicable in the case of other countries.

Some who agreed with the notion of the position objected on the grounds that it did not require ambassadorial ranking. This would be the first time that an ambassador-at-large would be assigned to deal with a specific country. Some senators found the split authority between the U.S. ambassador in Mexico and the ambassador-at-large to be disconcerting and pointed to a lack of clarity in the chain of responsibility and the lack of a direct counterpart in the Mexican hierarchy.[30] There were those who saw this as simply one more layer of bureaucracy in an already confusing morass of agencies, and evidence, more generally, of the failings of the Carter administration's foreign policy. Finally, questions were raised as to whether this was to be considered a permanent addition to the foreign service structure.[31]

Despite the many objections raised, a sufficient number of senators were convinced that U.S.-Mexican relations were indeed unique and deserving of a special approach. Krueger was approved

---

[30]There was some confusion on this point even among the principal actors. During the confirmation hearings, Krueger maintained that while he and the U.S. ambassador to Mexico were two ends of the same bridge (and would work together harmoniously), he would report directly to the secretary of state while the ambassador would report to the assistant secretary of state. Deputy Secretary of State Warren Christopher stated that, while he did not like to have to contradict Krueger, in fact all U.S. ambassadors report to the president and the secretary of state. Hearings on "The Nomination," pp. 14, 45.

[31]Deputy Secretary of State Warren Christopher was pushed on this point because some senators thought that the position had simply been set up to pay off political debts to Krueger and/or Lucey. Christopher stated firmly that it was a permanent addition to the bureaucracy and seemed to indicate that if Krueger was not approved, someone else would be nominated. Hearings on "The Nomination," p. 43. Had Congress been permitted access to PRM-41 it would have seen that the idea for such a position evolved out of this earlier review process. In fact, there were several other strong candidates in addition to Krueger and Lucey (the latter endorsed by Walter Mondale), including Thomas Enders (supported by Viron P. Vaky).

for the position and served as U.S. coordinator for Mexican affairs until his appointment was terminated on February 1, 1981, less than two weeks after the arrival of the Reagan administration.[32]

The Reagan Years: Informal Coordination

The new administration brought with it a tough, high-profile foreign policy designed to "make America proud again." The new mood was captured by Robert W. Tucker, who wrote of "the restoration of a more normal political world, a world in which those states possessing the elements of a great power once again play the role their power entitles them to play."[33] It was a world that would see the United States "return to the fundamental principle of treating—without apology—friends like friends and self-declared enemies as enemies."[34] This newly assertive foreign policy was accompanied by a harder line toward the Third World, and this was particularly evident in the commercial arena, where trade policy came to be dominated by the notion of reciprocity and "fair" practices.

When Reagan first took office, Mexico and its international creditors were riding a wave of oil-based prosperity. Two years after Reagan's election, the counterpart to the growing activism and self-assuredness of U.S. foreign policy was a deteriorated Mexico. The economic crisis of 1982 was the first turn of a downward spiral that—with few brief respites—gathered velocity over the next six years. A heightened sense of invincibility and moral superiority on the part of the United States contrasted sharply with a deepening sense of vulnerability and social decay in Mexico.

In the very early days of the Reagan administration—when Mexico was still viewed as a great investment, in the broadest sense of the word—Mexico was considered the linchpin of U.S. policy toward Latin America generally, and Central America in particular. There was much greater openness than there had been in the Carter administration to the idea of bilateral agreements and special

---

[32]Krueger was only the twenty-first ambassador-at-large in the history of the United States. Nine such posts were created during the tenure of President Carter.
[33]Robert W. Tucker, "The Purposes of American Power," in *Foreign Affairs* 59:2 (winter 1980/81): 273.
[34]"1980 Republican National Convention Platform," in the *Congressional Record*, Proceedings and Debates of the 96th Congress, Second Session, July 31, 1980, p. 39.

treatment for Mexico, and serious consideration was given to the notion of a North American Common Market.[35]

Mexico's refusal to support U.S. policies toward Central America was the product of a long tradition of independent foreign policy and real disagreement over U.S. policy objectives in the area. It was a thorn in the side of the Reagan administration which—alongside growing disillusionment regarding Mexico's economic future—eventually led to an explosion of frustration and anger on the part of the Reagan administration over the Camarena case in early 1985. The next year and a half was a period of marked deterioration in the bilateral relationship. Every aspect of Mexican behavior seemed to irritate some group in the United States, and day-to-day policy developments—from elections to budgets—were the subject of exhaustive scrutiny. By the time Senator Jesse Helms held his inflammatory hearings on U.S. foreign policy toward Mexico, there was little enthusiasm for Mexico in political circles in Washington or financial circles in New York, and public opinion was highly critical.[36]

Growing U.S. interference in the Mexican domestic agenda during the Reagan administration was the product of a variety of factors. Increased U.S. involvement in reshaping and bolstering the Mexican economy, paired with intense frustration over Mexico's unwillingness to respond to U.S. regional security concerns, led to the belief that the next step in protecting U.S. interests was to weigh in on the issues of political reform in Mexico. The decision to push for political "opening" was made more appealing by the fact that at that moment the only viable electoral challenge to the PRI—albeit solely at the regional level—was the conservative National Action party (PAN).

At the same time, U.S. Ambassador John Gavin was determined to change the nature of the interaction between the two countries and insisted, for example, on the appropriateness of his meetings with opposition figures in Mexico. Further, there was a coincidence of interests among some U.S. liberals and conservatives who joined

---

[35]It should be noted that minority opinion held that Mexico was "the next Iran" and postulated the need for increased U.S. attention to potential political instability in Mexico.
[36]Hearings before the Subcommittee on Western Hemisphere Affairs, Committee on Foreign Relations, United States Senate, 99th Congress, Second Session, on the "Situation in Mexico," May 13, June 17 and 26, 1986.

in condemning electoral abuses and corruption in Mexico, thus providing a measure of public support for stepped-up official U.S. pressure on Mexico. On the Mexican side, this was paired with a weakened bargaining position resulting from the country's economic situation; underestimation of Mexico's margin of maneuver vis-à-vis the United States on the part of Mexico's leaders (especially with regard to the debt negotiations); and growing grassroots pressure within Mexico for political reform, given added impetus by the civic organizing that took place in the wake of the 1985 earthquake.

During this period, Reagan's management style lent itself to an ad hoc, case-by-case approach to U.S.-Mexican relations. A decision was reached to prune the bureaucratic mechanisms for dealing with the bilateral relationship, to increase reliance on informal contacts, and to promote local and private-sector participation. The Office of the U.S. Coordinator for Mexico was disbanded, and the Consultative Mechanism was completely restructured.[37] The bureaucracy still played a crude coordinating function, but the absence of formal coordination promoted the appearance of new means by which to manage the relationship: informal "special coordinators" sprang up.

John Gavin was a particularly strong-willed ambassador with excellent access to the White House inner circle. He frequently sidestepped normal channels to bypass his State Department superiors. A combination of arrogance and skill enabled him to hold effectively most of the reins of U.S. policy-making toward Mexico. As a result, he exerted a tremendous impact on the course of the bilateral relationship during his tenure.[38]

The deterioration of the Mexican economy led to the emergence of a second informal coordinator, Paul Volcker, chairman of the Federal Reserve Board. Until his departure in late 1987, Volcker was a strong advocate for Mexico in Washington. Exhibiting a much greater depth of knowledge about Mexico than was customary in the nation's capital, Volcker stressed the severity of Mexico's economic plight and underscored the need for attention to broader, long-term U.S. interests in that country.

---

[37]The Consultative Mechanism and its nine working groups were replaced with a single Binational Commission headed by the U.S. secretary of state and the Mexican foreign secretary. A Joint Commission on Commerce and Trade was also formed but disappeared midway through the second Reagan administration.
[38]Gavin was replaced as U.S. ambassador by Charles W. Pilliod, whose low-key negotiating style won praise in both countries.

Assessment of the Carter and Reagan Experiences

Though the approaches were different and the objective conditions of U.S.-Mexican relations dramatically dissimilar, both the
Carter and Reagan administrations found coordination to be
indispensable. Even when unplanned, special coordinators
appeared. Each administration had its share of successes and failures, but the failings of the Carter administration were attribut-
able less often to the management style designed to guide U.S.
policy-making toward Mexico than to the circumstances in which
it was forced to operate. The failings of the Reagan administration,
on the other hand, were frequently the by-product of the unreliable nature of informal coordination.[39]

Bureaucratic structure does not define the objectives of U.S.
policy, but rather develops in response to those objectives. U.S.
policy-making is enhanced when structure and policy complement
one another, but this was not the case during either the Carter or
Reagan administration.[40] The Carter administration designed a
bureaucratic structure well-suited to special treatment of Mexico
but utilized a global approach when formulating policy.[41] The
Reagan administration, on the other hand, was well-disposed
toward bilateral agreements with Mexico but lacked the bureaucratic structure that would have enhanced such an approach.

The Office of the U.S. Coordinator worked particularly well
with the Departments of State, Interior, Justice, Health, Education
and Welfare (HEW), Housing and Urban Development (HUD), the
NSC, and the Immigration and Naturalization Services (INS), and
less well with Energy, Agriculture, Commerce, the Office of the

---

[39]There are several difficulties involved in evaluating the two administrations. The
first derives from the need to assess the validity of counterfactual claims. Krueger
maintains, for example, that the bilateral relationship would have been more
conflictual had he not been in office, in that he was able to head off certain problems. Secondly, although difficult to demonstrate, the Reagan administration—
particularly during its first four years in office—lost out on certain opportunities
because of an inability to develop and implement policy in a coherent and
coordinated manner. A final difficulty is that some of the successes of the Reagan
administration had their origins in initiatives undertaken by the Carter
administration.
[40]For more on the relationship between strategy and bureaucratic organization in
U.S.-Mexican relations, see Richard E. Feinberg, "Bureaucratic Organization and
United States Policy toward Mexico," in *Mexico-United States Relations*, ed. Susan
Purcell (New York: Academy of Political Science, 1981), pp. 32-42.
[41]This tension was foreshadowed during congressional testimony (and in particular that of Assistant Secretary for Latin America Viron P. Vaky) in October 1978.
See Hearings "Major Trends and Issues in the United States' Relations with the
Nations of Latin America and the Caribbean."

United States Special Trade Representative (USTR), and Treasury.[42] The latter agencies were more likely to go off on their own and avoid consultation.[43] Even within the Department of State, there was one egregious example of a lack of cooperation between the under secretary of political affairs and Krueger's office that led ultimately to virulent exchanges between the two countries regarding Mexico's decision not to readmit the Shah of Iran.

The record of the Office of the U.S. Coordinator for Mexican Affairs is mixed. Krueger himself felt that his greatest successes lay in helping to negotiate the final agreement on the sale of Mexican natural gas to the United States, his participation in trade negotiations with Mexico, and his arrangement of the 1980 grain sale to Mexico.[44] There were notorious failures as well. They included the Ixtoc fiasco (in which Krueger was involved as coordinator designate),[45] Mexico's decision in 1980 not to enter the General Agreement on Tariffs and Trade (GATT), the U.S. embargo of Mexican tuna, the debacle of the Shah of Iran, and the failure of the U.S. Congress to act on Carter's immigration proposals. At times, there was confusion over who was responsible for what part of the bilateral relationship. "The Office of the U.S. Coordinator probably worsened Mexico's situation in reality. It relegated Mexico into a sort of bureaucratic limbo that was worse than that of any other country."[46]

Some of the problems associated with the office derived from a perceived lack of clout stemming from its location in the Department of State, insufficient clarity in the definition of Krueger's role,

[42]Personal interviews with C. Fred Bergsten, Guy F. Erb, Robert Krueger, Stephen Lande, Doris Meissner, and Paul Storring. See also Hearings before the Subcommittee on Inter-American Affairs of the Committee on Foreign Affairs, House of Representatives, 96th Congress, Second Session, "Update: United States-Canadian/Mexican Relations," June 17 and 26, 1980 (Washington, D.C.: U.S. Government Printing Office, June 26, 1980).
[43]The assistant secretary of treasury for international affairs (during Krueger's tenure) stated "The Office of the U.S. Coordinator for Mexican Affairs was a failure.... Krueger could not come in and tell me what to do and he knew it." Personal interview with C. Fred Bergsten, January 6, 1986.
[44]Krueger felt that if he had not been based in Washington, the natural gas deal and the grain agreement would not have taken place. Personal interview with Robert Krueger, December 8, 1986. See also Hearings, "Update: United States-Canadian/Mexican Relations," pp. 27-61.
[45]In June 1979, an exploratory Mexican oil well blew out, producing a major oil slick which threatened massive pollution damage to beaches in Texas by mid-August. The United States—through Krueger—publicly asked Mexico for payment for damages. Mexican government officials indicated they should have been consulted privately and refused to honor the request.
[46]Personal interview with Larry Storrs, July 13, 1981.

the peculiarities of the personalities involved, bad chemistry between Carter and López Portillo, bureaucratic turf battles, the lack of prior consultation with the U.S. Congress, the absence of a U.S. ambassador in Mexico during the first six months of Krueger's tenure, confusion in Mexico over the existence of "two ambassadors," and the premature demise of the office with the arrival of the Reagan administration. More importantly, it was a less than auspicious moment to launch a major new bureaucratic initiative which demanded priority attention for Mexico. A series of major crises was beginning to envelop U.S. foreign policy-making, and Mexico fell by the wayside.

One overriding success of the entire process, however, is routinely overlooked. It guaranteed—intentionally or not—that energy would be just one among many issues on the bilateral agenda. From the way in which the PRM-41 exercise was first framed to its final bureaucratic guise, the emphasis was on the diversity of U.S. interests in Mexico. Energy concerns, while clearly of deep-seated importance, were not allowed to overwhelm the overall bilateral relationship, thus quelling fears of U.S. operations to "secure" Mexico's oil fields. There was recognition of Mexico's need to "go slow."

U.S. policy-making toward Mexico during the Reagan administration relied on informal coordination. Unfortunately these arrangements sometimes broke down at points of crisis, just when centralized coordination and consultation were most needed. A separate difficulty, also related to the lack of formal mechanisms of coordination, was that on more than one occasion the ambassador's maverick behavior and volatile temperament damaged the tenor of the relationship. Had Gavin been forced to participate in a process that required greater consultation, the relationship would have been less erratic.

In addition to lost opportunities, three cases during the Reagan administration underscored the dangers of bureaucratic fragmentation and the unreliable nature of informal, intermittent coordination. The first arose in 1982 when, in the absence of a coordinated policy toward Mexico, the Reagan administration found itself helping to bail Mexico out of a debt crisis while simultaneously engaging in an increasingly contentious series of trade disputes that exacerbated Mexico's foreign exchange problems.

The second case centered on the way in which the Camarena incident was handled. The Drug Enforcement Administration (DEA) and the Customs Service carried out a series of punitive measures, including a partial closure of the border, that were later the source of problems for other parts of the U.S. bureaucracy. These two agencies capitalized on the growing frustration with Mexico, which characterized the U.S. government's attitude more generally, to launch a "get tough on Mexico" offensive that was to last until mid-1986. Ambassador Gavin is reputed to have attempted to calm the waters, but it proved impossible for him to manage fast-moving events on three "fronts"—Washington, Mexico City, and the border—simultaneously.

The third episode was that of the Helms Senate hearings in mid-1986. The hearings highlighted monumental disorganization among the various U.S. agencies and a lack of cooperation between the executive and legislative branches. While one part of the Department of State attempted to have the hearings postponed or canceled, another wanted to use the opportunity to push Mexico on a variety of points. The presentation by the Department of Treasury was surprisingly upbeat, while those made by the DEA and Customs Service were quite hard-line. While the motives for displeasure with Mexico—both within the administration and on Capitol Hill— would not have disappeared, it is unlikely that this exercise in congressional grandstanding could have caused quite as much damage to the bilateral relationship had there been a greater degree of coordination within the executive branch.

Despite marked deterioration in U.S.-Mexican relations between early 1985 and mid-1986, significant agreements were reached. Following Mexico's entry into GATT in August 1986, a bilateral framework agreement for commercial interaction and an innovative debt swap were negotiated in late 1987. And, although it is unlikely to have a net positive impact on the bilateral relationship, passage of the Simpson-Rodino immigration bill was a major domestic achievement for the Reagan administration.

These achievements do not, however, constitute an argument for ad hoc management of the relationship. To a large extent, they derive from the interaction of a strong (in both economic and political terms) U.S. administration, eager to flex its foreign policy muscles, and a weakened bilateral partner. They are testimony to the gravity of the Mexican economic crisis and the presence in Mexico, after 1982, of the most pro-U.S., pro-private sector president in over fifteen years. From the perspective of the Reagan administration, even more could have been achieved in the areas mentioned above had there been a coherent policy toward Mexico and a centrally coordinated process of policy implementation. Other advances would have been possible in areas in which the Reagan administration was noticeably less successful, such as narcotics. The Reagan administration enjoyed certain successes, almost in spite of itself, due to the declining fortunes of its neighbor.

Comparison of the Carter and Reagan experiences shows that—whatever the content of policy—the absence of centralized management of U.S. policy-making toward Mexico can endanger the pursuit of U.S. interests in the bilateral relationship. With effective coordination, it is more likely that new policy initiatives will surface and receive attention. Because there are means by which to efficiently move new ideas through the bureaucracy, opportunities can be grasped more quickly. Further, it is possible to link issues comprehensively. In the absence of formal coordination, informal coordination will arise, but it will be less reliable.

In terms of Mexico's pursuit of its interests vis-à-vis the United States, there are costs and benefits to a well-coordinated and coherent U.S. policy process. On the one hand, clear U.S. policy guidelines would clarify for Mexico where it stands in relation to the United States. If those policies were perceived as generally enlightened, coordination would be viewed positively since it would enhance the prospects for implementation and reduce the risks of damage to the relationship from the sort of maverick bureaucratic maneuvering that characterized the Reagan administration. On the other hand, in issue areas characterized by disagreement between the two countries, Mexico would find its ability to play off one part of the U.S. bureaucracy against another substantially reduced.

The mixed record of both administrations derives in part, of course, from the nature of the beast itself. It is not so much that the two countries do not understand each other—and this is particularly true at the governmental level—but rather that they disagree fundamentally in a number of areas. Thus, no bureaucratic arrangement will guarantee a harmonious relationship. The best that can be hoped for is to design a mechanism that will increase the prospects for a good working relationship: one that will avoid unnecessary conflict, manage unavoidable conflict as efficiently as possible, and enhance the potential for cooperation.[47] Secondly,

---

[47]For more on the design of a bilateral framework for dispute settlement, see Guy F. Erb and Cathryn L. Thorup, "U.S.-Mexican Relations: The Issues Ahead," Development Paper 35 (Washington, D.C.: Overseas Development Council, November 1984), particularly pp. 29-30.

domestic problems and foreign policy crises in other regions of the world can always produce a siren's call capable of distracting the attention of U.S. policymakers. Again, the best that can be hoped for is an arrangement that makes it as bureaucratically difficult as possible to neglect Mexico.

POLICY RECOMMENDATIONS

The leaders elected in 1988 in both the United States and Mexico will face the daunting but inescapable task of setting new terms for bilateral interaction. While it is true that U.S.-Mexican relations extend beyond government-to-government relations, it is also true that the policy guidelines set forth by the administrations of Presidents George Bush and Carlos Salinas de Gortari will to a large extent still determine the tone, pace, and direction of the overall relationship well into the 1990s.

Paying attention to U.S.-Mexican relations has always been unavoidable for Mexico. Events of the past ten years—the growing strategic importance of Mexico to the United States and the rising complexity of the relationship—have made this true for the United States as well. Now that both countries simultaneously face the prospect of severe economic downturn, the costs and benefits of joint development strategies must be reassessed. The sociopolitical costs—to both countries—of Mexico's seemingly endless economic downturn must also be taken into account.

It may be that the moment has been reached in which Mexico's leaders believe that the country has no choice but to tie its economic fortunes even more closely to those of the United States— at least for the immediate future. The repercussions of such a move—which in many respects had, of course, already begun under de la Madrid—are as yet unpredictable, but they will be of such magnitude that every aspect of U.S.-Mexican relations will be up for grabs. Whether this will produce greater bilateral conflict or enhanced cooperation over the long run is impossible to judge.[48] What is clear is that U.S. policymakers are faced with the task of clarifying once again what it is they want from the bilateral relationship and how to achieve it.

---

[48]For more on this point, see Adolfo Aguilar, "Mexico: The Presidential Problem," *Foreign Policy* 69 (winter 1987-88): 40-60.

Past experience leaves many questions unanswered. While it is evident that centralized management of U.S. policy toward Mexico is desirable—the costs of bureaucratic incoherence are demonstrably far too high—it is less clear exactly how this should be accomplished. Neither the experience with formal coordination nor that with informal coordination was particularly successful. Yet the approaches failed for very different reasons.

Informal coordination fell prey to the fact that by its very nature it was unreliable and more susceptible—because there were more points of entry—to special interest pressures. Formal coordination failed less on its own merits than as the victim of inexperience and circumstance. This was the first time that such an ambitious approach had been attempted, and the effort was truncated before the learning process was complete. It was also initiated at the worst possible moment, both in terms of the U.S. election calendar (which meant not enough attention was going to be paid to Mexico or to the Office of the U.S. Coordinator for Mexican Affairs) and in terms of U.S. foreign policy (which quickly was consumed by Iran).

The fact that formal coordination did not work under the specific circumstances of the Carter presidency should not be construed as a final judgment on the viability of central management. It is sufficient reason, however, to avoid resurrection of that particular formula. Even if it were possible to win congressional approval for such an effort—a highly dubious proposition at this point—it would be tainted by the problems associated with the Krueger experience. Given past administrative history, the nature of the discontinuities in the bilateral relationship, and the precariousness of current U.S.-Mexican relations, new policy alternatives are in order. The following options range from the elaboration of a comprehensive framework for U.S. policy toward Mexico to more narrow suggestions for improvement.

The first task awaiting the Bush administration is to clarify U.S. policy toward Mexico. A review of current policy is more effective early on in an administration. Undertaken later, it will exhibit a greater tendency to rationalize the status quo. A new team will be able to maintain a greater degree of distance from the policies that are already in place and to be more innovative in their recommendations. Elaboration of a clear, coherent policy for U.S.-Mexican relations is the indispensable first step to effective management of the bilateral relationship.

The bureaucracy needs a clear awareness that paying primary attention to Mexico and cooperation among agencies in the development and implementation of policies is an administration priority and that, simply put, there is no other alternative. It is not enough to merely let it be known that Mexico is "important." There are always new crises that require attention, new areas of the world that seem all-important; for Carter it was Iran, and for Reagan it was Central America. Mechanisms must be put into place that will ensure consistent priority attention to the management of U.S.-Mexican relations. Further, it is helpful if these measures are developed and implemented prior to a significant downturn in the relationship. By the time Krueger's office was established, U.S.-Mexican relations were so deteriorated that a principal bureaucratic function was glorified damage control.

The basic idea behind all of the following options is that they afford Mexico a permanent place of priority in the U.S. bureaucratic structure and make it more difficult to downgrade its importance after the initial glow of presidential *abrazos* dims.

Executive Branch

The principal institutional failing of the previous attempt at coordination was that some agencies were reluctant to participate and immediately sought ways to circumvent the process. This was due in part to a perceived lack of clout that derived from basing the coordinator in the Department of State. Other agencies saw the process as "belonging to State," while many foreign service officers viewed Krueger—a political appointee—as "not one of our own."[49] One alternative would be to base a coordinator—who would not have to be a high-profile ambassador-at-large in this case—in the National Security Council, thus giving that person the imprimatur of the White House. This individual could be a behind-the-scenes coordinator, rather than the very visible—and at times confusing—"second ambassador."

The disadvantage of such an approach is that it immediately sends a signal that Mexico's primary importance to the United States derives from security concerns, a thought of little comfort to those in both countries who would prefer to ground the bilateral

---

[49]Personal interview with Robert Krueger, December 8, 1986. Krueger himself feels that it would have been better if the Office of the U.S. Coordinator for Mexican Affairs had been based in the White House.

relationship in less dramatic—and crisis-oriented—criteria. Secondly, it shifts the NSC's mandate from that of adviser to the president to taskmaster of the bureaucracy. Moreover, although locating the position in the NSC and avoiding the ambassador-at-large ranking would obviate the need for Senate confirmation, it is still unclear how much bureaucratic support such a move could command. The history of turf battles between the Department of State and the NSC alone indicates the type of problems that could be expected.

A second possibility is that of a bureaucratic reorganization that would group Mexico and Canada at State (a Bureau for North American Affairs), the NSC, and possibly other agencies as well.[50] A move of this sort would arouse opposition from those who did not want to see Canadian affairs separated from Europe or Mexican affairs separated from Latin America, but it might be well-suited to managing the sorts of economic problems these three countries will face during the course of the next administration. Such a major administrative upheaval would be contentious not only in the United States, but in Canada and Mexico as well, and would have to be preceded by careful, informal consultations with domestic interest groups and with both neighbors.[51] Such a move would not, however, respond to the need for interagency coordination.

A third alternative would be to afford Mexico a higher place in the existing bureaucratic structure of either or both the Department of State and the NSC. In terms of State, this might entail appointing a deputy assistant secretary for Mexico. With regard to the NSC, it would mean giving a staff member sole responsibility for Mexico. A co-stewardship of the bilateral relationship by the two agencies is a third possibility. Whichever option is pursued, the individuals responsible for U.S.-Mexican relations will need a greater depth and breadth of education and experience than has been the norm. An individual who speaks Spanish is not equally well-equipped to work on Mexico, Peru, or El Salvador. In-depth

---

[50]This idea has surfaced several times in the past but thus far has usually aroused more dissent than approbation. One notable exception has been the Office of the U.S. Special Trade Representative where this bureaucratic arrangement has been quite successful.

[51]The Mexican Foreign Ministry has its own Office of North American Affairs and therefore might support a bureaucratic counterpart in the U.S. Department of State. Canada—having just agreed to a proposed new free trade arrangement with the United States—is less enthusiastic, however, about including Mexico in any sort of trilateral arrangement.

knowledge of Mexico and the history of U.S.-Mexican relations would enhance the work of U.S. policymakers, whether based in Washington or at the U.S. Embassy in Mexico.

The fourth and most modest option would be to establish a permanent senior interagency group that would meet regularly and perform a collective coordinating function.52 Some of the same decisions would have to be made in terms of where it would be based and how it would be staffed.

The choice among these alternatives must be based both on the substantive merits of each and on the political feasibility of implementation. It is desirable to base the coordinating mechanism in the White House because of the latter's relative skill in addressing the domestic/foreign policy interface and the perceived legitimacy of its efforts to set trade-offs among a wide variety of interests. Given the drawbacks associated with establishment of the coordinating mechanism in the NSC, the best alternative is to appoint either an assistant to the president for Mexican affairs or an assistant to the president for North American affairs.

Basing the coordinating mechanism in the White House would provide clout—without the need for congressional approval for ambassadorial ranking—but it would still require political support. Approval of a move to establish such a position would be more likely with the option of an assistant to the president for North American affairs. Not only would the onus of a failed past experience be avoided, but many who would not support a special arrangement for Mexico alone could be convinced of the need for centralized direction and control of North American affairs. Those who favor specialized attention to either Mexico or Canada would be unlikely to object to such a move if the alternative was no such mechanism for either country.

Congress

One of the principal conceptual failings of the Office of the Coordinator for Mexican Affairs is that it took insufficient account of non-executive branch ties with Mexico. Not only did it not plan

---

52The Reagan administration had such an interagency group, but it met only irregularly in response to special events such as presidential visits and meetings of the Binational Commission.

for systematic input from the Congress (although one of the attractions of Krueger was that, as a former U.S. congressman, he was reputed to have good ties with Capitol Hill), but Congress was actually alienated by the lack of prior consultation regarding the entire procedure.53 Other outside interest groups were similarly excluded from formal participation.

Any planned bureaucratic restructuring of the bilateral relationship should take into account the inevitability of growing congressional involvement in U.S.-Mexican relations. The most ambitious approach would be to establish subcommittees on Mexican affairs or on North American affairs under the Senate Foreign Relations and House Foreign Affairs committees. Given past congressional opposition to attempts to single out specific countries for special attention, such a move would be difficult but more likely to succeed if both countries were included. A second recommendation would be the systematic inclusion of observers from the appropriate committees of the House and Senate in an executive branch interagency group.

Improvement of congressional information-sharing on Mexico and Mexico-related issues is indispensable. The Mexico-United States Interparliamentary Commission is a valuable bilateral activity, but it tends to attract those who already have some understanding of the complexities of U.S.-Mexican relations. All too many members of Congress are unaware of the broader issues at stake in the bilateral relationship since their first loyalty is to the more parochial interests of their constituents. At a minimum, programs to improve the level of knowledge on Capitol Hill regarding Mexico are needed. In this sense, establishment of a U.S.-Mexico caucus would constitute a useful tool for educating Congress on the nuances of the relationship and its impact on domestic constituents.

A final suggestion is to structure greater interaction between the Department of State and both the House Foreign Affairs Committee and the Senate Foreign Relations Committee. Both are natural allies for the Department of State that are approached only

---

53Both Krueger and Robert Pastor stated that Congress never understood the role of the coordinator. Personal interviews with Robert Krueger (December 8, 1986) and Robert Pastor (June 22, 1981). One congressional staff member stated, "The Office of the Special Coordinator was a joke. What was it for? Congress didn't buy the administration's explanation." Personal interview with Barry Sklar, July 13, 1981.

extremely rarely. There is a tendency for State to work with more parochial committees, such as Commerce, in lieu of the broader-based ones. By the same token, it would be useful to have a permanent staff person assigned to Mexico on both the Foreign Affairs and Foreign Relations committees.

Outside Actors

Special arrangements need to be set in place for liaison with external (i.e., non-governmental) actors. First, the coordinating mechanism should include an individual solely responsible for border management concerns. This would facilitate interaction among the local, state, and federal levels and would enhance the design and implementation of strategies specific to the distinctive concerns of the border area. This individual would also bear responsibility for coordinating the border-specific activities of the various federal agencies that deal with Mexico.

A second staff member of the new administration's coordinating mechanism for Mexico should be assigned exclusive responsibility for liaison with special interest groups, including cross-national interests. This would permit a two-way flow of information between the coordinating agency and representatives of these groups and facilitate the hard bargaining required.

This could be the first step toward a more ambitious project of public education. It is vitally important to gradually consolidate a national constituency for coherent, long-range planning on U.S.-Mexican relations. While the governments usually understand each other very well, the same cannot be said of public opinion in the two countries. It is not enough that elites in the United States and Mexico come to understand each other; the public in each country remains generally poorly informed about its neighbor.[54]

In the United States, there is no consistent and widely supported view of U.S. national interests regarding Mexico. The failure is compounded by the diversity of domestic constituencies

---

[54]"What Americans Think: Views on Development and U.S.-Third World Relations" (Washington, D.C.: Overseas Development Council and InterAction, 1987); William Stockton, "Mexicans, in Poll, Call U.S. a Friend" (see table "The View from Mexico: Attitudes About the U.S."), *New York Times*, November 17, 1986, p. 1; Enrique Alduncín Abitia, *Los valores de los mexicanos* (Mexico: Fundación Cultural Banamex, 1986).

which inhibits consensus among U.S. officials and the public at large on appropriate policies toward Mexico. From the perspective of U.S. policy-making, until there is a body of public support for enlightened policies toward Mexico, trade-offs will be difficult to achieve. Further, when both countries face simultaneous economic downturn, outbreaks of anti-Mexico sentiment will become the norm rather than the exception unless a common interest in cooperative economic development and conflict management is more generally perceived as being in the U.S. interest.

A third suggestion is that the coordinating mechanism establish a formal link with an outside advisory group, comprised of U.S. academics, private-sector representatives, and non-governmental policy specialists, to provide regular consultation. Informal discussions with a binational group such as the Bilateral Commission on the Future of United States-Mexican Relations might complement this process and ensure the introduction of a greater diversity of ideas into the U.S. policy apparatus.

The final recommendation is the creation of a rotating position in the U.S. Embassy in Mexico, to be staffed by an academic or nongovernmental policy analyst for a period of one to two years. These specialists in U.S. relations with Mexico could contribute significantly to the resource pool of the embassy—providing a broader historical perspective on the bilateral relationship—and, at the same time, gain first-hand exposure to "real world" diplomacy and politics.

Managing U.S-Mexican Relations: Summary of Recommendations

To facilitate the design and implementation of a comprehensive strategy for the management of the bilateral relationship, the following steps are recommended:

- Appointment of an assistant to the president for North American affairs. This individual would be in charge of leading the elaboration and implementation of U.S. policy toward Mexico and Canada, and would be supported by a deputy assistant for Mexican affairs and a deputy assistant for Canadian affairs. Under the deputy assistant for Mexican affairs it is recommended that staff positions be created for: (a) congressional liaison; (b) border area management; and (c) public affairs (particularly liaison with special interest groups).

The assistant's mandate would go beyond that of "coordinating" policy toward North America. The individual would be responsible for: clarifying national priorities in this area and highlighting the linkages among issues; building a domestic consensus on U.S. policies toward Mexico and Canada; negotiating trade-offs among competing domestic interests; establishing a framework for conflict resolution; and providing the sustained central management necessary for the design, advocacy, and implementation of policies. Finally, the assistant—in conjunction with each deputy— would be responsible for ensuring that comprehensive bilateral consultations with both Mexico and Canada be undertaken by the respective U.S. ambassadors and appropriate Cabinet officials.

- Establishment of a North American Interagency Group. Participants would include the senior officials involved in North American affairs in each agency and would be facilitated by a restructuring of these agencies to reflect a North American focus. In addition to the full range of executive branch participants, the meetings would be attended regularly by an observer from each side of Congress.

- Formation within the Senate Foreign Relations and House Foreign Affairs committees of Subcommittees for North American Affairs. This would be paired with a program to improve the level of expertise on U.S.-Mexican relations within the U.S. Congress and to enhance cooperation with the executive branch.

- Appointment of an outside advisory group to consult on a regular basis with the Office of the Assistant to the President for North American Affairs.

- Creation of a one-year, rotating position for an adviser within the U.S. Embassy in Mexico to be filled by a U.S. academic or policy analyst.

The United States and Mexico are in the midst of a major realignment in their relationship. That it is a shift of necessity rather than choice makes it even more important that careful thought be given as to how best to structure this new interaction. The direction of the bilateral relationship will be at great risk if left to ad hoc management of the vagaries of international economics and domestic interest group politics. Bilateral consultation is a key component to an effective working relationship, as is a reassessment in both countries of traditional policy approaches. This paper has explored the lessons to be learned from U.S. bureaucratic experience, in an effort to draw out the prospects for an administrative reform aimed at the creation of a coherent machinery for managing U.S.-Mexican relations.

Good process cannot replace good policy, but enlightened policy is irrelevant in the absence of a well-devised strategy for implementation. The experiences of the last ten years show only intermittent success in both arenas. It is now up to the Bush administration to explore ambitious and innovative approaches to the bilateral relationship that build on past experience to break new ground in U.S.-Mexican relations.

III

CASES

7

U.S. and Mexican Policies toward Central America

Claude Heller

For the last few years, the situation in Central America has been one of the principal foreign policy priorities for both Mexico and the United States. At the same time, as a result of different concepts about the nature of the regional conflict and the ways to solve it, it has been one of the main points of divergence between the two governments. It is a subject which affects the bilateral agenda but which goes beyond it and has great repercussions upon all inter-American relations.

The affirmation that Mexico's government has undertaken intense diplomatic activity which has favored Nicaragua and has consequently gone against the interests of the United States is often held in official U.S. circles. Moreover, Mexico has been given credit for having the ability to significantly affect the actions of the Contadora Group of which it is a member, along with Colombia, Panama, and Venezuela. A detailed examination of the events of the last five years would undoubtedly allow the reaching of different conclusions about that assertion, which, in Mexico's opinion, is a severe distortion of the facts.

The first three parts of this work aim to determine the terms of what has become the focus of disagreement between Mexico and the United States, in order to suggest, in a fourth section, some conclusions for the immediate future.

BACKGROUND

If we try to systematize the differences between the two governments, a first approach is to point out the existence of differing perceptions of the Central American crisis at the end of the seventies. This is not the first time that Mexico and the United States have had differences on the subject of inter-American relations. It has occurred in other critical situations—such as the cases of Guatemala in 1954, the Cuban revolution at the beginning of the sixties, the Dominican crisis of 1965, and the rise to power of the Unidad Popular in Chile in 1970. The distinguishing feature in this case is that Mexico did not limit itself to stating its point of view regarding the events but, for the first time, decided to play an active role in the region, individually and in conjunction with other Latin American countries.

When President Miguel de la Madrid took office in December of 1982, Mexico had defined several lines of action which would allow it to generate new diplomatic initiatives in Central America. In 1979 Mexico had already defined the Central American region as one of its basic priorities for its international action, and it had read well the implications of the events taking place at its southern border. At the same time, Mexico's relations with Central America would inevitably affect its relations with the United States, given the latter's weight and influence in the region. Thus, not only would Mexico and the United States have a different diagnosis of the crisis, but above all, the design of an active presence by the López Portillo government became an important variable with which the Reagan administration had to contend.

From 1979 to 1982 Mexico's foreign policy toward Central America turned around three fundamental axes which established the starting point of its initiatives. First, Mexico maintained that the regional crisis was a product of the people's legitimate struggle to change anachronistic power structures and that lagging economic and social development was the origin of the conflicts in the area. This diagnosis would be directly opposed to the one being formulated in the United States at the end of the seventies.

Mexico's rupture of diplomatic relations with the government of Anastasio Somoza in May 1979 and the active opposition to the formation of an inter-American peace force during the seventeenth meeting of the OAS were the first signs of the design of an action which gave flexibility to the management of traditional principles of foreign policy and to the practical exercise of that policy. The final throes of the Somoza regime in mid-1979 and the United States' last attempts to prevent the ultimate triumph of the Sandinista insurrection offered the appropriate framework within which Mexico defined its conception of the Nicaraguan internal struggle. This conception would later be applied to the El Salvador situation in particular and Central America in general. Mexico openly rejected the theory of an external plot to explain the internal crisis. Even though it did recognize that the international ramifications of what was happening in Nicaragua might legitimately interest neighboring countries and other countries in the region, it deemed this to be secondary to the fundamental consideration that this was an internal, domestic problem, not an international matter. The people of Nicaragua had exercised the sacred right to rebel against tyranny in the same way that the Mexican people had done seventy years before.[1]

With the Sandinista triumph in 1979, the domino theory—according to which Nicaragua was only the first piece of Soviet-Cuban expansionist policy, which would next center its immediate action in El Salvador and Guatemala and finally in Mexico—started gaining strength in political and academic circles. Evidence in support of the theory was the rapidly growing political opposition—legal or "subversive"—in both countries. Using fear of the domino phenomenon as justification, governmental and paramilitary forces increased their systematic violence and repression. The October 1979 coup d état in El Salvador which brought down the government of Carlos Humberto Romero was, in reality, a preemptive blow aiming to cripple insurrection. It was, however, a political failure: in January 1980, members of the Salvadoran left resigned from the civilian-military junta which the United States wished to present as a centrist democratic reform option under attack from the extremes of both right and left. The realignment of political forces in El Salvador coincided with the 1980 U.S. primary elections, during which Carter was severely attacked for his Latin American policy. The triumph of Ronald Reagan in November 1980 reinforced the view of the Central American crisis as caused by external factors.

Second of the three axes which set the tone of all of Mexico's diplomatic initiatives was its support of political, negotiated solutions to the conflicts in the area. Mexico responded to the critical

---

[1]Speech by the Mexican minister of foreign relations, Jorge Castañeda, to the Seventeenth Meeting of OAS Foreign Ministers, Washington, D.C., June 21, 1979.

Salvadoran situation with an initiative that is undoubtedly the boldest initiative of its foreign policy in the last few years. Together with France, it issued a statement recognizing the alliance of the Farabundo Martí Front for National Liberation and the Democratic Revolutionary Front (FMLN-FDR) as a "representative political force willing to assume the obligations and rights of state." The joint statement urged the alliance "to participate in reestablishing the mechanisms of rapprochement and negotiation necessary for a political solution of the crisis."[2] Beginning in 1980, Mexico, together with nonaligned countries and some European countries, promoted a human rights resolution in the United Nations which recognized the need for dialogue between the government and the armed opposition to end the armed conflict in El Salvador. This Mexican initiative was in conflict with the policy of the Reagan administration. The latter presented the Salvadoran situation as a product of communist intervention in the region and proof positive of the East-West confrontation in Central America. In 1981 El Salvador held center stage in U.S. foreign policy, as was demonstrated by the White Book prepared by the State Department, which spurred General Vernon Walters' intense efforts to demonstrate to Latin American and European governments the interference of the Socialist bloc.

Reiterating the Franco-Mexican initiative's focus on the internal situation in El Salvador, Mexico's president offered the bases for a negotiated solution in the Managua proposals of 1982. He referred to the "three knots of conflict in the zone: Nicaragua, El Salvador, and, calling a spade a spade, relations between Cuba and the United States." In addition to restating the Mexican position on El Salvador and offering to help improve communications between Cuba and the United States, Mexico presented for the first time a series of suggestions relating to Nicaragua. The United States should discard the use of force, support the balanced reduction of forces in the area, permit the disarmament of the Somozan bands, and stop external aid to those groups. These steps would permit Nicaragua to renounce arms and stop building its military forces. Finally, according to the Mexican president, Nicaragua and its neighbors needed to adopt a system of mutual nonaggression pacts.

The so-called negotiated solution can also be found in the September 1982 Mexican and Venezuelan initiative, in which the two countries offered to explore ways to prevent the escalation of

---

[2]Joint Franco-Mexican statement on El Salvador, August 28, 1981.

conflict in Central America, particularly along the border between Honduras and Nicaragua.

The third of the axes defining Mexico's diplomatic initiatives in Central America was a policy of economic cooperation free of political conditions. The best example is the San José agreement with Venezuela, signed in August 1980, to supply oil under exceptional financial conditions. That agreement was also in sharp contrast to the policy of the U.S. government. Among the different options which the Reagan administration considered for Central America, the idea of a "Mini-Marshall Plan," initially suggested by Prime Minister Edward Seaga of Jamaica in meetings with the U.S. president, came to the fore. In the first quarter of 1981, the idea of a Central American and Caribbean plan led to a diplomatic initiative, by which the United States hoped to unite, together with Canada, the countries considered to be "regional powers"—Mexico and Venezuela. As of the second interview between Presidents López Portillo and Reagan in June of 1981, Mexico declared that its perception of the regional problems was different from that of the United States and established three conditions intended to prevent Mexico's involvement in an anti-communist plan that did not accord with Mexico's policy of cooperation for regional development. To that end, Mexico pointed out that the U.S. plan should be conceived in terms of real economic aid to the entire region and not as a political instrument of struggle against an entire ideology, that the plan not be designed as a complement to the military aid granted to some governments, and, finally, that all the countries in the region be beneficiaries of the plan without any automatic exclusions.

The year 1982 saw the development of a series of diplomatic initiatives related to Central America. De la Madrid's proposals in Managua in February were followed by a six-point plan which Honduras presented before the Permanent Council of the OAS; it covered military and security questions (regional disarmament, reduction of foreign advisers, supervision of contracted commitments, elimination of arms trafficking, and the establishment of a multilateral permanent dialogue to encourage political understanding and thus strengthen democratic and pluralist systems).

The most significant outcome of the '82 initiatives was a rapprochement between Mexico and Venezuela; relations between these countries had cooled because of their differences over the Salvadoran case and the Franco-Mexican statement. The initiative of September of 1982 on the Honduras-Nicaragua situation was a sign of a Latin American political desire to join forces for the peaceful solution of the controversies. Simultaneously the relations between the United States and Nicaragua deteriorated progressively, and the Reagan administration—in addition to supporting the role of the OAS—tried to isolate the Sandinista government.

So it was that in October of the same year foreign ministers interested in the furtherance of democracy in Central America and the Caribbean met in San José. Only Costa Rica, El Salvador, and Honduras were active participants. Countries considered non-democratic (Guatemala and Nicaragua) were excluded. Also present were the United States, British Honduras, Colombia, Jamaica, Panama, and the Dominican Republic, the last two as observers. The participants stated that it was the job of the governments "legitimized by the will of the people" to defend, encourage, and develop the democratic system and that the time had come to define the conditions which would permit the reestablishment of a lasting and stable peace in Central America. In the Final Minutes of the meeting, the ministers outlined their objectives of political democratization—as well as security objectives similar to those presented by Honduras before the OAS. Finally, they decided to create an electoral advisory body and establish the so-called "Pro-Peace and Democracy Forum" to achieve these objectives which "would be amplified through the incorporation or cooperation of other democratic states." The latter is a reference to Mexico and Venezuela who had refused to participate in the meeting at San José.

Throughout 1982, the government of Nicaragua reiterated the need for a bilateral negotiation with Honduras and an agreement with the United States. Despite talks held between high officials of the Department of State and the Sandinista government, no understanding was reached, and Nicaragua viewed the Mexican-Venezuelan initiative as a positive step which might permit a solution to the conflict.

From 1982 onwards, the various initiatives reflected not only different and even opposing perspectives on the Central American crisis, but they also set different conditions for its pacification. Tension continued between Nicaragua and Costa Rica and between Nicaragua and Honduras. The actions of irregular Nicaraguan forces, the intensification of the Salvadoran internal conflict, and the aggravation of social conditions provoked a massive flow of refugees across the borders separating these countries.

In broad outline, this was the regional situation when Colombia, Mexico, Panama, and Venezuela decided to undertake a new diplomatic initiative. The new diplomatic momentum was strengthened by changes of administration in Colombia and Mexico. In the first case, the rise to power of Belisario Betancourt led to a new direction in Colombia's foreign policy. In Mexico, the sexennial change of government brought the ratification and intensification of a view of Latin America as a priority and a natural area of action. This occurred at a time when the traditional mechanisms of the inter-American system had been weakened by the Falkland Islands War and its repercussions in hemispheric relations.

CONTADORA PEACE NEGOTIATIONS

On January 8 and 9, 1983, the foreign ministers of Colombia, Mexico, Panama, and Venezuela met on Contadora Island. Although several questions of interest to Latin America were considered during the meeting, the Central American situation was the central theme. In the joint communiqué issued after the meeting, the four foreign ministers pointed out that it was undesirable for the conflicts in the zone to be included in the context of the East-West confrontation and they agreed on the need to eliminate "the external factors which make them worse."[3] At the same time they issued an urgent call to the countries directly involved to resolve their differences through dialogue and negotiation. Without a doubt, the most innovative element was the analysis of "possible new actions" compatible with the principles of nonintervention and self-determination. The four countries reiterated their decision to continue the economic strengthening of the Central American countries through initiatives such as the San José Plan sponsored by Mexico and Venezuela. The joint effort on the part of Colombia, Mexico, Panama, and Venezuela had begun, and its main priority was to prevent the generalization of armed conflict in the region. The Latin American initiative generated conversations among the five Central American governments to set an agenda for negotiating an agreement.

From the beginning of the Contadora Group negotiations, Mexico held that the solution to the Central American crisis could

---

[3]Joint communiqué of January 9, 1983 in the Bulletin of the Ministry of Foreign Relations, Government of Mexico.

not be achieved without the participation of the countries with ties and interests in the region. Thus, the presidents of Colombia, Mexico, Panama, and Venezuela—meeting in Cancún in July 1983 to discuss the continuing deterioration of the regional situation— decided to inform President Reagan and Commander Fidel Castro about their deliberations and request their involvement in the peace process.

For the first time, the Contadora Group was stating clearly that its diplomatic efforts would not exclude any country and that U.S. and Cuban cooperation was essential for a realistic regional solution. However, the response was not very encouraging: not only were the differences in focus between the Reagan administration and the Contadora Group reiterated, but, more importantly, militarization of the region increased when the holding of joint maneuvers by the United States and Honduras was announced. In a letter written on July 21, 1983 to the presidents of Colombia, Mexico, Panama, and Venezuela, President Reagan mentioned four basic principles for the solution of the Central American crisis: (1) the reestablishment of democratic regimes as the only means for the reconciliation of the Central American societies; (2) the respect for nonintervention, "including the prohibition of support for subversive elements who want to destabilize other countries"; (3) the supervised retreat of all military and security advisers and a freeze on the acquisition of offensive weapons; and finally (4) economic collaboration in order to reach a level of growth to guarantee the basic needs of the people. But from a political perspective, the U.S. government expressed its reticence toward Contadora by pointing out that the OAS, as the regional forum of the hemisphere, was the appropriate mechanism "to insure that those who make promises, keep them." For his part, Fidel Castro communicated Cuba's full support for the Contadora negotiations and emphasized that Nicaragua was willing to negotiate the different subjects in the Contadora agenda. In the same vein, he pledged Cuban support for "any solution which might be acceptable to Nicaragua, to the revolutionary forces of El Salvador, to those in Central America who are struggling to walk the definitive road toward national independence and democratic transformations."

After Cancún it was possible to enter into direct discussions of the different proposals presented by Nicaragua as well as by the other Central American countries. In its fourth meeting, the Contadora Group joined with foreign ministers of the five Central American countries in Panama to approve a text entitled

"Document of Objectives." This paper reconciled, within the frame-work of the Cancún Statement, the positions contained in the Central American proposals. While the document did not repro-duce the specific presentations of each country to the letter, it did identify the fundamental points of agreement which might permit the countries in the area to live in harmony. After reiterating the basic principles of international law, the Document of Objectives enumerated a total of twenty specific commitments on matters that concern the Central American governments and that form part of the agenda approved by them in agreement with the Contadora Group. These commitments were as follows: promotion of expan-sion in the area; compliance with the principles of international law; respect for human rights; adoption of measures conducive to the establishment or improvement of democratic systems; accom-plishment of actions for national reconciliation; creation of politi-cal conditions designed to guarantee national security and the integrity of the nations in the region; control of the military buildup in all its forms; proscription of foreign military bases; reduction and eventual elimination of the presence of foreign military advisers; establishment of mechanisms for the internal control of arms trafficking; elimination of arms trafficking to persons, organi-zations, or groups who try to destabilize governments; proscrip-tion of the use of its own territory in actions against other govern-ments; abstention from the support of terrorist acts; establishment of communications systems for the purpose of preventing incidents; help for and protection of refugees; promotion of economic and social development programs; revitalization of the mechanisms of economic integration; negotiation of external monetary resources; and greater access to international markets and mechanisms for technical cooperation. Lastly, the Document of Objectives included the commitment to initiate negotiations to prepare for signing the agreements and adopting the judicial mechanisms necessary to formalize and develop the objectives mentioned and to insure the establishment of adequate systems of verification and control.

Contadora activities in 1984 were oriented toward negotiating a multilateral judicial agreement based on the Document of Objectives. After intense diplomatic efforts, the Contadora Group prepared a draft treaty called the Contadora Pact for Peace and Cooperation in Central America. It included the points of agree-ment reached in negotiations among the Central American govern-ments, as well as proposals for an equitable commitment in areas where no agreement had been reached. This pact undoubtedly reflects a Latin American conception of the solution to the regional conflict. It contains commitments related to political, economic, and social matters, as well as those of security in Central America.

In regard to the political aspects, the Central American governments would make specific commitments to national reconciliation, protection of human rights, democratic electoral processes, and parliamentary cooperation. The Contadora treaty's chapter on security contained commitments designed to end violations of international law such as arms trafficking, support for irregular forces, terrorism, and subversion. It likewise proposed the proscription of a foreign military presence under any guise (international military maneuvers, foreign bases, and military advisers) and the initiation of negotiations on arms control and reduction. The 1984 Contadora pact also established an ad hoc committee to evaluate and preserve commitments in the areas of politics and refugees, as well as an International Commission of Verification and Control on the subject of security. A final protocol, open to the signature of all the states wishing to contribute to peace and cooperation in Central America, aimed to assure the international community's respect for the peace treaty.

Nicaragua's announcement that it was willing to sign the pact disconcerted the U.S. government. Although the Reagan administration did not abandon its rhetorical support for the Contadora Group, from that moment on it began to express doubts and reservations about the peacemaking process. The other Central American governments, who stated their agreement in principle with the treaty, soon fell under pressure from the U.S. government.[4] The *Washington Post* reported months later the existence of a secret National Security Council document which states, among other things, that the United States had been successful in blocking the latest "Mexican-Nicaraguan" efforts to precipitate the signing of an unsatisfactory agreement and that the initiative was now in the hands of the other four Central American governments. The article also mentioned the need to exert strong pressure on Guatemala, whose government seemed closer to Mexico's negotiating position, perhaps because of its problems with guerrillas in the border zone between the two countries.[5]

---

[4] The U.S. press provides illustrations of this. See, for example, the following articles: Robert J. McCarthy, "U.S. Urges Allies to Reject Contadora Plan," *Washington Post*, September 30, 1984; John M. Goshko, "Modify Contadora Plan, U.S. Urges Latin Allies," *Washington Post*, October 2, 1984.

[5] Alma Guillermoprieto and David Hoffman, "Document Describes How U.S. 'Blocked' a Contadora Treaty," *Washington Post*, November 6, 1984.

Facing the risk of a diplomatic vacuum which might favor forceful solutions, the Contadora Group agreed to continue negotiating the pact in view of the observations and objections presented by the Central American governments present at the October 1984 meeting in Tegucigalpa (Nicaragua was not in attendance).

Throughout the diplomatic process, the government of Mexico has reiterated the double nature of the Central American crisis, pointing out that the conflict is not limited to the Central American countries, but also involves relations between the United States and Nicaragua. Mexico's insistence that the solution of the regional conflict depends on the achievement of a regional agreement which satisfies the legitimate concerns of Costa Rica, El Salvador, Guatemala, Honduras, and Nicaragua and which normalizes U.S.-Nicaraguan bilateral relations has resulted from that consideration. The interdependence between these planes had been partially recognized when the Contadora treaty was negotiated as a multilateral instrument and when bilateral talks began between the United States and Nicaragua in Manzanillo in June of 1984, after President de la Madrid's state visit to Washington.

In 1985, the negotiation process met a serious obstacle. The deteriorating relations between Washington and Managua would affect the entire regional negotiation. Once the possibility for a speedy signing of the pact faded, U.S. diplomacy decided to apply greater pressure on Nicaragua under the so-called "two-track" policy that would combine diplomatic and military actions. Arguing that Nicaragua was trying to substitute a joint regional agreement within the framework of Contadora with a bilateral agreement with Washington, the United States suspended the Manzanillo talks. Another element that made it difficult to reach a negotiated solution was U.S. aid to the Nicaraguan counter-revolution.

On April 4, 1984, President Reagan announced a so-called peace plan for Nicaragua that had as a starting point the signing of a pact by the "Nicaraguan resistance" in San José on March 1. This pact proposed a cease-fire in exchange for an agreement with the government of Nicaragua to start a dialogue, mediated by the Bishops' Conference of the Catholic church, aimed at restoring democracy through honest elections held under international supervision. Reagan proposed that the members of the "Democratic resistance" extend the deadline for their cease-fire proposal to June 1 and promised to request humanitarian—not military—aid for the Nicaraguan counter-revolution from Congress in the amount of fourteen million dollars. This offer would be valid while the cease-fire proposal was being negotiated by the Nicaraguan government, but if an agreement was not reached within a sixty-day period, the U.S. government would then lift the aforementioned restriction and renew its request for military aid.

President Reagan emphasized in his proposal that, in agreement with the twenty-one points contained in the Document of Objectives, the U.S. government sought the following four objectives: Nicaragua's compliance with its commitment to democracy formulated before the OAS in June of 1979; the end of Nicaragua's aggression against its neighbors; the removal of the thousands of military advisers from the Soviet bloc, Cuba, the PLO, and Libya; and the reestablishment of Nicaraguan military parity with its neighbors. The special representative of the president of the United States for Central American affairs, Ambassador Harry Schlaudeman, presented the proposal to the Mexican government, as well as to the other member governments of the Contadora Group.

The Mexican government pointed out that while President Reagan's initiative to push for a cessation of hostilities might be a step forward in the solution of the conflict, the internal processes of national reconciliation and the corresponding conversations between the internal groups of each Central American country were questions that were beyond the scope of the Contadora Group, since nonintervention was one of the basic principles of its negotiations. Under this governing standard, President de la Madrid asserted that dialogue and negotiations had to take precedence over hostilities in settling the internal conflicts in the Central American countries.[6] In any case, the government of Nicaragua refused the plan based on its unwillingness to negotiate with the Contras.

On May 7 the U.S. government decided to adopt a trade embargo against Nicaragua in reprisal for the policies of the Sandinista regime and for President Ortega's trip to Moscow after Congress had denied the request for military aid to the Contras. The government of Mexico responded that economic repression was incompatible with the objectives of the Contadora Group and the principles of international law contained in the Charters of the United Nations and the OAS.[7] At Nicaragua's request, the U.N. Security Council approved Resolution 562 (1985), which urged all countries to refrain from taking any political, economic, or military

---

[6]Press release from the Presidency of the Republic, April 8, 1985.
[7]Ministry of Foreign Relations Bulletin, March 3, 1985.

steps against any nation in the region if those measures might hinder the Contadora peace objectives, and invited the governments of the United States and Nicaragua to resume the Manzanillo talks with a view toward formalizing their relations and promoting regional détente.

The growing confrontation between Nicaragua and the United States was accompanied by incidents on Nicaragua's borders with Costa Rica and Honduras. Given these circumstances, it is easy to understand that the resumption of negotiations on the Contadora pact faced several obstacles. In June of 1985, at the peak of its confrontation with the United States, Nicaragua called for revisions in the negotiation agenda in light of the approval of aid for the Contras by the U.S. Congress. In September the Contadora Group unveiled a new version of the pact and agreed to convene a meeting of plenipotentiary representatives to complete the negotiations on three pending points within forty-five days after October 7, 1985. The three points were: control and reduction of arms, mechanisms of execution and follow-up on the subject of security and policy, and military maneuvers.

The new version of the peace treaty contained modifications that tried to bring together the positions of Nicaragua on one side and Costa Rica, El Salvador, and Honduras on the other. Despite this important conciliation effort, the new draft was unsatisfactory to the Reagan administration to the extent that it affected U.S. security interests; the U.S. view appears in a study published by the Defense Department.[8] According to this analysis, the setting in motion of the commitments concerning military bases, removal of foreign military advisers, reduction of international military maneuvers, a freeze on the acquisition of arms, and a cessation of aid to irregular forces—issues included in the September 1983 Document of Objectives—would alter U.S. policy toward Central America. Similarly, the proposed verification mechanisms were inadequate and would allow Nicaragua to shirk its responsibilities. Moreover, experience demonstrated that communist countries such as Nicaragua did not respect commitments assumed in peace agreements, as witnessed in Southeast Asia. The Department of Defense study arrived at the conclusion that Nicaragua would eventually violate the agreement for the purpose of maintaining military superiority and promoting unrest in Central America, while the United States and its allies in the region would be forced

---

[8]U.S. Defense Department, *Prospects for Containment of Nicaragua's Communist Government*, May 1986, RPP.

to adopt new measures in response. Furthermore, with the failure of the Contadora pact, the United States would be forced to increase its military presence in the region at a high financial cost.

On the other hand, Nicaragua's dissatisfaction with the direction that the multilateral negotiation had taken was evident, since it could not accept a Contadora pact which, in order to be acceptable to the United States, affected its own fundamental interests. In the opinion of the Sandinista government, Contadora was running the risk of becoming a cover for the aggression of the United States. While the Contadora efforts made it appear that peace was at hand, the United States actually escalated the military buildup by furnishing SAM-7 land-to-air missiles to the Nicaraguan Contras at the end of 1985. This led President Ortega's government to request that Contadora suspend the discussions on the pending aspects of the pact and take urgent and direct actions before the government of the United States to end its aggression against Nicaragua.[9] Ortega proposed that the Contadora meetings be postponed until May 1986, taking into consideration upcoming elections and consequent changes of government in Costa Rica, Guatemala, and Honduras. The toughening positions made it impossible for the General Assembly of the United Nations to pass a resolution supporting the peace efforts in Central America, the U.N.'s first failure in this regard since 1983.

Because of the deteriorating Central American situation and the risks involved if a political vacuum were created in the region, the Latin American governments determined to undertake a new initiative: on January 12, 1986 the Contadora Group and its Support Group approved the Caraballeda message. This was the first joint action since Argentina, Brazil, Peru, and Uruguay had decided in August of 1985 to actively support the Contadora effort. The Caraballeda Message was a proposal to create political conditions favorable to the resumption of diplomatic negotiations. Its fundamental political value—in addition to reiterating the principles upon which the Latin American diplomacy of the last few years has been sustained—consisted of defining a group of actions which were to be developed simultaneously.

These actions included the resumption of negotiations leading to the signing of the Contadora peace treaty, the cessation of

---

[9]December 5, 1985 letter sent to the Secretary General by the president of the Republic of Nicaragua. Official UN Document A/40/993 and 5/17674 of December 6, 1985.

external support for irregular forces and insurrectionist movements, a freeze and reduction of the arms buildup, suspension of international military maneuvers, and a progressive reduction and eventual total removal of foreign military advisers and foreign installations, as well as steps promoting national reconciliation and guaranteeing complete human rights and freedom. In addition, the Contadora Group and the Support Group offered their services to promote "new actions of national reconciliation under the terms of the legal framework in effect in each one of the countries"; accepted the proposal made by the Guatemalan president-elect for the creation of a Central American parliament; and, finally, encouraged the reinstatement of talks between the governments of the United States and Nicaragua, for the purpose of settling their disputes and identifying possible areas of understanding. Days later, as President Cerezo took office in Guatemala, the Central American foreign ministers issued a statement of support for the initiatives and actions proposed in the Caraballeda Message.

Even though the State Department did not comment on the U.S. government's position on the Caraballeda Message until January 17, 1986, four days earlier a White House spokesperson stated that the Reagan administration had no intention of resuming talks with Nicaragua in Manzanillo. The U.S. concern was to determine if President Ortega's signing of the Guatemala Declaration signalled a change in Nicaragua's position, that the Nicaraguan government would agree to return to the Contadora treaty negotiations and would be willing to adopt "new measures" to promote national reconciliation. In any case, the United States held that Nicaragua should promote internal reconciliation and start talks with the "armed opposition" as a prerequisite to resuming bilateral talks. Likewise, the March 1985 proposals by the "Democratic resistance" to initiate talks mediated by the Church, call a cease-fire, and lift the state of emergency were held to be valid.

The U.S. reaction to the Caraballeda Message was initially disconcerting; later it was an open rejection, arguing that the signing of the Contadora pact should continue to be the central element of the negotiations. After that, the Reagan administration, in a severe distortion of the nature of the Contadora Group's diplomatic initiative, held that military aid to the Nicaraguan Contras would permit Contadora to reach its objectives. By combining diplomacy and military pressure, the United States would force Nicaragua to make concessions in the internal as well as the regional area.

In compliance with the Caraballeda Message, the eight Latin American foreign ministers decided to negotiate with the government of the United States. On February 10, 1986, they traveled to Washington to meet with Secretary Schultz. During the meeting they reiterated that the cessation of outside support for irregular forces constituted an essential contribution to peace.[10] Insisting that national reconciliation in Nicaragua was the fundamental subject, the United States held that the Caraballeda Message should be taken as a whole and not in its component parts; therefore the nine steps outlined in the document should be undertaken simultaneously, without giving greater importance to one over the others.

The Reagan administration discarded the path offered by the new initiative. From a Latin American perspective, a positive response from the Reagan administration would have permitted the initiation of negotiations with other governments, particularly that of Nicaragua, which had expressed interest in the proposal as long as the application of all the included points were considered—in particular, the resumption of the talks between Nicaragua and the United States.[11]

The Reagan administration's rejection of the initiative was clear when it announced its decision to pursue congressional approval for military aid to the Nicaraguan Contras. Moreover, the new special envoy to Central America, Ambassador Philip Habib, was emphatic in his rejection of the proposal on his first visit to the countries of the Contadora Group. In a letter to the presidents of the countries which made up the Contadora Group and the Support Group, President Reagan emphasized the political aspects of the Caraballeda Message, that it was essential for Nicaragua to agree to develop a process of national reconciliation.[12] The Reagan administration set aside the proposals contained in the Caraballeda Message—described by Special Representative Habib as an "unbalanced" document[13]—arguing that the negotiation should revolve around the Contadora peace pact. The United States would

---

[10]Information bulletin about the meeting of Contadora and Support Group Foreign Ministers with Secretary of State George Schultz. Mexican Ministry of Foreign Affairs, February 10, 1986.
[11]Communiqué from the Office of the President of the Republic of Nicaragua, January 16, 1986.
[12]Letter from President Reagan to the President of Mexico, February 10, 1986.
[13]Visit to Mexico by U.S. Special Representative for Central America, Ambassador Philip Habib, April 28, 1986.

be willing to support the signing of a treaty as long as it were comprehensive, simultaneous, and verifiable.

Mexico reiterated its position that negotiation within the framework of Contadora depended in a very large measure on the expansion of bilateral relations between the United States and Nicaragua. The Mexican government also proposed informally that a Latin American country (not to be Mexico, because of its involvement in the Contadora Group) might be able to contribute to the establishment of a mechanism of dialogue between the two governments. The proposal was not accepted because the Reagan administration continued to maintain that bilateral talks were not a solution, that a bilateral approach only helped Nicaragua evade its internal responsibilities. The United States still saw the Central American conflict as the result of the Nicaraguan internal conflict and the threat that Nicaragua represented to its neighbors, and not a conflict with the United States. Hence Contadora was, in the opinion of the U.S. government, the propitious framework for developing an adequate response to the Central American problem.

The diagnosis of the White House continued to be diametrically opposed to that of the Mexican government which found no legal basis for compelling a legally constituted government, like that of Nicaragua, to negotiate the political power of the country with a group of irregular forces supported from the exterior.

However, the Caraballeda initiative broke the impasse created at the end of 1985 by resuming negotiations on the pending items of the Contadora pact.

THE CENTRAL AMERICAN PEACE PROCESS

Regional negotiations in 1986 centered on reaching agreement on the subjects of arms control and reduction, the mechanisms for execution, and follow up on the subject of security and policy and international military maneuvers.

The analysis of several international reports shows that the military buildup in Central America has been on the increase since the middle of the seventies. Since 1980, the arms race in the region has received new impetus from the intensification of internal conflicts (El Salvador and Guatemala) as well as from the worsening of bilateral tensions between Central American countries

(Honduras and Nicaragua) and between Central American countries and regional powers (Nicaragua-United States). This steady military buildup has been expressed in the acquisition of arms as well as the increase of military aid provided by other governments. Concurrently, constant international maneuvers have allowed the introduction of new weapons, the creation of a logistic infrastructure which enables the launching of large-scale military actions in a short period of time, and the permanent presence of a growing number of foreign troops and advisers in the region.

The military buildup is region-wide, not the exclusive practice of one or more countries. All the Central American armed forces have grown in terms of number of troops and combat ability. The armed forces of El Salvador, Guatemala, and Honduras have doubled since the beginning of the decade. A similar trend can be seen in Costa Rica, which, although it has no regular army, does have a Civil Guard and a Rural Guard. Regular Nicaraguan forces grew notably after the triumph of the Sandinista revolution; according to President Ortega's media briefing in July 1987, the defense budget increased in the 1980-86 period from 20.4 percent to 38.5 percent of the total national budget.

Interestingly, international reports differed little in their estimates of the size of the regular forces. The central problem is in the classification of paramilitary forces, regardless of the name given to them by each country. In any case, if only regular forces are considered, Nicaragua has obvious numerical superiority over its neighbors. Nicaragua's point of view on the causes which have justified this difference will be mentioned below.

The quantitative growth of the Central American armies has been accompanied by a second, no less important trend consisting of increased outside participation in support of Central American militarization. Foreign military aid to Central America generally increased considerably from 1980 to 1986-87. So it is that U.S. aid to the region, with the exception of Nicaragua, increased from $126.8 million dollars in 1983 to $254 million in 1987. El Salvador and Honduras are the principal recipients of this aid. The increase in economic aid during these same years was from $625.4 million dollars to $1 billion.[14] For its part, Nicaragua received Soviet

---

[14]Information contained in the letter sent by U.S. Ambassador to Mexico Charles Pilliod to the newspaper La Jornada, Mexico City, July 14, 1987.

military aid which, according to U.S. sources, reached between 250 and 300 million dollars in 1984.[15]

It is in this framework that in 1986 the Contadora Group tried to encourage the negotiation of the pending items of the Contadora treaty on the subject of security. Throughout its diplomatic negotiations, the Latin American initiative has tried to include the different issue areas which affect the regional situation in the negotiations.

In 1983, the Document of Objectives approved by the five Central American governments included a united commitment on the subject of security to be considered for incorporation into a regional agreement. After a lengthy process of negotiating the Contadora Pact on Cooperation and Peace in Central America, an international legal instrument, the Contadora Group presented a final version on June 6, 1986 which included agreements reached and proposals that might reconcile positions in those matters over which it was not possible for the five Central American governments to concur.

Contadora has held that the Central American arms buildup cannot be isolated from all the political factors that make up the problems of the region. That is why it has recognized the interrelationship that exists among the various negotiated points. As it now stands, the Central American military situation is characterized fundamentally by the following factors:

- Modernization and expansion of the armed and security forces in the countries in the area, particularly in El Salvador and Nicaragua.

- Consolidation of the Honduran air force and the creation of a relatively powerful air force in El Salvador.

- Consolidation of the U.S. military presence in Honduras, a country which does not have an internal or external conflict, unlike El Salvador and Nicaragua, and the creation of an unparalleled infrastructure in the region.

- Military presence of countries belonging to the Soviet bloc in Nicaragua through advisers and military aid.

---

[15]Central Intelligence Agency information collected by Charles R. Babcock and Bob Woodward, "Covert Aid Salvage Try Under Way," *Washington Post*, April 16, 1984.

- The existence of irregular forces against Nicaragua who operate in border areas of neighboring countries and who count on support from outside the region.

- The presence of an armed opposition in El Salvador and the intensification of the civil war.

- The existence of guerrilla movements in Guatemala.

Within the framework of the regional crisis, a deep divergence developed regarding regional military balance. Since 1981, Nicaragua has been accused of carrying out a military buildup that threatens the stability of neighboring countries and the entire region. Some argue that the firepower of the Sandinista Popular Army and the inclusion of large sectors of the population in this army through various groups (Patriotic Military Service, irregular battle battalions, militia, etc.) upset the balance between Nicaragua and its neighbors.[16]

Added to the charges of military imbalance, levelled basically by some governments outside the region and their allies in Central America, is the foreign military presence. It has been claimed that the presence of Cuban military advisers and other security elements from Socialist countries confirms the East-West nature of the Central American conflict as well as the subversive or destabilizing objectives of arms trafficking and support for guerrilla movements of the neighboring countries. A third and final element is the military ties established through Socialist bloc military aid to Nicaragua.

As of 1984, Nicaragua abandoned its original proposal for an arms freeze. The Nicaraguan decision was the result of the CIA mining of its ports, the growing role of the Contras, and the U.S. military maneuvers in Honduras. Faced by the impossibility of a bilateral agreement with the United States, Nicaragua rejected the thesis of military balance under the premise that it would not be valid to compare its military strength, considered individually, with that of its neighbors, without taking into account alliances that

---

[16]According to 1986 estimates, regular troops, militia, and interior ministry units add up to about 100,000 men. Most of the fighting is done by the irregular battalions (BLI), which number from 15 to 20. Close to 20,000 Sandinista soldiers, almost all of them in the BLI, carry out the struggle against the Contras. See Stephen Kinzer, "Sandinistas Have an Edge in Size, Speed and Strength," *New York Times*, July 20, 1986.

operate in the Central American region. Within that framework, Nicaragua defined a security doctrine to address the potential threat represented by the conflict with the United States, not confrontation with the Central American countries. This opinion has evidently not been shared by Honduras, whose government has justified its military alliance with the United States as a guarantee against what it considers to be the Sandinista threat.

The Contadora Group has been open to these different perceptions and, consequently, the negotiations have to deal with all questions which are of legitimate interest to the countries. The proposals of the Contadora Group have been directed toward two main areas of negotiation. The first, an area which includes all the relative commitments of the foreign military presence, encompasses the following:

• Regulation and proscription of international military maneuvers.

• Elimination of foreign military bases within 180 days and express prohibition of their establishment.

• Gradual withdrawal of foreign military advisers and registration of those who perform functions of a technical character associated with the maintenance of military equipment and establishment of limits.

The final objective is to guarantee elimination of all the modalities of military presence which affect stability and confidence in the area.

The criteria developed by Contadora have been incorporated into the second area of negotiation, regarding the following subjects:

• Regulation of national military maneuvers by adopting measures to develop confidence among the Central American governments themselves, including, among other elements, not holding maneuvers in border areas, inviting observers, and giving notification of the maneuvers.

• Commitments on the subject of direct communications systems.

• Commitments on the subject of the prohibition of all support for irregular forces which utilize the territory of one country for the purpose of attacking another.

- Commitments on the subject of the prohibition of arms trafficking.

- Commitments on the subject of terrorism, subversion, and sabotage.

In regard to the control and reduction of the arms buildup, the following commitments are presented:

- Prohibition of the introduction into the area of weapons which qualitatively or quantitatively modify weapons inventories.

- Prohibition of the use of lethal chemical, ecological, radiological, and other weapons which may be considered noxious or have an indiscriminate effect.

To that foundation are added the commitments on the subject of weapons and military troops which make up one of the central elements of the negotiations. In regard to the difficulties in the definition of the so-called military balance, for the aforementioned reasons, the Contadora Group established a relationship in its proposal between international military maneuvers and the definition of the maximum limits of weapons. It is thus that the Contadora pact establishes the following commitments on the subject of international military maneuvers:

- For a period of 90 days from the time the peace treaty goes into effect, international military maneuvers that imply the presence in their respective territories of armed forces belonging to countries from outside the region will be suspended.

- At the end of the 90 days, the parties to the agreement, taking into consideration the recommendations of the Commission for Verification and Control, may extend said suspension until the time the maximum limits on weapons and troops are reached, as set forth in the pact. In case no agreement is reached regarding the extension of the suspension, military maneuvers would be subject to different regulations established in the pact.

These regulations tend to limit the number and duration of the maneuvers (one per year and for no more than fifteen days at a time) as well as the number of participating troops. Moreover, another clause provides that maneuvers are not to be held within a 50-kilometer strip adjacent to the territory of a nation which does not participate in the maneuvers, unless express consent is given by that country.

• When maximum weapon and troop limits are reached, military maneuvers which imply participation of countries from outside the Central American region will be proscribed.

On the subject of weapons and active troops, the treaty provides for holding the negotiations in two stages:

• The first stage consists of a weapons freeze (parts excepted), delivery of inventories to the Verification and Control Commission, and the elaboration of necessary technical tests (duration of stage, sixty days).

• In the second stage (thirty days), the parties shall establish maximum limits while accepting the possibility of extending the negotiations and accepting the limits suggested by the Verification and Control Commission.

It should be pointed out that the last proposal of the Contadora Group in June of 1986 picked up the principle included in the Costa Rican and Guatemalan proposal to formulate a "base build-up table to establish verifiable levels of active troops and war matériel." Using data from that table, the different weapons would be classified and a maximum percentage would be established for each country. According to this proposal, those countries whose level of military development exceeded 100,000 points would reduce their weapons within ninety days. For its part, Nicaragua presented a list of military items that it was willing to "reduce, limit, regulate, and do without" in the framework of the negotiations.[17]

The Contadora Group proposed that the aforementioned table contain basic criteria (such as territorial extension, population, distance from border to border, military expenses in relation to the gross national product, technological level, etc.). It similarly established new criteria for distinguishing between weapons "subject

---

[17]This list includes: all types of military airplanes; all types of military helicopters; military airfields; battle tanks; heavy mortars over 120 m; self-propelled anti-aircraft guns; multiple-missile launchers over 122 m; artillery over 160 m; self-propelled artillery; surface-to-surface missile launchers installed on warships; warships over 40 m long or displacing more than 100 metric tons; international military maneuvers; foreign military bases; and foreign military advisers.

to control" and weapons "subject to reduction," which could facilitate negotiations among the Central American governments.

Finally, the Contadora Group gave particular importance to the subject of verification and control of the commitments the Central American governments assume. Throughout the negotiations, the creation of mechanisms for enforcement and follow-up of the Contadora agreements were proposed, including the Verification and Control Commission. This Commission would comprise representatives of nations whose impartiality is acknowledged, as proposed by the Contadora Group and accepted by the five governments.

After several meetings at the level of representatives, the Contadora Group delivered a final version of the treaty on June 6, 1986 which contained the proposals mentioned and which might serve to reconcile positions on those matters over which it was not possible for the five Central American governments to reach agreement. The draft of the treaty contained the entirety of the substantive commitments on all the subjects included in the 1983 Document of Objectives. It aimed for balance and fairness to all parties and took account of the proposals presented by the Central American governments.

The Contadora Group declared the substantive negotiations concluded and proposed to go on to a new stage in which agreements could be made about several operative questions which, once resolved, would facilitate the implementation of the treaty. Upon delivery of the pact, the Contadora Group pointed out the need for a political atmosphere that would allow for the signing of the agreement. To this end, the Group asked the Central American governments to pledge not to let their national territories be used by subversive groups or irregular troops to attack another country, not to become members of military or political alliances that insert the regional crisis in the framework of the East-West conflict, and not to give military or logistic support for the irregular troops which operate in the region.[18]

The Central American governments expressed their respective degrees of disagreement with the final proposal of the Contadora Group. Costa Rica, El Salvador, and Honduras in particular emphasized that the pact did not guarantee implementation of the substantive commitments. These governments proposed that the

---

[18]Message of Panama, June 7, 1986.

negotiations continue, particularly in regard to limitations on weapons and active military troops, and, in agreement with the U.S. position, they sought stronger mechanisms for the verification of the political provisions.

Nicaragua, on its part, held that the June 7, 1986 version of the pact was the only document which might allow a speedy and effective conclusion of the negotiation process toward peace in Central America. For the Sandinista government, it was fundamentally important to create political conditions that would make negotiating possible, in particular the cessation of Contra aid.

As was the case in 1984 and 1985, events were making negotiation more difficult. As of June 1986 the search for a peaceful solution to the Central American conflict reached another impasse. Several events interacted to exacerbate the situation, particularly congressional approval on June 25, 1986 for one hundred million dollars in military aid to the Nicaraguan rebel troops. Two days later, the International Court of Justice ruled in favor of the complaint which the government of Nicaragua filed in 1984 against the United States for violation of international law.

Regional negotiation became impossible given the deterioration in relations between Nicaragua and its neighbors: dialogue stopped; border incidents increased; a vast supply network for the Nicaraguan counterrevolution was put in place (as would later be revealed by the Irangate crisis); the military buildup in El Salvador, Honduras, and Nicaragua continued in both quantitative and qualitative terms; and military maneuvers were carried out in Honduras with U.S. participation.

In 1986, the U.S. government continued to criticize the Contadora process, alleging that the proposed peace treaty did not adequately deal with political topics related to national reconciliation and democratization. Moreover, it considered that the problems of verification of the agreements had not been adequately solved. The Reagan administration also opposed other initiatives of the Contadora Group, such as the creation of a commission between Costa Rica and Nicaragua designed to prevent incidents along the border. The United States argued that partial solutions favored Nicaragua and would lessen the pressure on the Sandinista regime to commit itself to broad negotiations of the key questions.[19]

---

[19]Document outlining the U.S. government point of view, testimony by Ambassador Habib before the Senate Foreign Relations Committee, February 5, 1987.

An assessment of recent diplomatic measures leads to the conclusion that the United States not only viewed the Contadora process with distrust and skepticism, but even went so far as to consider it an obstacle to its own Central American policy. The Reagan administration always preferred the OAS as the appropriate forum for dealing with the Central American conflict and concluded that Contadora's efforts, particularly Mexico's, were a hindrance to imposing democratization upon the Nicaraguan political system. The Contadora plan seemed to lose inertia in mid-1986, but during 1987 regional negotiations were resumed thanks to the introduction of new initiatives. The first of these came in November of 1986, when the secretaries general of the United Nations and the Organization of American States presented to the Central American, Contadora, and Support Group governments an initiative aimed at complementing and consolidating the peace efforts. Both international officials alluded to the "range of services that the U.N. and the OAS could offer," recognizing that these could come into play only if the two organizations received authorization from the appropriate agencies of both entities and the parties reached a preliminary agreement. The most relevant aspect of the initiative referred to "establishing an appropriate civil and/or military presence" to enforce the political and military agreements that have been part of the regional negotiations and that were included in the Contadora pact. As an outgrowth of the initiative and of the situation on the border between Honduras and Nicaragua, the Contadora and Support Groups decided to visit Central America in January 1987 and invited the secretaries general along to explore opportunities for resuming the negotiations.

The U.S. government did not see any value in the new Latin American initiatives and took it upon itself to encourage the Costa Rican government to take on an active role.[20] After the president of Costa Rica unveiled the Arias Plan on February 15, 1987—at the meeting of all Central American presidents except Daniel Ortega, who had not been invited—Mexico and the other seven Latin American countries took no diplomatic actions that might stand in the way of a peace agreement. On the other hand, they did state that the participation of all five governments, bar none, was an essential condition for reaching an agreement that would take into account the legitimate interests of all parties. Nicaragua and, to a certain extent, Guatemala held that the so-called Arias

---

[20]Ambassador Habib's testimony provides eloquent insight into the origins of the Arias Plan and the U.S. government's misgivings regarding the role of the Contadora Group and the Support Group.

Plan should be considered within the framework of the Contadora initiative.

For the Reagan administration, the Arias initiative made it possible to pressure Nicaragua and at the same time remove the Contadora Group from the regional negotiations. Nevertheless, some parts of the Arias Plan—particularly those dealing with the cease-fire and the suspension of aid to irregular forces—were a source of concern for the U.S. government.

On August 7, 1987, the presidents of Costa Rica, El Salvador, Guatemala, Honduras, and Nicaragua reached an eleven-point agreement known as the "Procedure for Establishing Firm and Lasting Peace in Central America." Based on President Arias's initiative, this document had been refined by the other Central American governments in two meetings of their foreign ministers, the first of which was attended by the Contadora Group.

The Procedure incorporates the main political and security commitments of previous agreements, some of which were to have gone into effect on November 5, 1987. Building on this foundation, it provides that the five Central American governments, with the Contadora Group in its role as mediator, would resume negotiations on the pending points of the Contadora agreement with regard to security, verification, and control. Moreover, the agreement gave rise to the International Verification and Follow-up Commission—comprising the secretaries general of the UN and OAS and the foreign ministers from the Central American, Contadora, and Support Group countries—as the body to oversee compliance with the agreements and make a progress report to the Central American presidents in January of 1988.[21]

Once again—as in 1984, when Nicaragua announced its willingness to sign the Contadora pact—the signing of a peace agreement took the Reagan administration by surprise. Days before the August 7 meeting in Guatemala, the U.S. government had notified the Central American governments about a "bipartisan" proposal that had the approval of then-House leader Jim Wright. The so-called Reagan Plan was not even considered during the gathering of presidents in Guatemala, during which attention focused on the Central American governments' observations concerning the Arias Plan.

---

[21]The Commission was dispatched five times between August and December of 1987. In addition, during a meeting held in Caracas on December 10, 1987, it was decided to resume the above-mentioned negotiations as of February 1988.

The Reagan administration stated from the outset that the agreement was insufficient and rejected the steps taken by the Nicaraguan government to comply with it in regard to freedom of the press and national reconciliation. It deemed the adopted measures to be cosmetic and announced that it would ask Congress for $270 million in military aid for the Nicaraguan Contras. Further, President Reagan stated to the OAS that the agreement failed to assuage U.S. concern for security in the region.[22]

The U.S. government has raised the same objection to all Central American proposals, including the Contadora agreement: that it considers that no diplomatic move has solved the problem of democracy in Nicaragua. And yet, the measures announced on November 5, 1987 by the Nicaraguan government—to arrange a cease-fire, set up an amnesty program, and call off the state of emergency—seemed to open up the possibility of a resumption of the Managua-Washington dialogue. However, the U.S. government's position had not changed significantly at the end of 1987. The Reagan administration continued to insist upon aid for the Contras as an essential means of pressing for the democratization of Nicaragua and ignored the commitments undertaken in Guatemala—an end to outside assistance for irregular forces and no use of one nation for carrying out actions against a neighboring state.

The arms buildup received new impetus with the U.S. government's decision to modernize the Honduran Air Force by providing it with twelve F-5 combat planes. This U.S. decision represented a change in the policy of not introducing combat aircraft into Central America. By increasing its total number of planes to sixty—including Brazilian Toucans and U.S. A-37s, the Honduran air force became a factor in discouraging aggression by the Popular Sandinista Army.

In contract, Nicaragua has no combat air force; its Soviet Mi-24 and Mi-25 helicopters basically provide counterinsurgency capabilities. In 1986, Nicaragua was to have tripled its air force by receiving fifteen new helicopters and six to twelve "flying tanks," as the Mi-24 helicopters are known.[23] Later reports indicate that Nicaragua negotiated with the Soviet Union at the beginning of

---

[22]Speech by President Reagan to the OAS, October 7, 1987.
[23]Stephen Kinzer, "Nicaragua Said to Seek More Soviet Helicopters," *New York Times*, April 7, 1987.

1987 for a third delivery of new helicopters (previous deliveries having been in May of 1985 and October of 1986) as a result of intensified fighting against rebel forces. According to military and diplomatic sources, the Popular Sandinista Army has between forty and fifty helicopters, most of them Mi-17s, while the Pentagon estimates the figure at fifty-seven. Not to be forgotten is the U.S. veto against Nicaragua's acquisition of MiGs or equivalent aircraft, whose presence would not be tolerated and would provoke their immediate destruction.

According to specialized sources, during November 1988 Nicaragua likewise was to have received Soviet-made S-14 ground-to-air missiles that would increase firepower against the planes transporting arms from Honduras to the counterrevolutionary forces. Soviet military aid continued in 1987, including the delivery of new helicopters, anti-aircraft guns, armored vehicles, anti-tank guns, and large amounts of ammunition.[24]

The subject of the military buildup has taken on new prominence since a high-level Sandinista official who fled to the United States revealed that Nicaragua had a 1991-95 military expansion plan which, in addition to counting on Soviet aid, would increase its total troop strength to 600,000.

Added to the arms buildup are ongoing international military maneuvers and the permanent outside military presence. During the first half of 1987, new U.S.-Honduran joint military maneuvers took place involving 22,000 U.S. soldiers. The General Terencio Sierra exercises, which lasted from January 10 through May 10, 1987, were carried out in the Yoro Department and in northern, eastern, central, and western regions of the country. It bears mention that at least 4,000 U.S. troops and only 150 Hondurans took part in these maneuvers. Highly placed Pentagon spokespersons characterized the U.S. military presence in Honduras as "temporary, yet indefinite" and indicated it would require a $65-million investment for the construction of new facilities.[25] With the Central American agreement signed in Guatemala, however, these plans have run into opposition in Congress.

---

[24]Stephen Kinzer, "Sandinista Forces Are Said to Triple Stock of Copters," *New York Times*, July 10, 1986. Doyle McManus, "U.S. Stresses Over Soviet Weapons sent to Nicaragua," *Los Angeles Times*, July 20, 1987.
[25]Testimony by General John Galvin, commander of the U.S. Southern Command, before the Senate Appropriations Subcommittee as reported by Joanne Omang in "Funds Sought for Honduras Bases," *Washington Post*, April 7, 1987.

Military assistance to the Nicaraguan rebels is a key factor promoting an eventual armed conflict. It is obvious that the millions of dollars approved by the U.S. Congress for military expenditures contribute to the level of irregular warfare. Military analysts agreed last year that the intensity, frequency, and scope of Contra actions would grow to the extent that new deliveries of weapons and equipment were made. Likewise, it was considered likely that the Contras would receive new weapons that would increase their firepower and allow them to offset the present superiority of the Popular Sandinista Army.

Even though it is acknowledged that the Nicaraguan rebel forces are unlikely to defeat the Nicaraguan armed forces, we can overlook neither the fact that a war of attrition or "low intensity" war goes on, nor the possibilities of a scaled-up conflict. Because Nicaragua's borders with Costa Rica and, above all, Honduras are the main areas of tension and armed encounters, there is a risk that the armed forces from those countries might become directly involved in the fighting.

In light of the above, the Central American conflict could take on the following, not necessarily mutually exclusive, modalities:

• Occupation of part of Nicaraguan territory by the Contras. The Atlantic seaboard would be the most likely area for an action of this sort. The operation would have U.S. logistic support and make possible the Reagan administration's proposed establishment of a "provisional government" on Nicaraguan soil. All such attempts to date have failed.

• Stepping up the war of attrition through rebel attacks against military and strategic installations as well as civilian objectives. The Contra military presence within Nicaragua would thus be gradually strengthened.

• Intensification of border fighting, which could eventually lead to armed clashes between Honduras and Nicaragua. In March 1986, the Popular Sandinista Army carried out incursions into the neighboring country to thwart Contra offensives and destroy their camps. A similar incident took place in December of the same year. Since 1983 there has been a risk that a bilateral incident may trigger a larger scale conflict.

• Finally, more overt U.S. military participation, with varying degrees of involvement, cannot be excluded. Along these lines, as far back as 1985, the U.S. press itself revealed the existence of alternate Pentagon plans that range from "surgical" bombing strikes aimed at destroying strategic and military centers and the economic infrastructure, to armed intervention either directly or in support of the conventional forces of its allies in the region. Obviously no Central American country could undertake armed conflict with Nicaragua on its own.

CONCLUSIONS AND PERSPECTIVES

Over the past five years, Mexico has spoken out against acts that implied a flagrant violation of the basic standards of international law. Substantive differences between Mexico and the United States, which went beyond the Contadora framework, were aired in international organizations, particularly within the United Nations. Thus it was that in 1984, when Nicaraguan ports were mined by the CIA, Mexico denounced the escalation of military actions, destabilization, and the economic blockade against Nicaragua in the Security Council of the United Nations.[26] Such acts not only constituted an assault against law and order but also undermined the Contadora Group's efforts.

In May of 1985, Mexico addressed the Security Council over the commercial embargo decreed by the United States against Nicaragua, including the cancellation of air and sea traffic between the two countries. (Interestingly, the U.S. government took these steps aimed at modifying the Sandinista regime's behavior and assuring peace in Central America after President Ortega's trip to the Soviet Union and other countries of the Soviet bloc.) The Mexican government maintained that, under various U.N. and OAS resolutions, this was a matter of coercive economic measures intended to bully the sovereign will of a state. The Mexican representative likewise reminded the international bodies that his government's essential thrust was to guarantee in the Central American region the right to self-determination and its practical corollary, political pluralism, which allows each state to achieve full sovereignty in its political and economic processes as well as complete freedom in its international relations.[27]

---

[26]Speech by Mexico's alternate delegate to the U.N., April 2, 1984.
[27]Speech by Mexico's permanent representative to the U.N., read to the Security Council on May 9, 1985.

One of the most serious frictions occurred in November of 1986. The Nicaraguan government had earlier filed suit against the United States in the International Court of Justice, but the Reagan administration announced it would not recognize this Court's jurisdiction on the Central American situation. At Nicaragua's insistence, the Security Council met on October 22, 1986 to consider that country's complaint of U.S. noncompliance with the Court's decision. In its sentence the Court had stated that U.S. military and paramilitary activities in and against Nicaragua, including its aid to the Contras, were contrary to international law. In particular, the Court decreed that the U.S. government was violating its obligations under international law not to intervene in the internal affairs of another state, not to violate the sovereignty of other states, and not to use force against other states. This most elevated international tribunal likewise reminded the United States of its obligation to compensate Nicaragua for the damage caused and reminded both parties in the dispute of their duty to come up with a solution to their differences by peaceful means and according to international law.

The Mexican delegation to the United Nations took part in the Security Council discussion in order to explain its position in favor of full enforcement of the sentence. The draft resolution submitted to the consideration of the Security Council called attention to the obligation of all member states to comply with the Court's decisions in all litigations in which they are parties and stressed the fact that, by virtue of international common law, countries are under obligation to refrain from intervening in the internal affairs of other states. In its operative provisions, the draft likewise urgently called for the full and immediate application of the decision of the International Court of Justice. Nonetheless, and despite eleven votes in favor of the draft (and three abstentions—France, Great Britain, and Thailand), it failed to pass because of the United States' veto. The U.S. veto moved Nicaragua to request that this item be included on the General Assembly agenda. True to its legal tradition, Mexico once again felt obliged to participate in the discussion.

The exceptional nature of Nicaragua's petition to the Security Council deserves mention at this point. This was the first time in history that the Council met under the terms of Article 94 of the United Nations Charter, which provides that if one of the parties in litigation should fail to abide by the obligations imposed upon it by a Court decision, the other party may turn to the Security Council. If, in turn, the Council deems it necessary to do so, it may make recommendations or adopt measures designed to enforce the decision. In Mexico's opinion, ignoring Article 94 would have been tantamount to a refusal to dispense international justice, to the detriment of all nations.

With the obstruction of the procedures provided for in the Charter, it was to be expected that the Assembly would take up the question. During the discussions, the Mexican delegation stressed the irregularity involved in allowing a permanent Security Council member to vote when it is party to a controversy being studied by the Council, particularly if that dispute has been brought before the International Court of Justice and the latter has pronounced a binding sentence. Accepting this state of affairs would amount to declaring that the permanent members of the Security Council, Charter provisions notwithstanding, are not subject to the jurisdiction of the International Court of Justice and may disregard its decisions by the unilateral recourse of vetoing Security Council resolutions proposing measures to enforce the judgments or, as in this case, simply exhorting the parties to carry them out. Aside from political considerations regarding the Central American question, Mexico's position was intended to draw attention to the serious hazards involved in noncompliance with the Court's sentences and to the fact that the United Nations Security Council is, in practice, becoming incapable of taking steps supporting their full enforcement. By a vote of ninety-four in favor (including Mexico), three against (including the United States and Israel), and forty-seven abstentions, the General Assembly passed the same draft resolution that had originally been placed before the Security Council. The United States criticized Mexico's active participation in the discussion on this question.

Mexico and the United States have a common interest in the Central American peace process. Both governments have justified their policies toward the region by arguing that what happens there affects their national interests. Solution of the Central American conflicts, the installation of democratic governments able to meet the needs for economic and social development, demilitarization of society, control of the arms buildup, and peaceful coexistence among the nations of the region are shared aspirations. The differences between Mexico and the United States stem from divergent viewpoints on the causes of the regional conflict and the terms in which its solution should be approached.

At the same time, it should be acknowledged that both governments, as a function of their individual characteristics and their differing degrees of influence, have had a different perception of the role that they must play in the life of the region. The first such difference appeared in regard to the very substance of the negotiation. Since 1983, Mexico has attempted to achieve, within the Contadora framework, a negotiated settlement that recognizes the legitimate rights of the five Central American states, including Nicaragua. This has been an attempt to foster understanding on all matters of common interest from a starting point of full respect for the principles of nonintervention and self-determination.

At no time has the Mexican government questioned the legitimacy of the governments of the area, nor much less has it attempted to establish a change in the political regime of any of the Central American governments as a condition for reaching a regional agreement. Implementation of the Contadora agreement would imply specific obligations for each Central American state, including Nicaragua, but with unwavering respect for national sovereignty. Mexico has maintained that peace in Central America will be possible only to the extent that judicial order is restored and countries' basic interests are assured by means of a system of mutual concessions that do not impinge upon their sovereign rights.

For Nicaragua, the Contadora pact specifically means the obligation to abstain from any act of destabilization against its neighbors, to end support for rebel movements, to disallow foreign military bases on its territory, to remove Cuban military advisers and those of other nationalities, and, lastly, to halt its military buildup.

For Honduras, implementation of the peace treaty would mean non-use of its territory by the Contras and cessation of all political, military, and logistic support for the Contras, as well as controlling the U.S. military presence in its various manifestations (bases, advisers, and military maneuvers).

From the Salvadoran point of view, the treaty places special emphasis on the restriction of arms trafficking, a basic feature mentioned by the Duarte government with regard to the threat of destabilization that the Nicaraguan government would represent.

Throughout the Reagan years, the U.S. administration was disinclined to support regional negotiation, and the central objective in its strategy was the removal of the Sandinista regime, not the modification of some of the regime's policies. It is important to note that in 1982 U.S. demands on Nicaragua referred basically to the need for Managua to modify substantive aspects of its foreign and defense policy: ending aid to subversive movements in the region, breaking off military and security ties with the Socialist bloc, and reducing Nicaraguan military power to levels that would allow for the reestablishment of regional balance. Starting in 1985, once the electoral process that carried President Daniel Ortega to power had been held, U.S. demands expanded to include the topic of democratization and dialogue with the counterrevolutionaries as prerequisites for any negotiation.

It should be stressed that the Reagan administration did its best to discredit the November 1984 Nicaraguan electoral process by discouraging the participation of the Nicaraguan Democratic Coordination and other independent opposition candidacies as well as any possible preelection understanding with the Sandinista government. In fact, the White House rejected the result of the election, the validity of which had been certified by a wide range of international observers, some of whom are little suspect of sympathizing with the Sandinistas.[28]

As far as the regional negotiations were concerned, Contra aid and military pressure inevitably conflicted with the Contadora approach. The Reagan administration had misgivings about the Contadora Group's efforts for several reasons. In the first place—and this factor may well have been underestimated—it represented the Latin American states' first attempt to play an independent role in their sphere of influence, which could not but affect their policy in the region.

Moreover, Mexico had adopted individual diplomatic initiatives during 1981 and 1982 that did not coincide with U.S. policy. Now, with the creation of Contadora, and later of the Support Group, it could project its regional policy more forcefully. Doing so produced reciprocal effects, however. The peacemaking efforts shared with Colombia, Panama, and Venezuela led Mexico to moderate its support for Nicaragua and for the Salvadoran opposition.

In any case, Mexico has been perceived by the United States as the moving force behind the regional process and as the

---

[28]According to official results, 75 percent of the potential voters took part. Of these, 63 percent voted for Daniel Ortega's candidacy and 64 percent voted for the Sandinista candidates to the National Assembly. Recognized opposition parties won 35 of the 96 seats in the Assembly. See, among others, reports by the British Liberal party, the Socialist International, and the Latin American Studies Association (LASA).

Nicaraguan government's main source of support. Because of this perception, the United States in effect blocked the Contadora negotiation, viewing the pact as contrary to U.S. interests. Not only was the negotiating process not given the chance to prove its merit—or, for that matter, the advantages that it might offer U.S. interests in the region—but political communication between the Reagan administration and the Latin American governments deteriorated further.

Contrasting perceptions of the Central American conflicts have led to differing criteria for approaching their solution. The United States has emphasized the factors of ideological confrontation and has therefore tried to place different national processes in the framework of the East-West conflict. Differences with Latin America countries have not been limited to differing assessments of the events in Central America; they extend to practical approaches, where the U.S. government has chosen to ignore and even hinder the peace initiatives undertaken by the Contadora countries and later by the Support Group. A case in point is the January 1986 Caraballeda Message, by means of which the eight Latin American countries opened up a new channel for a negotiated settlement of the conflict.

In any case, the insensitivity shown the Latin American proposals on an issue of acknowledged regional importance and dimensions widened the existing gap in inter-American relations. The governments which make up Contadora and the Support Group have not given up stressing the need for a peaceful solution that respects the legitimate rights of all Central American states. The military escalation that started with the approval of U.S. military aid for the Nicaraguan rebel forces has been one of the main factors standing in the way of peacemaking efforts.

U.S. backing for solutions based on the use of force has also applied to the Salvadoran conflict, to the detriment of a political solution supported by various Latin American governments and reflected in the human rights resolutions approved by the U.N. General Assembly over the past two years. The bottom line is that none of the Central American conflicts that existed when Ronald Reagan took office has been solved. On the contrary, the situation has gotten worse.

Since 1981, inter-American relations have deteriorated so drastically that some have questioned the bases upon which the inter-American system is founded. The search for Latin American solutions at the beginning of the decade also came about as a reaction to the OAS's inability to respond to regional aspirations for independence, the most obvious example of which was the Falkland Islands War. Then the Central American crisis and the formation of the Contadora and Support Groups showed that the inter-American forum is far from offering an appropriate atmosphere for negotiation. The persistence of a Cold War approach that holds the OAS to be an instrument for imposing or legitimizing solutions by force in bilateral controversies between countries in the region has wiped out that possibility. U.S. government reservations regarding the Cartagena Protocol of Reforms and their interpretation demonstrate the chasm that exists between the Latin American proposals and the present U.S. government's perception of the situation in the hemisphere.

The Reagan administration's conception of political regimes automatically dismissed the struggle being engaged in by various Latin American political movements. In the case of Central America, this justified intervention in the internal affairs of El Salvador and Nicaragua with the excuse of outside aggression and Soviet bloc presence. Latin America has unequivocally held that, although it shares concern for regional democratization, at no time are interventionist policies which violate international law justified. Contrary to what several Central American governments have at times stated, Contadora has not been interventionist; on the contrary, it has attempted to mediate legitimate interests on the basis of non-intervention and strict respect for self-determination of the people.

True acceptance of political pluralism as the fundamental basis of inter-American relations continues to be one of Latin America's central objectives. The aim of including Latin America and the Caribbean in contemporary international relations must also be added to the above. The nature of the ties which Latin American countries establish with other countries or groups of countries, particularly with the Socialist bloc and the movement of non-aligned countries, has been a source of friction and even of controversy since the U.S. government has tended to consider these ties an intrusion into its sphere of influence.

The Central American crisis is a long-term crisis that can be guided toward resolution but not solved all at once. Events have concentrated attention on Nicaragua while the economic and social situation has gotten worse throughout the region. Civil war in El Salvador continues its course after eight years, while the burden of the armed forces concurrently demonstrates the limits of the democratization process and of reform policy in Guatemala and Honduras. The vulnerability of Central American political development, combined with the external factors that condition it, will demand that the United States and Mexico continue to pay particular attention to the region. Given these circumstances, it is essential that a common ground of understanding between the two governments be found. The Central American peace process will move forward only as greater cooperation between Mexico and the United States can be established.

Do real possibilities of a greater rapprochement on the topic of Central America exist? An affirmative answer to this question seems to depend on three essential factors. First, the United States needs to acknowledge that Mexico has its own interests in Central America. The Mexican government has defined its commitment to a negotiated solution as a function of a foreign policy based on principles and on the preservation of her sovereignty and independence. The spread of violence and political instability, foreign military presence, and the risks of outside intervention impact Mexican development. One clear expression of this has been the mass movements of refugees. Official U.N. figures—which are very conservative—indicate that there are 175,000 refugees in Mexico, of which 120,000 are Salvadorans and 45,000 are Guatemalans. Since 1983, and especially since the election of President Vinicio Cerezo, relations between Mexico and Guatemala have improved appreciably, both on a bilateral level and within the Central American peace negotiations. This has meant a significant improvement over the tenuous communications that had characterized relations between the two countries since 1954.

Mexico's foreign policy regarding Central America was interpreted by the Reagan administration as a series of actions designed to oppose U.S. interests, when in reality it is vital to Mexico's national security. The United States should understand that the Mexican government determines its international policy according to its own interests, interests which may or may not coincide with those of other countries.

Mexico and the United States have differed profoundly as to the procedures for achieving regional peace. It would seem that from the U.S. perspective, the foreign policy of the de la Madrid government was overly naive with regard to the evolution of the Nicaraguan regime and to Central American revolutionary movements, particularly El Salvador's. In truth, what has at times been overlooked is that the Mexican government has fostered negotiation of the Central American conflict not only out of adherence to the principles which serve as the basis of its international actions, but also because of the conviction that solutions by force, far from solving the conflict, would make it worse. Mexico perceives the Reagan administration's Nicaraguan policy, far from encouraging a flexible attitude on the part of the Sandinista regime, as favoring its internal radicalization and its inflexibility at key times in the past five years of the negotiating process. In this sense, in Mexico's view, the U.S. government's fundamental interests in Central America might be better assured through diplomatic means.

The recent Central American experience has itself proved enlightening as to the political cost incurred through the use of force. The 1954 foreign intervention in Guatemala, which led to the overthrow of President Arbenz in the name of anti-communism, was a fundamental factor in the process of militarization which Vinicio Cerezo's government is now attempting to overcome. After eight years of civil war in El Salvador, it has become likewise evident that its internal pacification requires genuine dialogue with the FMLN-FDR alliance.

Second, based on acceptance of Mexico's legitimate interests, the United States should acknowledge that Mexico is a force in the region that can play a basic role in the normalization of Central America. Her tradition as a land of asylum, the stability of her political system, and the consistency with which she has defended her foreign policy qualify Mexico as an exceptionally good liaison with Cuba and Nicaragua as well as with opposition groups in some Central American countries, especially El Salvador. It is not a question of Mexico's taking on the job of mediation, but rather of her being able to contribute to the establishment of channels of communication and to provide points of view that promote a climate of regional coexistence.

Third, it is essential that Mexico continue to recognize that the United States has strategic interests in the region and that provision must be made for the inclusion of the conflicts in the framework of the East-West confrontation. Mexico, however, will continue to consider that this should be accomplished through negotiation. Violation of the principles of nonintervention and self-determination by the people would provoke new and constant frictions between the two countries.

Establishing regional security for Central America depends fundamentally upon the conclusion of a bilateral agreement between the United States and Nicaragua which includes both governments' basic perceptions and concerns. This agreement should address, among other issues, the topic of foreign military presence in its various manifestations (maneuvers, bases, and advisers) as well as a commitment not to destabilize the area's governments.[29]

Culmination of the regional negotiation is an equally important complement. The draft of the Contadora pact and the August 7, 1987 Guatemala agreement contain the basic elements for doing so. Reaching bilateral agreements among the Central American governments themselves is also important to the extent that it would facilitate the prevention and settlement of border incidents. All of these are feasible, realistic elements in a negotiated political solution guaranteeing regional stability and security, recognition of the legitimate interests of all the Central American states, and full compliance with international law.

As a fourth and central factor, interjecting the Central American crisis into inter-American relations as a whole should be discarded. One way or another, events since 1979 have shown the tremendous difficulties that the United States has had in tailoring its policies to the social change which has taken place in several Central American countries. The U.S. concept of hemispheric security which has prevailed to date has been a basic factor shaping the independence of the Latin American countries' national processes. Joint security, as understood since the signing of the Inter-American Mutual Assistance Treaty, has produced a framework for justifying U.S. intervention in the region.

Thus it is that the existence of governments unpalatable to U.S. interests has traditionally been perceived as a threat to U.S. national security, and therefore as a threat to the security of the hemisphere. A Cold War mentality has held forth which interprets any plan for social transformation with a nationalistic content as an automatic threat to U.S. interests. The experience of recent decades has shown the cost that Latin America has had to pay as a result of the close identification drawn between nationalism and communism. In this way, by linking the national security of the United States to the political nature of the Latin American regimes, the various popular, democratic movements exercising their right to self-determination have been stripped of legitimacy. Moreover, democratization has been used as an argument to discredit nationalist processes that

---

[29]The August 1987 U.S. plan contains elements pointing in this direction.

do not coincide with U.S. foreign policy objectives. A clear example of this is the insistence on turning the "four Central American democracies" against the Sandinista dictatorship, when Costa Rica may well be the only one of the four countries to meet the minimum qualifications of the Western concept of democracy.

Over the past five years, Latin America has made a tremendous effort, within the complex inter-American framework, to redefine its interests and establish its priorities. The Contadora experience has, without doubt, been the clearest expression of a new conception of a system of Latin American security. The proposals which it has generated in the Central American context may have viable applications in other areas of Latin America and the Caribbean. Its conceptual validity may be a starting point for the Latin American debate.

This is not a question of suggesting a new regional security which ignores the geopolitical factors of the region, but rather of defining a new treaty between Latin America and the United States. Revising the terms of inter-American relations, particularly those among the key nations involved in hemispheric security, is not necessarily antagonistic to U.S. interests. On the contrary, there exists a need to lay foundations, mutually acceptable to Latin America and the United States, that will make it possible to reduce conflicts and effectively settle the various controversies that not only persist but are escalating.

These elements should be taken into account in developing a concept of regional security that responds to Latin American aspirations. Some fundamental criteria for doing so might be the following:

- Latin America's security should be compatible with strict respect for self-determination by the people and for the sovereignty and independence of all states.

- Latin America's security cannot be used to mold the internal process of any country in the region and will be better assured to the degree that the region's dissociation from the global East-West confrontation is maintained.

- Latin America's security will be better assured to the degree that political pluralism is accepted as the cornerstone of inter-American relations.

- Latin America's security will be better assured to the degree that all states, no matter what their internal political regime, accept commitments that secure the common interest and preserve their legitimate rights.

- Latin America's security is not confined to the strategic-military arena, but rather should encompass the political, economic, and social substrata that lie at the root of the various conflicts in the region.

A fresh approach to the Latin American situation requires an analysis of the various circumstances that affect national security and that generally arise over interrelated questions such as border conflicts, the military buildup and the foreign military presence, the impact of the East-West conflict upon Latin America, nuclear proliferation, and colonial questions. These are some of the questions that will be on the inter-American relations agenda in the coming years. Mexico and the United States have differed throughout a complex diplomatic process in which opportunities for peace have often been ignored. It is therefore essential that Mexico and the United States pick up the dialogue on the basis of recognition of their respective national interests.

POSTSCRIPT

The events which occurred in the months after this essay was written did little to alter the focus of the paper, and in no way modified its conclusions. The Central American situation underwent a further phase of deterioration in 1988, primarily because of the absence of an independent and impartial verification mechanism and a failure to respect the provisions of the Esquipulas III Accords. Further exacerbating the regional context were the breakdown in the Sapoa Accords of March 23 between the Nicaraguan government and the Contras (the most important national component of the Esquipulas process), diplomatic incidents between Nicaragua and the United States, the civil war in El Salvador, an extremely tenuous stability in Guatemala, and the continuing presence of U.S. military in Honduras.

In light of these factors which worked against a peaceful resolution of the Central American conflict, Mexico made a declaration on July 30, 1988 to the effect that the positive effort of the Sapoa Accords was being "hindered by interests which continued to rely on intervention, intolerance, and force." Tne administration reiterated its position that the normalization of relations between the United States and Nicaragua was a prerequisite for easing regional tensions.

The implementation of the Esquipulas Accords has been blocked by a lack of constructive participation on the part of countries with ties to and interests in the region. Without their cooperation and active support, the commitments made by five Central American governments may prove unviable. But despite this impasse, the arduous process of negotiation embodied in the Contadora, Esquipulas, and Sapoa agreements has built a foundation on which to erect pacification in Central America, once the obstacles introduced by external interference have been removed, and once a new phase of inter-American relations has begun. The latter will depend on support from the new executive and legislative powers in Mexico, the United States, and several Central American countries, as well as vigorous leadership within Contadora.

8

Mexico and the Soviet Union: Tangled Metaphors for U.S. Foreign Policy

William H. Luers

The dramatic changes that have taken place in the world over the past two years will have a profound effect on the types of issues that preoccupy the United States in its foreign relations in the 1990s and beyond. Some of the most important changes have taken place in the Soviet Union and in Mexico—nations that played such major roles in the evolution of how the United States thinks about its foreign relations. Mexico and the Soviet Union are metaphors for tangled U.S. foreign policies over North-South and East-West issues. As Mexico and the Soviet Union both have begun to deal with the issues of democracy and decentralization in their societies in 1988, the United States will find itself having to deal with a more complex but possibly less frightening world. This essay is about the changing roles of the Soviet Union and Mexico in shaping the American view of the world and about how the United States might prepare itself to better manage its relations with Mexico.

The U.S.-Mexican bilateral relationship is like none other in the world. It is intense, extremely important, and yet peculiar. The overriding peculiarity in the relationship stems from the low level of awareness in the United States about the high level of impor- tance this bilateral relationship holds for U.S. interests. The United States deals with symptoms of its problems with Mexico, but it has not had to deal seriously with Mexico as a nation. In sharp contrast, the United States' other intense and peculiar bilateral relationship is with the Soviet Union. It is the compulsive super-consciousness of the importance of the Soviet Union that has formed an almost Manichaean mentality in the United States toward foreign affairs. Because it is a nuclear superpower, the Soviet Union demands U.S. attention, and because it is "communist," it totally engulfs the American imagination.[1] For a variety of reasons Mexico and the Soviet Union—so different from each other—have played central roles in shaping and illuminating the weakness of twentieth-century American foreign policy. These nations have posed two powerful challenges for the United States as it has struggled to define and give continuity to its role as a great power over the past fifty to seventy years. A look at the special features of the U.S. effort to cope with these two countries tells us a good deal about the flawed nature of the foreign policy process in the United States.

The especially troubling aspects of these two bilateral relationships are rooted in history. As World War I was ending, the issues of how to influence, how to relate to, and whether to intervene in the Bolshevik and Mexican revolutions became as important to President Wilson and his advisers as the challenge of defining the new U.S. role in a Europe of imploded empires. Then, after World War II, as the United States sought to put in place a world democratic order free of conflict, the Cold War and the relentless resource tug of the Third World created the real agenda for U.S. foreign policy for the next four decades. If the Soviet Union has been our principal Cold War antagonist in all of the military strategic issues and our major political competitor since World War II, then Mexico has clearly come to symbolize all other Third World countries in imposing on the United States the importance and the human drama of the resource and equity issues of the developing world. The Soviet Union defines the East-West issues as Mexico defines those of North-South for the United States.

Yet, for many reasons, the United States, its policymakers, and its institutions have found these two nations and the problems they present particularly difficult to understand and to deal with coherently. Developing policies toward the Soviet Union and Mexico has regularly proven to be unusually divisive for the American political system. This paper seeks to outline briefly some of the similarities and differences in the challenges which these two

---

[1]Throughout this essay I have used "American" rather than "North American" as would be more appropriate in discussing the U.S.-Mexican relationship. I have done this not for political reasons but to simplify the discussion.

great nations pose to the United States—one a distant superpower antagonist, and the other a troubled, culturally distinct neighbor.

It is the thesis of this paper that the United States has been inept in its dealings with Mexico and the Soviet Union for a prolonged period of time, during which the monopolistic ruling parties of each pursued largely steady and predictable foreign policies. But today, in 1988, we are witnessing profound changes that could lead to greater internal divisions in both nations and, perhaps, to greater swings and surprises in their external relations. Although Gorbachev's Russia and Salinas's Mexico may be more unpredictable, the decline of revolutionary pretensions and the emergence of pluralistic forces in open contention for the first time represent important, even dramatic, new opportunities for the United States to deal with the real issues, rather than with mythologies, which impact our vital interests with Mexico and the Soviet Union.

These changes will also require the American political system and its foreign policy process to deal more realistically with the complexity of international relations and to seek a more balanced and integrated approach to the perennial conflict between the challenges of North-South and East-West priorities in our foreign policy. As the Soviet Union and Mexico become ever more consumed by their internal process of reform, economic development, and internal divisions, the United States may have to place more emphasis on the Mexican relationship and allow itself to be less obsessed by its Soviet counterpart. These two nations have so influenced the way Americans think about the world that any profound changes they experience will inevitably affect the United States.

THE UNITED STATES VERSUS RADICAL REVOLUTIONS

The United States has not found it easy to deal with radical revolutions in the twentieth century. Our problems in dealing with the Bolshevik and Mexican revolutions seventy years ago form a pattern that has shaped official and non-official American thinking. Why do radical revolutions so enrage Americans and move us to action—action that is often extremely damaging to U.S. interests? What is at the bottom of this anti-communist or anti-revolutionary attitude that, probably more than any other single factor, defines the way Americans think about the role of U.S. power in the outside world?

There are many explanations for this particular American attitude, none of them wholly satisfactory. We are said to oppose
radical, particularly Marxist-Leninist, revolutions because:

— The United States, as the most powerful democracy and one of the few nations with a "global
vocation," has a strategic obligation to contain
Soviet Communist power in the world—or, in
earlier days, the challenge of other threatening
powers such as Nazi Germany.

— Or, U. S. private commercial interests have traditionally influenced U.S. foreign policy, particularly in the Western Hemisphere. The U.S.
domestic pressure to intervene, to sanction, and
to isolate radical regimes, therefore, is often to
protect U.S. investment and trade interests which
are inevitably threatened by radical regimes.

— Or, Americans believe in private enterprise,
democracy, and spiritual freedom. Autocratic or
dictatorial governments that crush or do not permit these basic political and economic freedoms
are offensive to Americans. The United States has
traditionally had a large element of morality and
messianic commitment to spreading democracy
in the conduct of its foreign relations. Belief in
American "exceptionalism" and in the "American Century" has been a factor.

— Or, bureaucratic politics and special interest
groups have occasionally played a role in shaping official U.S. government reaction to and
intervention in radical revolutionary situations.

— Or, Americans are uninformed, isolationist, and
naive about the world beyond our borders. We
do not speak foreign languages and—despite our
varied ethnic, racial, and religious nature—we
understand little about the problems and cultures of foreign lands. Americans, therefore,
respond with simple gut reactions to external
challenges and problems.

All of these factors have played some role in this century in
determining U.S. public and official reaction to revolutions. My own

bias and study suggests that on balance the strategic reasons have generally been more important than the economic interests in decisions to intervene—with some outstanding exceptions (Guatemala)—and that the value issues (democracy, law, and human rights) were more important than naiveté and ignorance.

In relation to Mexico and the Soviet Union, all of these explanations have played a role in determining American attitudes toward those revolutionary regimes at various times in the past. But other factors have played major roles in contemporary times. The Soviet Union's growing military and strategic nuclear power in the past twenty-five years has tended to overshadow all other considerations. And Mexico's exploding population and its interaction with the population of the United States in the past two decades has dramatically changed the focus from concern about Mexico and its revolutionary pretension to concern about Mexico as part of the U.S. domestic agenda. Yet the historic beginnings of these two revolutions and their impact on the United States are important to recall.

The Mexican Revolution was the first profoundly disturbing experience of its type for the United States. "The Mexican Revolution, to put the issue in its broadest context, represented the first serious challenge to the international order established by the industrial nations after the middle of the 19th century."[2] The U. S. government, through its embassy and its multiple other sources in Mexico, tried to understand, devise policies, influence the most favorable (we thought) forces, make decisions on financial or military intervention, and explain to the American public the disorder, xenophobia, and cruelty that was taking place in that neighboring country while U.S. officials simultaneously tried to explain the social and economic inequities that could justify these dramatic changes across the border. This history of the United States—fumbling yet finally reaching an accommodation with the Mexican national phenomenon—which Americans have never understood or appreciated would be repeated time and again throughout the rest of the century. On each occasion, whether in China, Cuba, Vietnam, or Nicaragua, the United States seemed to react with particular outrage at radical revolution—indeed a level of outrage that time and again would move us toward intervention and divide us domestically.

---

[2]Lloyd C. Gardiner, "Mexican Revolution," in *Woodrow Wilson and a Revolutionary World, 1913-1919*, ed. Edward S. Link, (Chapel Hill: University of North Carolina Press, 1982), p. 4.

No revolution shaped the thinking and foreign relations of the United States more than the Bolshevik revolution. By the time the Russian Revolution was in full flower, Woodrow Wilson could draw on the experience gained in his dealings with the Chinese and, particularly, the Mexican revolutionaries. He thought he had learned the limits of power and the problems of intervention in the internal process of such traumatic events. Also, "he came to recognize that the Mexican Revolution was not merely a personal struggle for power but also a major social upheaval comparable to the French Revolution."[3]

Despite these lessons, the United States under Wilson did participate in interventions in the Soviet Union, and the United States could not come to terms with the Bolsheviks until fifteen years after the revolution. Even after Roosevelt established diplomatic relations in 1933 and after the two nations fought together to defeat Nazi Germany, Soviet power and the threat of the expanding "Red revolution" shaped the containment foreign policy of the United States for the entire postwar period.

This is not to say that the Mexican and Russian revolutions were identical phenomena, or that the Mexican Revolution was communist, or that the United States was not justified in making some strenuous efforts to contain Soviet expansion. Indeed, there are probably more differences in the revolutions than similarities. What happened in Mexico was uniquely Mexican, and it contained little that was exportable or even relevant to other nations. The Bolsheviks, on the other hand, saw their revolution as only the first stage of world revolution. Moreover, the Mexican Revolution, while bloody, did eventually bring order and prolonged economic growth to that society. The Russian Revolution was bloody enough, but it turned into Stalin's revolution a decade later, resulting in the death of perhaps 20 million more Soviets, even before the horrors of World War II.

The two longest ruling political parties in the world today are the Communist Party of the Soviet Union and the Institutional Revolutionary Party (PRI) in Mexico. However, their shared longevity belies profound differences. The Soviet ruling revolutionary party has been dictatorial, ideological, increasingly expansionist,

---

[3]Betty Miller Unterberger, "Russian Revolution," in *Woodrow Wilson and a Revolutionary World.*

and closed. The Mexican ruling revolutionary party has been autocratic, monopolistic, inward-looking, and modernizing.

Octavio Paz, in his essay "The Philanthropic Ogre," has much to say about the similarities and differences between Russia and Mexico:

> In Mexico as in Russia at the turn of the century, the historic goals of the intellectuals and also those of many prominent groups and the enlightened bourgeoisie can be epitomized in the word "modernization" (industrial development, democracy, technology, laicism, etc.). In Mexico as in Russia, when faced with the relative weakness of its own bourgeoisie, the central agent of modernization has been the state. Finally, as in Russia, our state inherited a patrimonial regime—that of the viceroys of New Spain. Yet there are two basic differences.
>
> First, the brief but ineradicable democratic period of the Restored Republic (1867-76), which interposed itself between the state of New Spain and the modern state. Second, while the totalitarian state wiped out the Russian bourgeoisie, subdued the peasants and the workers, exterminated its political rivals, murdered its critics and created a new ruling class, the Mexican state has shared its power not only with the nation's bourgeoisie but also with the cadres who control the great unions. As I have pointed out, the relationship between the various Mexican governments, the leaders of Mexico's workers and peasants, and the bourgeoisie is ambiguous, a sort of unstable alliance that is not without quarrels, especially between the private and public sectors. All this can be summed up in one basic difference that contains all others and is paramount: whereas in Russia the party is the true state, in Mexico the state is the substantial element, and the party is its arm and instrument. And so, although Mexico is not really a democracy, it is not a totalitarian ideocracy either.[4]

---

[4]*The Labyrinth of Solitude* (New York: Grove Press, 1985), pp. 386-387.

Despite these important differences in the nature and evolution of the "revolutionary" systems that prevailed in Mexico and in Russia in 1917, the revolutionary origins and the political dominance and pretensions of the self-styled heirs to those two revolutions have helped shape and condition generations of North Americans in their dealings with and intolerance toward these two most important nations in American foreign relations.

Problems of U.S. Public Policy

While the United States has had similar attitudinal problems in relation to these revolutionary nations, the realities of dealing with the Soviet Union and Mexico have raised completely different sets of issues. The Soviet Union and Mexico each symbolizes most effectively polar opposite types of problems that have competed for the attention of U.S. policymakers, at least since the end of World War II. Each case demonstrates different aspects of the mounting U.S. problem in dealing effectively with the strong mix in our foreign relations: the so-called North-South and East-West sets of issues. First let us look briefly at how the Soviet Union and Mexico symbolize these two issue sets.

The principal determinant of U.S. foreign policy for over forty years has been the containment of Soviet communism. In 1947 George Kennan sought to capsulize in one work, and one short brilliant article, a national security policy for the still-neophyte world power. Containment became for the United States an ideology, a national purpose and global mission. Containment simplified the complex world for insular America and gave coherence to policy formulation. But it also led to excessive and yet ineffective use of force in Vietnam, to interventionist policies in other regions, and to obstructing the United States' capacity to deal with an increasingly diverse and internally divided communist world. Even if you believe that the struggle to contain communist expansion was a just cause, you must agree that it obscured for us the broader, increasingly complex world outside the context of the struggle against communism.

Every American has clear thoughts on communism, yet very few Americans have had any substantial contacts with the people or even the issues of the communist world. American students are taught to hate and to fear Marxism-Leninism, but they do not study Marxism-Leninism in school to learn how to deal with and understand this major twentieth-century political force. The issues involved in dealing with the Soviet Union, therefore, tend to be abstract (communism), exotic and compelling (Kremlin power), ideological (no private enterprise or religion), and frightening (nuclear weapons and war). These are the weighty issues that focus the mind and dominate the media, but they are also esoteric and arcane for most Americans who have neither the time nor the preparation to probe their complexities. Therefore Americans tend to fall back on their instincts and political attitudes—anti-communism.

In dealing with the Soviet Union, U.S. policies have tended to be inconsistent, reflecting the schizophrenia of the American body politic, its fear and distrust of Soviet communism and its powerful desire to reduce the likelihood of nuclear war. Americans are distrustful of contacts or agreements with the Soviets, yet believe the Soviets cannot be ignored. U.S. foreign policy since World War II has been shaped by surges of accommodation with this powerful unknowable adversary followed by periods of revulsion from it.

American public opinion influences the conduct of our relations with the Soviet Union only in the most general terms. Presidents from Eisenhower to Reagan have been largely successful in garnering popular support when they have tried to lead the American people toward agreements with the Soviet Union. It is only when they exceed the limits of good judgment or try to deceive the American people (as Nixon did in trying to use détente to save his presidency from the Watergate scandal) that public opinion backfires. Conversely, of course, when American presidents respond to some negative Soviet behavior, leading the American people back into the Cold War—a more simplistic and intellectually comfortable environment—the American majority follows.

The set of issues that plague U.S. policymakers who deal with Mexico is entirely different. Domestic politics and public opinion govern every issue in the complex network of bilateral relations. Virtually no American has an overall concept of Mexico and the importance of the U.S.-Mexican relationship, yet each American has some contact with Mexico or Mexicans that shapes individual thinking. Americans feel strongly about these issues and will vote, lobby, and act on their views. Such issues are migrant workers or immigrants, trade or agricultural produce, drugs or border contraband, tourism or "tacos," gas or petroleum, money or debt. There is no country in the world with which the United States has a more complex or broader human and material interaction than with Mexico. The bilateral relationship with Mexico therefore becomes a reflection of the diversity and tension within our own national agenda.

The contrast with the Soviet Union is dramatic. The issues with Mexico tend to be material (not abstract), mundane (not exotic and compelling), practical and real (not ideological), and productive or disruptive (but not frightening). In our relationship with Mexico we are inconsistent, and often ineffective, because we tend to deal separately with individual issues while ignoring or being unable to grasp the overall nature of this intimate but troubling partnership in North America. We deal with Mexico much as we deal with our own domestic agenda—at the state and local level.

The making of U.S. foreign policy is complicated by these radically differing sets of issues and by the different roles of public opinion and political process; but more to the point it is complicated by the institutional complexity of the conduct of U.S. foreign relations. A scholar of the U.S. government could easily list the principal agencies which determine U.S. relations with the Soviet Union but get utterly lost in the morass of detail and rationale for trade and export controls, weapons systems and targeting, arms negotiations and intelligence data and estimates, and the multiple arcane subjects that define the U.S.-Soviet relationship. Those who dominate policy and procedures in dealing with the USSR in the United States are a relatively small number of individuals with access and information and (ideally) expertise and professional experience. This group is little influenced by public opinion or by the complex domestic political process. Within the executive and legislative branches there has evolved a cadre of "experts" who claim to understand the arcane issues and who seek to monopolize the formulation of policies toward the Soviet Union.

There are several problems here, however. First, the Soviet experts in the United States realize that knowledge is power and are not above manipulating data and proposals for political or personal reasons. Tensions over arms control have defined some of the most vicious and legendary struggles for power in Washington. Second, many individuals in key slots are overnight experts brought into key jobs because of their political loyalty and ideological purity rather than for their understanding of the Soviet system, the Russian language, trade issues, or arms control concepts. Indeed the politicization of U.S.-Soviet relations has resulted in a depleted, demoralized, and dispersed cadre that was once the cream of U.S. government and academic professionals.

Therefore, the management of U.S.-Soviet relations is centralized in the hands of a relative few, who have a strong influence on decision-makers and are relatively unresponsive to public opinion or political process. The fact that the knowledgeable community is rather small, however, has over the years tended to so frustrate the "outsiders" that other bureaucratic elements have increasingly become engaged, and the U.S. Congress, with its multiple committees and opinions, has in the past twenty years come to demand ultimate control by blocking agreements in such areas as arms control and trade. Congress's largely negative role in relation to U.S.-Soviet relations is a reaction to this perceived elitist monopoly over the complex issues involved.

By contrast, the conduct of our relations with Mexico is dispersed so broadly among so many different federal, state, local, and private entities that no one individual can be in charge or pretend to have an overview. From the small businessman and mayor in a border town to the state governor and corporate executive, to congressional committees of every sort and virtually every agency and department of the executive branch, each has a particular agenda that relates to and influences relations with Mexico. In most cases, individuals involved probably understand their particular piece of the Mexican puzzle but care little about how their particular effort might affect other aspects of the relationship.

There can be no "policy" toward Mexico anymore than there can be a "policy" on the local issues of the fifty states. In many states, particularly near the border, the domestic U.S. and Mexican-U.S. agendas are similar. Therefore a U.S. president cannot try to enunciate a "policy" toward Mexico, such as one is expected to announce a policy toward the Soviet Union. What a president can and must do is define the tone of the relationship and try to coordinate better the work of the principal entities and give general direction to the government on the large issues.

The overall style and tone of the relationship depend on the president, since no bureaucratic gerrymandering can reduce the power of the president to correct or seriously damage the public atmosphere in which the complex relationship is carried out. Whereas a president can really affect the substance of U.S.-Soviet relations through direct guidance to the relatively small cadres involved in reaching agreements, the president can, by and large, merely influence the degree of attention the United States gives to U.S.-Mexican relations and a few of the larger issues (such as debt and financial matters).

No American president can arrive at the White House with sufficient comprehension of the complexity of this relationship with Mexico, but he can hope and try to protect his administration from committing a series of errors or overly bold policy initiatives in the first few months that could sour the bilateral environment and thereby limit the possibility of managing problems in the years ahead. It is simply too much to expect a transition team or a new national security group to prepare a new president for the awesome complexity of the agenda with Mexico or for the fact that the president can probably not hope to solve many problems in four or eight years—only to manage them a little better than his predecessor and integrate the U.S.-Mexican agenda more effectively into overall U.S. foreign policy.

Finally, there is yet another factor which curiously affects the U.S. thinking about and management of these two vastly different relationships: that is the nature of the American specialists and scholars who write about and influence policy. There is a division between those foreign policy experts, journalists, and academicians who concern themselves with East-West issues and those who concern themselves with North-South issues. The East-West specialists, who have tended to dominate in the State Department, the NSC, Defense, and every other agency of government involved with national security since World War II, focus on arms and arms control, NATO and alliance politics, defense strategies, and Soviet power and policies. When presidents and secretaries of state have begun to think about foreign policy, East-West issues were central for many historical, cultural, and logical reasons. No U.S. president or secretary of state has come to office with knowledge of or experience in Latin America since World War II.

The North-South group of specialists are relatively new to academia, journalism, and government. They focus on Africa, Latin America, and South Asia, international financial institutions, bilateral aid, development economics, commodity trade, non-proliferation, military coups, human rights, and social justice. The difference in mind-sets between Sovietologists and Latin Americanists is most striking. One only needed to attend meetings of the American Association for the Advancement of Slavic Studies (AAASS) and its counterpart, the Latin American Studies Association (LASA), over the past 20 years to discover that the participants' vision of foreign policy and U.S. society are at opposite poles of the American political spectrum. The Latin Americanists are often influenced by the Latin vision of us—severely critical of the U.S. government and the U.S. private sector, sympathetic to and supportive of Latin criticism of the United States, worried about people and development problems. Ironically they tend to exaggerate the U.S. ability to shape events in the region. They also tend not to want to be too critical of Latin American countries or governments for fear of evoking hostile reactions and being cut off from access to officials who react quickly and emotionally to criticism from the north. Even though the Mexicanists, as a special subgroup of the Latin Americanists, are often more inclined to be critical of Mexico and its autocratic political system, there is, nonetheless, a sharp contrast between the Mexicanist and Sovietologist in experience and world view.

The Russian-East European specialists have tended to be extremely critical of the Soviet Union, communism, and revolution. They are not given to idealism, are hardnosed about the limits of U.S. policy, and convinced that there are virtually no issues so important as those involved in the U.S.-Soviet relationship. Soviet specialists and Europeanists in general give low priority to North-South issues and tend to be either patronizing toward those who do or, worse, instant experts when they engage the issues. These two groups do not relate easily in policy debates either in or out of government.

Because of this tension between the North-South experts and East-West experts and because of the fact that their language and world views are so very different, there have been few successful efforts to integrate competing demands in making coherent U.S. policies for resource allocation and in determining the United States' appropriate role in the world. As long as the Cold War continued, containment policies, with their interventionist implications, governed U.S. priorities even in those cases in which straight "developmental" policies might well have worked better. This division, even tension, between the humane and power issues in foreign affairs is a reflection of the tensions within American politics and values. It is, therefore, not surprising that somehow the Soviet Union and Mexico have come to symbolize the foreign policy expression of this domestic debate. Yet as the Soviet Union and Mexico themselves take on more diffused and less polarizing roles, how will, and should, the United States begin to deal with the new realities in foreign affairs?

MANAGING U.S. RELATIONS WITH MEXICO AND THE SOVIET UNION

The way the United States manages its relations with these two countries is influenced by the way Mexico and the Soviet Union themselves deal with the outside world. The contrasts and similarities in the way Mexico and the Soviet Union relate to their foreign relations are striking:

— The Soviets consider national security and their military power of primary importance in national policy; the Mexicans give low priority to national security and military issues.

— Soviet foreign relations are closest with those nations which are military client states; Mexico has virtually no military relations with other states.

— Soviet power dominates its neighbors, particularly in Eastern Europe, and the Soviets became increasing interventionist after World War II; Mexico has traditionally played a minor role in relation to its smaller neighbors in Central America and the Caribbean and is ideologically and effectively non-interventionist.

— Until very recently the Soviet Union has paid only lip service to the United Nations and its institutions and has had little presence in the major international economic institutions. Mexico actively and effectively pursues its role in international organizations and considers them the front line of Mexican foreign relations. Mexico places a high priority on "world order" and international law, while the Soviet Union, like a great power, prefers unilateral action.

Yet there are striking similarities in Mexican and Soviet approaches to foreign relations which often align them against the

United States internationally and bilaterally and which tend to present similar sorts of problems to U.S. policymakers:

— The Soviet Union and Mexico are run by single dominant political parties the leadership of which have the ultimate say on all policy issues. U.S. officials, therefore, must deal through a single hierarchical, Byzantine-like, closed political structure in each country. This is disturbing and at the same time simplifying for the United States. We find that the stability of the structure of power enables us to know who answers the "hot line," but ultimately we encounter a high level of difficulty in dealing with closed systems, given the openness and pluralism of the American system.

— On a related topic the ruling parties of the Soviet Union and Mexico each lean heavily on their revolutionary origins and ideologies to sustain legitimacy, and each party retains its authority through pursing often radical rhetoric with regard to the future, to capitalism, and to the United States. The United States is a nation much more interested and involved in the political process than revolutionary promises.

— The Soviets and the Mexicans both have a special obsession with the United States and with its citizens. That feeling toward Soviet Russia and Mexico is not reciprocated by the large, diverse, largely insular Americans who, while anti-communist, traditionally have limited understanding of the cultures, languages, and motivations of the major foreign nations. This situation presents asymmetries and opportunities in both relationships.

These similarities and differences are intellectually interesting. They should also somehow lead the United States to a better understanding of how it can structure its government in the future to manage these extremely important bilateral relations better than we have in the past. What, moreover, can we say about the future in light of this effort to contrast and compare the impact of the Soviet and Mexican nations on U.S. foreign policy?

First and most important, some of the problems with the Soviet Union may be on their way to being corrected. The Cold War may be coming to a close. The most dramatic developments in international relations that have occurred since World War II seem to be happening in the late 1980s in the Soviet Union. The reforms which Mikhail Gorbachev is trying to put in place could have a direct impact on some, but not all, of what we have examined in this paper. Gorbachev seems to wish to achieve some of the following:

— A more pluralistic political system, in which a reform "process" (*perestroika, glasnost,* new thinking) gradually replaces ideology as the guiding principle of the society.

— A more open approach to certain "market" ideas in economic development in the Soviet Union and abroad. Interestingly and ironically, the Soviet Union is considering as one step opening up some "free trade zones" for foreign manufacturers in Soviet border areas similar to the *maquiladoras* on the Mexican-U.S. border.

— A gradual reduction in world tensions through arms control.

Developments in Mexico in 1988 could also be far-reaching for that political system. With Carlos Salinas de Gortari as president and the PRI trying to retain control of its and Mexico's future, Mexico will be entering a period of possibly dramatic transformation.

— Mexico is likely to be more pluralistic politically—with all that implies for the PRI and other political forces, for the role of the Congress and the budget and legal process, and for the general level of internal information flow and debate.

— It is also likely to be somewhat less ideological about its own particular past, recognizing the growing similarities between its own development problems and those of its neighbors.

Mexico now will have to develop some new thinking, new rules of the game, and new habits for its complex society. The media, private sector, and other diverse institutions are finding very quickly that Mexico without the PRI in total control is apt to be a far more confusing, and more democratic, society.

It is indeed one of those striking ironies of history that these dramatic changes in Mexico and the Soviet Union should begin to happen at the same time, given the close coincidence of their revolutions over seventy years ago. Should the process of building democracy and decentralizing authority really take hold in Mexico and the Soviet Union, those societies will be changed in fundamental ways over the next decade. As Octavio Paz has written, however, "democracy is a political philosophy but it is also an apprenticeship and a technique." There will be a long hard road for the peoples of both these countries to absorb the implications of this "technique," this process called democracy. Will the Soviet Communist Party, even more than the PRI, be able to give up, to quote Paz again, "their vain and high-sounding language" and discontinue playing "their time worn games of power"? More importantly, will they be able to give up claim to absolute truths and their absolute claim to power? Paz remarks, "in open societies defeat is provisional, victory is relative."[5] Can the opposition groups as well as those in power in Mexico and the USSR avoid the need to seek total conquest and political annihilation of their antagonists?

We are witnessing in 1988 exciting times in Mexico and the Soviet Union, and if these trends prevail many aspects of our relations with these two "revolutionary," autocratic nations will change as well. But many aspects will not change, and some problems are likely to get worse as diversity and disorder, democracy and unpredictability, decentralization and balkanization begin to go hand in hand.

Let me try to summarize briefly what might change and what might stay the same or worsen over the next several years in our troubled relations with these two nations:

The Soviet Union is likely to become more inward oriented, less adventurous in foreign affairs, more inclined to international as opposed to unilateral resolution of conflicts, and more disposed toward arms control agreements. Nuclear war will recede but by no means disappear as a threat. The Soviet Union is becoming somewhat more open, accessible, divided, and understandable. It is beginning to become less enigmatic, less ideological, less

---

[5]"One Country's Crisis," *Los Angeles Times*, August 28, 1988, part V, pp. 1, 6.

self-congratulatory, less proud, more self-critical, and more practical about its own problems. The history of seventy years is becoming an unbearable burden for the party and for those who have ruled.

As this opening process takes on a life of its own, the Soviet economy is likely to get worse, the internal conflicts will become sharper among interest groups and nationalities, the traditional controls of empire will become strained; and the threat of retreat from reform or reaction to it makes the course of future Soviet policies and leadership more unpredictable.

Moreover, the "democratic process" in Soviet society will be slow and follow a different path from that of Western democracies. Some in the United States will become impatient with, confused by, and intolerant of the process, while others will be optimistic about the strength and direction of reform. Over the next decade, more of the U.S. population will become involved in the Soviet Union than ever before. Economic, financial, intellectual, political, and personal stakes in the outcome of struggle will develop in the United States. In other words, our relations with the Soviet Union will become less dominated by the few, and more the subject of broader and competing interests. Public opinion and human interaction will make this relationship less abstract, less frightening, and perhaps less an obsession over communism.

But for the foreseeable future, the Soviet Union will remain the major nuclear and conventional power antagonist of the United States; it will have close relations with dozens of communist and radical parties around the world; it will pay at least some attention to the Marxist-Leninist ideology; it will retain an oppressed but restive empire in the USSR and in Eastern Europe; and it will be supporting some of the cruelest dictatorships in the world, such as in Cuba, Ethiopia, and Cambodia.

In the case of Mexico the changes are likely to be of a similar nature. The president and the PRI will confront new popular and organized opposition to policies of economic sacrifice and continued privatization. The media, legal, and international communities will become bolder in critically examining the Mexican system, and regional and congressional resistance to presidential authority will grow. Moreover, the myths and realities of Mexican history will be more discussed as opposition parties compete openly to become heirs of the past or architects of the future. Decentralization and democracy will contribute to political confusion and perhaps great economic inequities.

What will not change in our relations with Mexico are the human realities, the economic disparity, the drug flow, the trade issues, the immigration questions, and, above all for the foreseeable future, the Mexican debt of over $100 billion.

The United States will have to face the same issues as in the past and in much the same way but with a central government in Mexico that is weaker and has fewer options. The U.S. government and other U.S. entities will, moreover, probably have to make some tough choices on how to deal with the growing power of opposition forces within Mexico. Another issue is what impact a more open relationship will have on our traditional relations with the PRI.

A PROPOSAL FOR MANAGING THE MEXICAN PARTNERSHIP

U.S.-Mexican relations are too important, too complicated, and too long-term to leave to the presidents of the United States and Mexico. This is one conclusion I draw from two decades of thinking about this bilateral relationship and in the context of my foregoing analysis about this ongoing and increasingly serious management problem. I now synthesize in six propositions the key issues which, I believe, make the management of this important relationship increasingly troubled. I then offer an unconventional, probably undo-able, proposal that follows from the deductive process. The proposal has the benefit of dramatizing the dimensions of the problem as I see it.

Proposition One. The national sanctity of sovereignty (and non-interference) is the most important legal principle of Mexican state policy, yet the nature of the evolving U.S.-Mexican relationship is, in reality, progressively eroding the sovereign rights of both nations and limiting the sovereign decisions available to both federal governments. The more the sovereignty of both countries becomes blurred, the more frustrated and publicly defensive the political leaders of each country become. Yet the process of erosion is relentless because of the almost unrestrictable flow across borders of people, products, drugs, capital, and even decision-making and politicking. This blending of these two giant and vastly different cultures and political systems is not only difficult, but against the laws of both nations. Yet, in fact, each nation is interfering constantly in the internal affairs of the other in ever new ways on a scale probably unequaled in the modern history of large independent states—we call it "interdependence" but it is reciprocal interference and mutual involvement.

As Mexico and the United States become more and more like one global yet bifurcated system, each government is increasingly fearful of these developments and their implications. The challenge for the future will be for the governments and governing elites of both nations to define and accept systems for managing the relations which can recognize the paradox of the relationship in which the principle of sovereignty must be maintained while it is progressively eroding in reality. This probably requires some radical steps toward building a new bilateral formula, not simply bureaucratic manipulations within the two governments.

Proposition Two. While it is certain that the United States and Mexico cannot have good or trouble-free bilateral relations in the foreseeable future, the positive elements in the relationship—notwithstanding the ineptitude of political leaders and diplomats— are remarkably enduring and binding. Our economic and political relations are extremely troubled but not warlike, annoying but not hostile, confrontational but hardly ever unresolvable. There has rarely been a bilateral problem we cannot find a way to manage or live with. The clashes come from differences in both style and substance: if we can deal with the conflicts in style, the substantive issues can be managed with the proper focus of government energies. The substantive issues are becoming more numerous and more serious. Most of these (debt, drugs, migration, trade) will be around for a long time. They cannot be managed unless the respective leaders comprehend the vastly differing perceptions on both sides of the border about the origins of these chronic bilateral problems.

At the same time, the areas of bilateral cooperation have a great potential for growth, not only in the widening border area but also throughout both societies in the areas of education, culture, environmental protection, resource usage, and conservation. The democratization and decentralization of Mexico could greatly improve the sense of common purpose between the two countries. The political leaders of both countries must be wise and informed enough to continue to press for the constructive programs even as one or more of the serious problems are becoming confrontational.

Proposition Three. The overall style and tone of the relationship ultimately depends on the abilities of the two presidents. As pointed out earlier, it is simply too much to expect of any transition team to prepare a president for the awesome complexity of the domestic and foreign agenda involved in the U.S.-Mexican relationship. President Bush is uniquely positioned among modern U.S. presidents to grasp the complexity of the issues because of his eight-year term as vice president.

But we must now build new structures for better long-term management. Critical to any serious efforts to facilitate the transition from an ill-informed outgoing president to a non-informed president-elect and his equally uninformed new team is the establishment of new institutions that provide continuity, advice, and a leaven for the mixture of optimism and despair that is present in every new encounter between American and Mexican presidents.

Proposition Four. Even though the U.S. president has enormous impact on the style and tone of the overall relationship, the variety of issues and the number of private actors—as well as federal and regional government agencies—that are deeply interested and involved in shaping U. S. policies toward and programs with Mexico are so vast that the White House cannot hope to determine or even effectively control the course of U.S.-Mexican relations. Even if the president were to limit his scope to trying to better coordinate the activities of the executive branch, as the Carter administration sought to do, the Congress, Federal Reserve, state governments, private sector, and even a few dissident departments of the executive branch would defy the coordinator and, if necessary, the president. This is not to suggest that better executive branch coordination of the president's policies is not eminently to be desired; it is simply not enough.

Proposition Five. The cultural and informational divide between Mexico and the United States is a major source of confusion and disruption in the relationship. Major remedial steps must be taken to fill this gap if better communications and mutual respect between the two nations are the objective.

So much has been written on this subject that it is unnecessary to rehearse here once again the points of difference between the culture of Mexico and the culture of the United States. But several brief statements may help sketch the scope of the problem:

> — The differences go much deeper than language and reflect fundamental differences in world view.

— Mexico should not be perceived simply as a part
of or the gateway to Latin America. It is so different from the rest of Latin America and so
much more important to the United States that
it should be dealt with outside of or on the
margin of the inter-American system.

— The cultural divide results in vastly distorted
pictures on both sides of the border on the basic
question of what is culture. Each side harbors
stereotypical views of the cultural achievements
(or lack of such achievements) of the other.

In this environment perhaps the biggest failing is the minimal
amount or, worse, the distortion of information available on Mexico
and the United States in the other country. Senior officials, federal
and regional bureaucrats, leaders of the private sector, and opinion leaders in both countries frequently find it impossible to obtain
information on the wide range of activities, attitudes, problems,
pending legislation, executive actions, and cultural life that affect
the overall relationship.

Proposition Six. The foreign policies of Mexico and the United
States are often in conflict, yet there is little likelihood that these
fundamental differences can be reduced in the foreseeable future.
Whereas the United States is the major issue in Mexican foreign
policy, the obverse is not the case. Moreover, much of Mexican
foreign policy is shaped by its economic-financial predicament as
well as by its self-image as a revolutionary nation. When U.S. and
Mexican government policies, views of international law, and
perceived national interests come into direct conflict, as they have
in recent years over Central America and in the past over certain
other problems such as Cuba, the complex U.S.-Mexican bilateral
agenda will be affected negatively. The Central American set of
issues are particularly traumatic in this regard.

Yet there is little utility in exaggerating the role these differences play in the ability of both countries to get on with the major
bilateral issues. Mexico's dissension from the United States in the
global context and in international organizations is often an
important portrayal of its national sovereignty in the face of the
mightier North American power. Mexico, moreover, has not chosen
to be a major political actor in the Western Hemisphere but has
positioned itself forcefully and effectively in international agencies

and organizations outside the inter-American system. While the tension that flows from these differences over foreign policy could well result in one or both sides moderating their positions, ultimately foreign policy differences are much less important to both countries than the effective and steady management of the bilateral relationship.

The foregoing propositions outline what is a particularly outstanding example of the U.S. problem in managing relations with one of the most important nations to U.S. interests in the world. Because the problem is so acute and is evidently getting more so, radical changes should at least be considered. The following recommendation, therefore, is put forward in the belief that it will respond to many, although not all, of the problems brought out by the foregoing analysis and propositions.

> *The United States and Mexico should form a "Council of Mexico and the United States" that would function much like the multiple European Community institutions.*

The Council would be composed of:

- A small *Executive Branch* made up of Mexicans and Americans which would monitor the bilateral relationship. The Executive Committee in the Executive Branch would comprise six individuals, three from each side. The Committee would lead the Executive Branch, and the CEO of the Committee would rotate every year between Mexico and the United States. Appointments to this body would be made by the executive branches of each country; the senior appointed executive on each side would be a former senior official (president, vice president, or cabinet member) with extensive prior experience with the bilateral relationship. The Executive would:

  — Monitor the entire range of issues in the bilateral relationship, advise the two governments of ongoing or pending problems, make recommendations to each government on possible solutions or courses of action.

  — Publish a weekly bilingual information bulletin available to all which would provide full, balanced, informative coverage of the range of activities on both sides of the border relating to the bilateral relationship. The bulletin would include reprints of important recent articles and editorials affecting or commenting on U.S.-Mexican relations.

— Stimulate and carry out expanded programs of cultural exchange and interaction including the expansion of the training of Mexicanists in the United States and U.S. specialists in Mexico, give greater attention in each country to the history and the culture of the other, etc.

— Prepare and train experts on U.S.-Mexican relations for future roles in the governments and private sectors of both countries.

• *An Assembly,* which would meet twice a year for a week or less, once in Mexico City and once in Washington. Each side would send fifty delegates to the Assembly, to be drawn from the legislatures of each country, from the regional or state governments, and from the private sector. The Assembly would air problems and make proposals to the Executive of the Council and to the legislatures of Mexico and the United States on measures to improve the relationship or to solve problems.

• *A Judicial Body* composed of judges from both countries which would receive cases of obscure or dual jurisdiction and which could make findings on disputed legal issues between the two countries.

The "Council of Mexico and the United States" would be paid for by the two governments; its programs (the bulletin and exchanges) would be paid for with funds raised from private sources or from subscriptions. The appointments to the Executive Branch (perhaps a total of thirty on each side, including staff) would be staggered every two years to ensure continuity and, ideally, to isolate the appointees from the political process.

The *disadvantages* of such a proposal are numerous:

It will be seen as too costly, redundant, unworkable.

Its powers would be ambiguous and its role would likely become an additional center for dispute rather than problem solving.

The same objectives could be achieved more efficiently by strengthening the pertinent institutions
in each government.

However, the *advantages* of some such radical approach are
overriding:

It would provide a high profile and knowledgeable
super-lobby in each country that would provide
continuity in the relationship, but it would not
significantly detract from the sovereign rights of
each government.

Although it could be costly, the cost of not doing
something of this type could be greater.

Although such a Council might be troublesome for
the executives and bureaucrats of each country, the
Council could serve as a lightning rod and intermediary during times of trouble and serious mis-
understanding.

The Council of the United States and Mexico would assist the
United States and its people to pay more consistent and informed
attention to this relationship.

CONCLUSION

The United States is now facing a much more complex world
than it has for the past seventy years. Over the near term at least,
the issues of most concern are not the spread of communism in
the Third World, the growth of Soviet military power and nuclear
overkill, and the strength of our military power and alliances. The
more crucial issues seem to involve identification of a new U.S.
role in a world in which U.S. military power is no longer as vital
to world stability as it was before. U.S. economic power has become
a major source of confusion, uncertainty, and concern for other
nations. New economic, political, and national forces in the world
(such as Japan, Southeast Asia, Europe in 1992, religious funda-
mentalism, drugs, terrorism, ecology, and debt) drive and define
our real concerns as never before.

How the United States rethinks its national priorities with
regard to its relations with the Soviet Union and Mexico is central

to its ability to adjust to the new agenda imposed by the world outside. The United States is much in need of "new thinking." It is not enough to say proudly that the ideas of pluralism, democracy, private initiative, and decentralization have won out over radical revolutions as the twentieth century comes to a close. Indeed, as the world becomes more committed to "pluralism," the United States must enhance its understanding of what that means outside of our borders.

As communism, Soviet Russia, the Bolshevik revolution, and the "red threat" take on a more manageable dimension and a more human face, the United States will have a tough time distinguishing between real, illusory, or transitory change. This will not be an easy task, nor do we face a period of transition that is danger free. There may be a reactionary resurgence to Gorbachev's reform process that will return the Soviet Union to a more aggressive posture. Yet it seems possible that the Cold War is almost over, and with it the policy of containment. Rethinking what that means will be very difficult, but it will also be essential for any new relationship with the Soviet Union and with Mexico.

Mexico's role in this "new thinking" of the U.S. foreign policy agenda could and should be central. Not surprisingly, as our obsession with Soviet Russia—now more pluralistic, more democratic, more internally divided—becomes less obsessive and less abstract, our relations with a more pluralistic, more democratic, more internally divided Mexico could and should become more important, more focused, and better understood.

About the Contributors

Jorge Chabat is coordinator of the Program for the Study of Mexican International Relations at the Centro de Investigación y Docencia Económica (CIDE) and a professor at the Universidad Iberoamericana. Born in Guadalajara, he earned his degree in international relations from El Colegio de México. He was the personal secretary to the rector of the Universidad Autónoma Metropolitana in 1981-1982, and from 1979 to 1981 he was a professor at the UAM's Iztapalapa campus. From 1982 to 1988 he was a professor at the Universidad Nacional Autónoma de México's School of Political and Social Sciences, and from 1981 to 1983 he was a member of the Advisory Commission on Entrance to the Mexican Foreign Service. He has written various articles on Mexican foreign policy, and he is presently coordinating a book on Mexican foreign policy under Miguel de la Madrid.

Guadalupe González received a degree in international relations from El Colegio de México and a master's degree in political sociology from the London School of Economics. At present she is Coordinator of the North American Studies Program at the Mexican branch of the Instituto Latinoamericano de Estudios Transnacionales (ILET). She has written many articles on Mexican foreign policy, particularly with regard to drug trafficking, oil, Central America, and U.S.-Mexican relations.

Rosario Green is director of the Commission on Foreign Affairs of the National Executive Council of the Partido Revolucionario Institucional (PRI). She studied economics and international relations at the National Autonomous University of Mexico, at El Colegio de México, at Columbia University in New York and at the Instituto para la Integración Latinoamericana (INTAL) in Buenos Aires. She has been a professor at El Colegio de México and, from 1982 to 1988, director of the Matías Romero Institute of Diplomatic Studies. Ms. Green has published ten books, including a prescient analysis of Mexico's foreign indebtedness—*El endeudamiento público externo de México: 1950-1973; Estado y banca transnacional en México*; and, most recently, *La deuda externa de México de 1973 a 1988: de la abundancia a la escasez de créditos*. She has written articles for academic reviews and journalistic media in various languages. Ms. Green has also been a consultant to the United Nations and to the Sistema Económico Latinoamericano.

Claude Heller has reached the level of Ambassador as a career member of the Mexican Foreign Service. One of the principal negotiators for the Contadora Group's efforts to achieve peace in Central America, he has occupied many different positions in the Ministry of Foreign Relations, most notably as General Director for the United Nations (1983-1987) and as Executive Director for Multilateral Issues (1987-1988). He has taken part in numerous international gatherings, and in 1988 and 1989 he was the Mexican delegate to the Human Rights Commission of the United Nations. He has authored diverse works on international policy issues and he has been a professor in various institutions of higher education.

William H. Luers has been President of the Metropolitan Museum of Art since 1986. Formerly, he served as Ambassador to Czechoslovakia from 1983 to 1986 and Ambassador to Venezuela from 1978 to 1982. In the Foreign Service from 1957-86, he also served in Italy, Germany, and the Soviet Union, and worked in the Department of State, Washington, D.C., in the Office of Soviet Affairs and as Deputy Executive Secretary, Deputy Assistant Secretary for Inter-American Affairs, and Deputy Assistant Secretary for European Affairs. He has been a Visiting Lecturer at the Woodrow Wilson School at Princeton University (1983), at Johns Hopkins University School of Advanced International Studies (SAIS) (1966-68 and 1973-75), at George Washington University (1975-77), a leading consultant to the Bipartisan Commission on Central America, chaired by Dr. Henry Kissinger, and a Director's Visitor at the Institute for Advanced Study, Princeton, New Jersey

(1982-1983). Mr. Luers has written extensively for newspapers and magazines on the Soviet Union and Eastern Europe, on East/West relations and on Latin America. He serves on the boards of various academic institutions, non-profit organizations and corporations.

Carlos Rico is professor and researcher at El Colegio de México's International Studies Center and an advisor to the North American Studies Program of the Instituto Latinoamericano de Estudios Transnacionales. He attended El Colegio de México from 1969 to 1972, receiving his degree in international relations. He completed his doctorate in 1980 in poltiical science at Harvard University. He has been a professor at the Universidad Iberoamericana, the Universidad Nacional Autónoma de México, the Centro de Investigación y Docencia Económicas, the Facultad Latinoamericana de Ciencias Sociales, Duke University, and the University of North Carolina-Chapel Hill. He was an advisor to Mexico's Foreign Relations Minister from February 1972 to December 1975, and he has been a member of the Mexican delegation in diverse international forums. He has published many books and articles on U.S.-Mexican and inter-American relations.

Lars Schoultz, a political scientist specializing in inter-American relations and United States policy toward Latin America, is director of the Institute of Latin America Studies at the University of North Carolina-Chapel Hill. Professor Schoultz is the author of *Human Rights and United States Policy toward Latin America* (1981), *The Populist Challenge: Argentine Electoral Behavior in the Postwar Era* (1983), and *National Security and United States Policy toward Latin America* (1987). He is a co-editor of *Latin America, the United States, and the Inter-American System* (Westview, 1980). His articles have appeared in a variety of journals, including the *American Journal of Political Science*, the *American Political Science Review*, *Comparative Politics*, *International Organization*, the *Journal of Politics*, and *Political Science Quarterly*.

Peter H. Smith is professor of political science and Simón Bolívar professor of Latin American studies at the University of California, San Diego. Born in Brooklyn, New York, he graduated from Harvard College in 1961 and earned a Ph.D. from Columbia University in 1966. A specialist on long-run processes of political change, Mr. Smith has written books on Argentina and on empirical methodology. His best-known work on Mexico is *Labyrinths of Power*, a study of elite recruitment and mobility. He has also co-authored a textbook entitled *Modern Latin America*.

Mr. Smith has served as a department chair and academic associate dean at the University of Wisconsin and at MIT, and he is past president of the Latin American Studies Association. He was professor of history and political science at the Massachusetts Institute of Technology before joining the faculty of UC-San Diego.

Cathryn L. Thorup is Senior Fellow and Director of the U.S.-Mexico Project at the Overseas Development Council, a policy-oriented, Washington-based forum for the exchange of ideas among key actors in the bilateral relationship. Prior to joining ODC in 1980, she lived in Mexico for six years, where she received a B.A. in international relations at El Colegio de México and worked as a journalist for the Mexican news magazine, *Razones*. Since receiving a Master of Science degree in economic history at the London School of Economics, Ms. Thorup has written extensively on U.S. policy toward Mexico, conflict management in U.S.-Mexican relations, and Mexican economic and political reform, and has edited *The United States and Mexico: Face to Face with New Technology*. She is a doctoral candidate in political science at Harvard University, a member of the Board of Directors of the Consortium for U.S. Research Programs for Mexico (PROFMEX), and a member of the Council on Foreign Relations.